Rene Lecler was born in Belgium, educated at the Sorbonne in France and has been a British citizen for over forty years.

A journalist and a writer, he worked for many years for various national newspapers and magazines before becoming, in 1958, Features and then Travel Editor of *Harpers & Queen*. As such he has travelled widely and repeatedly in 104 countries and is known as the 'doyen' of travel writers in Britain and the expert on exotic travel.

A Fellow of the Royal Geographical Society, he is the recipient of numerous international travel awards. He has written several books, including *The World Shopping Guide* and *The 300 Best Hotels in the World*.

He has recently moved to Cyprus but still contributes regularly to *Harpers & Queen* and is now their Travel Consultant.

A HARPERS & QUEEN PUBLICATION

A Guide for the
INDEPENDENT
TRAVELLER

Rene Lecler

WILLOW BOOKS
Collins
8 Grafton Street, London
1987

Dedication

For Chris Lawrence, who will never contribute
to tourism pollution.

Willow Books
William Collins Sons & Co. Ltd.
London . Glasgow . Sydney
Auckland . Toronto . Johannesburg

First published in 1987
© Rene Lecler 1987

Maps drawn by Michael Munday

BRITISH LIBRARY CATALOGUING IN PUBLICATION DATA

Lecler, Rene
The Harpers and Queen guide for the
independent traveller.
1. Travel—Handbooks, manuals, etc.
I. Title
910'.2'02   G151
ISBN 0 00 218223 8

Typeset by Ace Filmsetting Ltd., Frome, Somerset
Printed and bound in Great Britain by
Mackays of Chatham

CONTENTS

INTRODUCTION

Some years ago I recall meeting an eminent British High Court Judge in the middle of a pellucid lagoon on an island in the Indian Ocean. He wore Blimpish shorts, a disreputable straw hat and green wellies and spent his time turning over the stones with a stick to see what was underneath. Inevitably that evening we talked, though I felt like an intruder. He told me that this was his holiday style. Every year, he would go to a different part of the world, find a lagoon and get started. 'I simply love lagoons,' he told me rather sheepishly. I left him to his passion, convinced that I had found one of my heroes: a man who knew what he wanted, went there and got it.

Of course, you don't have to go to the tropics to do that. Travel 10 miles inland from Marbella and you are back in Spain. Take a wrong turning in France and discover a country you never knew existed. Find a beach in Greece with two people on it and walk to the next one because you don't like crowds. Examples abound and some are in this book. To miscoin a phrase, it is undeniable that all tourism corrupts and mass tourism corrupts absolutely.

The most eloquent condemnation of mass tourism can be found in Patrick Leigh Fermor's famous book, *Roumeli* (Penguin Books). As it is too long to quote and would take away from people the thrilling pleasure of reading one of the most beautiful travel books ever written, I won't do it.

Yet, Patrick Leigh Fermor is too wise to utterly squash what one might call the suntan-lotion-syndrome and he admits that this would be both unfair and impractical. No one has a god-given social right to deny other people their stupidities. So, they say, the world is being spoiled. Fortunately, the 'spoilers' have hardly begun. Indonesia for instance has over 11,000 islands but everybody goes to Bali. The rest of that wonderful country fortunately belongs to the Indonesians and to those of us who pass through, wonder and march on.

This book has two parts. The first is practical and tells you what you can and cannot do, where to go for help and information, how to cut corners, how to assemble the holiday of your choice as you would piece together a jigsaw puzzle and, above all, how not to take no for an answer. In so doing, and not without some acrimony, it explains the role played by the various working parts of the travel industry. The second part of the book is strictly motivational. It tells you why you should go to this or that country or area, who will like it and looks at some more unusual areas to visit that are seldom featured in holiday brochures.

It hints at a number of ways you can avoid the grasping fingers of commercialism – some commercialism is useful but too much of it is too much. Speaking for myself, I was completely put off by a very nice area of Papua New Guinea when I discovered that the famous local carvers now go to evening classes to learn how to make things suitcase-size, so that tourists could take them home effortlessly. This book will also tell you how to avoid the poisonous nostalgia of songs, books and plays. Do you really want to 'come back to Sorrento'? And are you desperate to go and look for Gauguin in Tahiti?

I do not know what the results of *A Guide for the Independent Traveller* will be. Naturally, I hope that lots of people will buy it and enjoy it. I already know that the 'commercial establishment' of the travel industry will hate it and blame me for letting the side down. No matter, why should we not tell the truth?

PART ONE

1 Choosing the Holiday

WHAT IS INDEPENDENT TRAVEL?

These days, the trouble with travel is travel agents, and tour operators (some of them). And airlines and hotels (also some of the time). And the countless people who stand between you and the world you want to see. It is not that they wish you ill but simply that they are convinced that they know what you want. This they cannot do because you are you, an individual with individual tastes, a person with a particular background and certain wishes – even if you are not always able to transform them into practicalities.

For some vague reason, you think that you might like to go to Outer Mongolia but your sense of what is possible tells you that Outer Mongolia is sure to be off limits, too far, too inaccessible. So you stop dreaming and that is basically your first mistake. Perhaps you should go somewhere nearer – southern Italy perhaps? The man who sells travel says to you: 'You don't want to go there, nobody ever does. There is nothing in southern Italy. Why don't you go to Rimini instead? I can fix it for you in a jiffy.'

Speaking for myself, and notwithstanding the fact that Rimini can be perfectly nice in certain circumstances, I have no more intention of going to Rimini than of flying to the moon. Yet the man who is supposed to be an expert tells me that I should. This is where the dream gets sold short and, let us face it: all travel is a dream, a kind of make-believe world in which, free of all fetters and restrictions, you float about between departure and arrival in a state of perpetual euphoria. Travel is what you imagine, what you would like, what tempts you. And you can perfectly well have it, providing you believe in your own instinct and cross the street away from the man who is trying to sell you something.

I have travelled far and wide and for a long time. As the song of the American marines goes: 'I have gone from the shores of Tripoli (that was long before Colonel Gadaffi) to the Halls of Montezuma' and, with my hand on my heart, I can say that I have usually been disappointed by the places to which I was taken and almost always exhilarated by the great and wonderful people and the fantastic sights I came across when I just followed my instincts.

Part of the engaging contrariness of human nature is that people never remember the generality of the bad but almost always recall the particularity of the good. They may pass comments on, say, Greece, or Spain, but they only become really poetic when they recall one incident, one unplanned episode. It may be the time when, having lost their way in Crete, they asked a mountain shepherd for directions, sat atop a stone wall, ended up sharing his lunch of country bread and Feta cheese, contributed an apple and a swig of wine and spent the rest of the afternoon recounting the days of the Cretan resistance in broken Greek and fractured English.

Or it could be the Sunday morning when they drove into some unknown Spanish village and discovered that it was the day of the annual *festa* when the statue of the local saint was being carried from and to the church and after which the whole village sat down to a gigantic, well nigh endless paella at long tables in the square. They were introduced to the mayor, the padre, the bride and groom to be, the oldest inhabitant and, by 7 p.m., they had become experts at drinking strong red wine from a skin. This, people remember. They may forget how they got there, or how someone had actually told them to go somewhere else but the particular incident remains for ever and often completely takes over their recollection of one country.

My own memories, thank goodness, are not made up of airports, or Concorde flights, nice as they are, or round-the-world tours run on rigidly set and adhered to itineraries. They consist of hundreds, possibly thousands, of individual happenings all over the globe, in places near and far, that in the end add up to make a kind of mental library which is quite priceless because only I know where the bird's-eye pictures are. So if I am asked, for instance, what Sicily is like, I will naturally oblige with, I hope, a fairly accurate picture of the great island. Yet, despite my professional training, the first thing that comes into my mind is the day when I lost my way (losing one's way is the greatest way to travel) in the great, parched centre of the island. My gastric juices told me that it was about time for lunch. But where? I passed a fairly large trattoria at the bottom of a field near the road and my mind registered the fact that there were no cars parked there although I should have looked at the back to see the two coaches that had come to rest in the shade.

I walked into a place that looked like a disused cinema,

with dummy bottles of the local wine hanging from ropes, last year's calendars on the walls, with pictures of the Pope of course, and roughly 200 people sitting down at long tables, eating and staring at me with disbelief. A waiter came up and I asked him if the place was open. He shuffled his feet the way Sicilians do so well, gestured at the throng and said, 'Naturalmente, it is Giuseppe's wedding'.

He gave me a small table near the door and, gingerly, I ordered my meal. Within a few minutes, a young man in his Sunday best approached me and asked who I was. A tourist from England. 'Ah,' he said, 'We love all tourists, but they never come here.' I almost felt like apologising for being there myself. He whisked me up the long room and gave me a seat at the end of the top table, clinked his glass and announced to everyone: '*Un turista dall' Inghilterra*'. A long sigh of disbelief passed through the crowd and everybody shouted '*Benvenuto*'. I tucked into the wedding fare and shook I don't know how many horny hands. By four o'clock, I knew the names of every brother and sister, uncle and aunt in the family. By five, I had toasted bride and bridegroom about 13 times – the exact count escapes me. By six, Giuseppe and his Marina had disappeared towards their life of bliss and I had made various attempts at leaving.

That, however, was not on the agenda. Where would I be going at this time? I explained that I had vaguely intended to spend the night in Caltanissetta. My neighbour threw his hands in the air. Caltanissetta? Mama mia, didn't I know that they were all thieves up there? They'd steal my watch off my wrist for sure. I would be much better staying there. The trattoria could give me a room. Later, after making a speech of thanks in Italian (to my eternal shame), I was conducted to a bedroom that smelled of crisp, linen sheets, wax polish and rosemary. The full moon shone outside the windows and the night breeze turned the leaves of the olive trees from green to shivering silver. Sicily? That's the Sicily I remember, or at least one of them.

So it is mostly people that make you remember places. Take the Caribbean. Everybody who has been to those blessed isles has a different memory. Some may be of cool daiquiris on hot beaches, or the steel bands or the sheer perfection of some top-class beach hotel. I have those memories too – wrapped up in affection and tied with strings of blue and gold. How come, then, that almost every island brings back to my mind someone I met? Take St Kitts – hardly among the Barbadoses of this world – an island not overly blessed with travel agents' adjectives. Yet, when I remember the Caribbean, and St Kitts in particular, I recall one day walking into a local boarding house in a small town for a meal. Plastic birds climbed up the walls, plastic covers hugged the chairs and plastic covered the long dining table too, which was littered with bottles of indigestible sauces and condiments and looked rather like jetsam on the beach.

Before long, another customer walked in, a huge black man with a great grin and arms like tree trunks. He sat at the other end of the table and for a while we said nothing. But one of the hardest things in the world is to say nothing when there are only two of you in the room.

So, eventually, we passed comments on the weather, which was hot, and on politicians, who should repair the roads. Out of politeness I asked him what he did for a living. He told me that he was a commercial traveller. I said it sounded interesting. What was he travelling in? His smile stretched from ear to ear and he replied: 'Ah sells false teeth.' I remarked that his visits must be short since there were not many dentists in these parts. He said no, he did not sell to dentists but to ordinary folk. Totally nonplussed, I put down my knife and fork and said: 'But surely, you can't do that! After all, people's mouths are different.' He said yes, of course they were. 'But I go into them villages and when I sees a man who needs my help I ram in the false teeth.' And, opening a large black Gladstone bag at his feet, he showed me that it was indeed full of false teeth, big ones, little ones, all grinning up at me. But, I asked, what happens if the customer has one tooth that gets in the way? He laughed. 'Easy' he said, 'I just knocks it out!' Now, this was many years ago but to this day, whenever someone mentions St Kitts to me, the first thing I remember is the false teeth man with the Gladstone bag.

Travel could be described as a landscape with people. The landscape is there, all the time, a kind of huge Cinerama reel which unfolds as one's memory reaches back and this constant film show, for the real traveller, is what makes travel. I don't care how technical people become about the Himalayas. For me, they will always be as I saw them on my first trip on the little train to Simla – like a series of gigantic ice cream cones reaching up into the sky. I remember the Temple of Apollo at Bassae in Greece's Peloponnese not for what it represents, architecturally and historically (I have learned about that since), but because of the picture it drew in my mind the first time I saw it just as a Greek shepherd led his flock of sheep through the noble ruins. It was like a Virgilian ode come to life.

Many people I know believe that a beach is a beach is a beach. I think they should stay at home and contemplate their back garden. Beaches are infinitely different, providing a rhapsody of moods. I realised this when I first went to Bermuda and noticed that the beaches were indeed pink. How odd. I sat down and began enumerating all the beach colours I could remember, which ranged from white to champagne to hot chocolate to the jet black of powderised lava. It was when I came to the types of sand that I lost count. As for the shape of beaches, each one is totally different, open to new interpretations, individually shaped by nature for the enjoyment of man. The quality of the pedalos and the alcoholic contents of the Planter's Punch are afterthoughts. Although these too can be nice.

Great vistas are also opinion-forming and memory-making. Years ago, driving south from Naples, I turned off into the rarely-visited region of the Cilento. Then, near a place called Torre Orsaia, I suddenly slammed on the brakes. High up over the Gulf of Policastro, the whole of Calabria lay before me giving a view to which no travel poster could possibly do justice. Cascades of great greenish-mauve mountains rushed down into the deep blue of the Tyrrhenian Sea as far as the eye could see. I stayed there for an hour, moved by the beauty of the world. The travel agent, of course, says that there is nothing worth while in southern Italy. I can tell him that I would not have missed my roadside stop for all the reductions and starred attractions in his many brochures.

RULES OF THE GAME

The first rules of the game for the independent traveller are simple. Leave your prejudices behind and go with a fresh mind even if you are a little frightened, like a small child going to school for the first time. The second rule, which is easy, is this: know what you want – even if you don't quite know what it is and once your decision is made, whether it is for a trip around the world or a fortnight in the Mediterranean, let no one, repeat no one, put you off. It is your life, your time, your money. All that the travel professional can really do is to offer you advice and, if he is in business, present you with a choice of opportunities. You should be so lucky.

With apologies to that well-loved magazine, the *Reader's Digest*, I am sorry if what follows sounds a bit like those footnotes you read in it so often. Yes, it is perfectly true that the beginning of wisdom for the independent traveller lies in his knowing himself and what it is he wishes to do with his leisure life. It is always a matter of surprise to me how many people don't. They may express a wish to see great cathedrals when in fact all they want to do is to have a beach for a fortnight of relaxation. There is nothing wrong with either but one should label the first piece of that jigsaw as 'self searching'. Do you want to tour Europe looking for Romanesque churches? Or do you really care only for convivial evenings in happy bars? Do crowds of holiday-makers upset you or do you prefer togetherness to alone-ness? Are you hooked on antiquity or does the thought of Egypt's 23rd Dynasty send you rushing for cover? Do you want to see or be seen? What is your boredom threshold when it comes to the countryside? When it comes to this particular holiday, do you see it as the fulfilment of a long-cherished personal dream, or do you just want to be left alone for two weeks?

This first bit of self-analysis is vital for the would-be independent traveller. It means the difference between success and failure. After all, if you don't know what you want, how can you possibly hope to find it? Be honest with yourself and, remember, it is your time and your money. Face up to the question: What makes you happy? The happiness of your spouse/companion is also vital. This is not just because you are unselfish but because you are selfish! There is nothing worse than spending your leisure time coping with complaints or arguments.

If you like to be exact and pedantic about it, label several pieces of the jigsaw puzzle with different notions and ideas, shuffle them together and see how they fit. Some of the time, several of the pieces will fit perfectly well together. If so, you are lucky. On the whole, it is expensive and time-consuming to search for the one holiday that will fulfil all expectations. It is really too much to ask. It is much better to adhere to some of the conditions and be happy with the result than to ask for the lot and get little.

GENERAL GEOGRAPHY

So, now one presumes that with the help of your jigsaw pieces you have arrived at some vague decision on the type of holiday/travel you are looking for. That, believe me, is a good part of the battle. You know roughly what you want but do you know where it is? Much will be said later about the crucial need for information but let us for the moment concentrate on what one might call 'general geography'. Most lay people are very bad at this. A great friend of mine persists in thinking that Australia is somewhere in the Far East, which is a logistical error that brings me out in goose pimples. When I point out to him that it is about as far from Hong Kong to Sydney as it is from London to the Persian Gulf, he smiles and says 'Yes, but it's all in the same part of the world, isn't it?' I am sorry but it is not. In my early travelling days, I was as guilty of this as everyone else. I once went to Sydney thinking that, since I was there, I might as well hop over to Tahiti. I was extremely embarrassed when I discovered that it (then) took seven hours to fly to Papeete. It happened several times. Once, in Brazil, I decided that since I was in Rio de Janeiro, I might usefully combine it with a side trip to the Amazon. Some side trip. It took me five hours to fly to Manaus, which is even in the same country.

One friend to whom I praised the delights of Salamanca, said to me: 'When we are in Seville, my wife and I will certainly drive there for the day.' I wished them luck. Another friend persisted in combining Spain and Morocco in his mind. They were next door to each other, weren't they? Yes, but they might just as well be on a different planet. Sailors are good at distances. So are airline pilots. But the vast majority of the general public are first-class duffers. So when they tell you that the world is getting smaller all the time, take it with a pinch of salt. Happily, it is still very large indeed.

LOGISTICS

Another thing that is difficult to grasp is what might be called travel logistics or, if you like, how does one get from here to there. People persistently tell me that they are going to do the Caribbean and when I ask them where, exactly, it is that they are going, the answer is usually the same: 'Oh, we'll hop from island to island, you know.' Can it be done? Of course, it can – barring government changes, airline schedule alterations, the weather, airport repairs, the charming vagaries of the West Indian mind, luggage going astray and a few other things. And if the travel agent who fixed up your ticket while reading last year's timetable is in London, it is no good raving at him from Point-à-Pitre. He won't hear you and neither will the girl behind the airline desk.

These general geographical and logistical items must also be taken into consideration when piecing together your jigsaw puzzle. But don't let that put you off travelling, or indeed being a true independent traveller. Just make sure, that's all. Make a practice of never believing anyone totally and of reading an air ticket as if it had been torn out of the Bible. Ask and ask again. Confirm and confirm again.

Always, but always, find out the name of the man who directed you, or misdirected you, in the first place. Make sure you have a point of reference.

THE SORRENTO SYNDROME

One of the other general pieces of the jigsaw has to do with what one might call 'folk memory' or the Sorrento syndrome and that is the business of places which have figured in famous songs, books and so on. Yes, Somerset Maugham did write about this country a long time ago. Has it changed? You can bet your last Singapore dollar that it has, so don't expect things to always remain the same — just for you. Equally, Robert Louis Stevenson lived in Samoa and Gauguin in Tahiti. They died there too, rather a long time ago. Wilfred Thesiger did cross the Arabian peninsula though today he might have to step around the parking lots and the oil pipelines. Generally, I would say that if your terms of reference are less than five years old, you are probably safe, though please don't quote me. If they are ten years old, they are probably dodgy and things won't be the same. But if you are intending to follow the footsteps of Lady Hester Stanhope to Palmyra, I would certainly urge you to do so, as long as you don't forget the generations of Kilroys in between.

One good way of determining how much a certain country or place has changed is to try and remember how your own country has changed. When Robert Louis Stevenson wrote about the Cévennes, for instance, hansom cabs and gaslight still flourished in London. What possible cause could one have for thinking that the other man's country has not changed in the same way? That is not a reason, however, for not going.

It is a reason for being cautious about your dream, lest it should shatter into a thousand fragments. If you think of your holiday aim as being one-third dream and two-thirds possibility you will not be far wrong. The world has changed — while you were not looking.

HOW LONG?

The next two pieces of the jigsaw puzzle concern time and money, which are valuable commodities. To this day, I am amazed at the number of presumably competent travel agents who tell me that if I book through them, I can see the Far East in 17 days from door to door, or go for a week's safari in East Africa. I know from experience that this is just poppycock. I know lots of people who have 'done' India in two weeks. Have they really? Or have they just had time to write a few 'wish-you-were-here' postcards home? I once asked a very wise old traveller how he liked to travel, and he replied, 'Slowly'.

Of course, it all depends on the kind of traveller you are. If all you want to get out of your holiday, apart from relaxation, is a quick reconnaissance, a surface impression, then a comparatively short time might be useful and appropriate. If you are looking for more, give yourself, and your destination, a real chance. Don't cut corners on the calendar or your diary. However much time a trip might be deemed to take while sitting at home and planning it, I have found it very useful in the past to add one-third or one-half more time, which may sound a lot but, believe me, it is not. I know only too well the problems that can arise, the things that can go wrong, the places you just wish you had had more time to see. Just as one should not be too mean with a budget, one should not scrimp and save on time. To enjoy your holiday fully, this is a false economy. If you don't have the time, do something else.

HOW MUCH?

Which, of course, brings us to the subject of money. How much is your holiday going to cost? Frankly, I don't know and I think it would be very foolish of me to make guesses since so much depends on your life style, your habits, your eating and drinking, your standards when it comes to hotels and comfort. Travel is not cheap (can anything that is worth while be called cheap these days?), but it is cheaper than you think.

Throughout its pages *A Guide for the Independent Traveller* will save you money and if you are prepared to follow the rules and do the fixing yourself, this is one thing, after many years, that I can actually guarantee. By fitting the bits of the jigsaw puzzle together, you will save money. How much? A good guess would be between 10 and 20 per cent of the tour operator's charge.

However, while this is important (if only because it will allow you to do more), it is not the whole point of this book. That, in the end, comes down to self-satisfaction, the certainty that by doing it yourself you will have travel and holiday opportunities not given to millions. Once, some years ago, I was lucky enough to be a fly on the wall at a meeting between the owner of a new hotel in Greece and the British travel agent who had just blockbooked one-third of his rooms. Quite naturally, the hotel owner was anxious to please the man who had brought him this lucrative business and he asked the travel agent many questions. One was about food. What kind of food would the travel agent's package customers like? The visitor looked at the Greek as if this was a totally superfluous question. 'Meat and two veg,' he said. I am glad to say that this is the very thing this book is not about.

2 Pieces of the Jigsaw

THE TRAVEL INDUSTRY

In the mind of the public, the two most visible parts of what is generally known as the travel industry are the travel agent and the tour operator, though the distinction is somewhat unclear. The tour operator initiates, organises and promotes a package holiday. The travel agent is essentially the retailer who sells his big brother's product in the high street.

Although there are exceptions, for example, tour operators who sell directly to the public, both sides of the industry are seen to be exceedingly polite to each other. Each maintains the most elaborate pretence of being indispensable to its partner and, of course, what is 'good for one is good for all' – always provided one is speaking of the industry side, not necessarily the members of the public. Privately, however, tour operators will readily suggest that travel agents are inefficient and ill-informed, both of which are sometimes true. The travel agent lives in constant fear of the operator's size and power and, like a half-tamed bird, is always screechingly pleading for more crumbs from the rich man's table. The tour operator complains that the travel agent is not selling his product well enough while the travel agent is certain that big brother is not giving him the means to do better.

Strange as it may seem in a world ruled by such disparate partners, both sleep between the same sheets and hide their multifarious misdeeds well away from the public eye. Fronting for both sides of the industry is one association – the Association of British Travel Agents, better known as ABTA. As is common in a world of big business riddled with cant and hypocrisy, ABTA is a fully paid-up member of the brotherhood of the soft sell. It is incredibly expert at passing itself off for what it is not.

By and large, ABTA claims to represent the whole of British travel abroad, which clearly it does not since 54 per cent of the 15 million Britons who go overseas on holiday every year never go near a tour operator and the number of non-buyers is growing – would-be customers are voting with their feet. As the self-appointed voice of British travel abroad, ABTA makes pronouncements accordingly. The uninformed media, taking their cue from a well-oiled propaganda machine, repeatedly headline the fact that, 'More Britons holiday abroad — ABTA' or 'British holidaymakers may get left out in the cold', that is if they don't go and book quickly (with an ABTA member).

But the role which ABTA most loves playing, though it never says so officially, is that of the benevolent uncle who always has the public's good at heart, which of course is totally untrue. ABTA is a pressure group, an out-and-out trade association whose sole responsibility is to look after the welfare of its members and these do not include you or me. ABTA is not in the business of consumerism. It does little or nothing to improve the quality of the travel product. It does not make any attempt to 'educate' either the seller or the buyer. It does not, in public, ever describe the alternatives to organised travel and certainly it never mentions the millions of people who wisely shun the services of its members.

Well aware of the fact that its avuncular mask must not be seen to slip, ABTA occasionally makes some effort to put its house in order. For example, it has tried to discipline its more wayward members by imposing a so-called code of conduct, a scheme which is as likely to succeed as attempting to clear the African jungle with a penknife or to turn cannibals into vegetarians. ABTA, very self consciously, declares its intention to make travel safe for all travel buyers and, if a member fails to honour his commitments to his clients, ABTA will foot the bill and quietly hush it all up — rather like saying that you will be safe from potential murderers if you walk down the middle of the street.

There is, of course, nothing intrinsically wrong with all this. Every trade has its own 'Protect old Joe' mafia. Supermarket owners protect other supermarket owners except when it is expedient to pounce at dead of night. Likewise, they will promote their 'own-brand' image to make you, the customer, feel that it is not only cheaper but better, without ever offering comparison tests or mentioning the fact that 100 small producers or manufacturers may have been put out of business while offerings were being made to the gods of gigantism. Anyone living in today's mass-oriented society does so at the peril of his own life style and if he is too weak or uncertain of his ground to oppose the trend, he is likely to forget the meaning of the word quality. And that certainly applies to the travel buyer of today.

ABTA's members naturally have a common sense reply to all this — at least it sounds like common sense. They say, 'If the travel buyer did not like our product, he would not buy it.' That is true. But, one might answer: 'Who is there who can tell him that there is a choice?' This is where *A Guide for the Independent Traveller* and travel writers and journalists, without their hand in the till, come in. If they like travel, if they know it and if they wish to share their knowledge with others, it is their duty to do so. Some do.

This being said, I would not like the readers to fasten on to the idea that I feel all organised travel is evil, or ill-meant, or bad value. Such is not the case. Over the last quarter of a century travel agents and tour operators, as well as airlines and hotels, have made it possible for hitherto untravelled millions to see something of the world. One simply feels, as indeed do millions of non-package buyers, that there are other aspects to travel beside two weeks in Torremolinos.

The following destinations were, for the record, the ten most popular with British tourists in 1984: Spain (nearly 4 million); France (almost the same); Italy (843,000); Greece (816,000); Portugal (503,000); Belgium/Luxembourg (486,000); Austria (434,000); Ireland (419,000); West Germany (397,000); and Gibraltar/Malta/Cyprus (379,000). The United States came twelfth and Switzerland took the thirteenth place. The top exotic destinations for British visitors were, in order: Thailand, Barbados, Kenya, Hong Kong, St Lucia, Antigua, India, Sri Lanka, Bali and Egypt.

If one blindly followed the philosophy behind this book, it could be said that these are reasons for not going to these countries. However, nothing could be further from the truth. 'Tourism pollution' depends on a huge variety of factors including: the time of year, the type of tourists, the facilities available and, above all, the small or large number of places to which the tour operator tries to lead you. In my own mind, not one of the above countries could truly be called 'tourist polluted' but each one has areas where there are really rather too many visitors and this is explained in the chapters devoted to the various countries. Do not despair.

TRAVEL AGENTS

To return to the component parts of the travel industry, let us take retail travel agents first. There are about 5000 in Britain and their historical pedigree is impeccable. The country's and the world's first travel agent was that pillar of the Midlands' Temperance Movement, Thomas Cook, who in 1841 took the world's first package tour on a rail day trip from Market Harborough to Leicester. Within a few years, Thomas Cook's empire had reached London, where he set up shop in Ludgate Circus, and had stretched to Rome and Venice, Paris and Vienna. He was the first to send off clients to the Egyptian pyramids, much to the annoyance of the British living there who had not known tourists before, the first up the Nile, and the first to South Africa.

What is indeed fascinating when reading Thomas Cook's story is how he never dared to organise his clients' leisure time. He was an agent which meant that he would advise them on the best way of travelling from A to B, book their rail ticket or steamship ticket and make sure they were met on arrival by a Thomas Cook agent who would look after their needs while on the spot. Cook never attempted to tell local entrepreneurs how to build their hotels. If he thought of booking clients into, say, the Old Winter Palace Hotel in Luxor, Mr Cook would march in, inspect the place from kitchens to bedrooms and say, yes, it would do. Thomas Cook was a friend and counsellor, a knowing hand, a man who could tell you how to avoid Egyptian baksheesh seekers or Indian rope trick illusionists. He cared for you.

One has the distinct feeling that if Thomas Cook came back to this life, he would be totally appalled by the travel agent of today. Thomas Cook would find that Britain's travel agents are now among the worst in the world, displaying a frightening lack of understanding of the public's needs and an almost total ignorance of the world. He, who knew the departure and arrival time of the Rajputana Express and even the kind of carriage to ask for, would find the inexperience of today's high street travel agent nothing but deplorable.

Where is the friend and counsellor of yesteryear? The travel agent of today – for the most part – has become a paper shuffler and computer key-pusher. His only value to you, the travel buyer, is that he is on your doorstep and it is only too easy to believe that he knows more about travel than you do. This is not so. He does not know how to serve his client and is interested only in displaying the tour operators' gaudy brochures on his shelves so that he can sell you a holiday that he has not sampled and collect the ten per cent commission, which the tour operator will pay him or indeed the nine per cent he receives for selling you an airline ticket. He pleads poverty and, admittedly, he is not overly paid for his labours, which might be fine in the case of a straightforward transaction but not so good if an inquiry demands a score of telephone calls, staff time, the setting up of a customer file and a lot of research. Without wishing to be hard on a particular set of people, most travel agents know next to nothing when it comes to advising you about a country or a resort.

When arranging my own travel, and for the sake of professional curiosity, I often call in, incognito, to consult one of my local travel agents before setting forth and not long ago I did so to inform the principal that I half intended to spend a holiday in Israel. What did he think? He advised: 'I wouldn't if I were you, there is a war going on there and people shoot at each other all the time.' 'You don't say,' I replied. 'Fancy that.' The next evening I recounted the incident to the Israeli Director of Tourism in Jerusalem. The poor man nearly had a coronary on the spot. 'My god,' he said, 'when I think of the money we spend and effort we make trying to educate these people.'

Travel agents are also at the mercy of their counter clerks, who are as badly paid as they are ill-informed. Their sense of geography is deplorable and their general knowledge abysmal. While researching this book, I was given the following gems of information by the counter clerks of travel agents in the home counties:

'If you know Italian, there is no language problem in Greece.' (Tell that to the Greeks.)

'Yes, it is a good idea to take a raincoat to Eilat.' (It will never get wet.)

'The best time to visit Bangkok is between May and September.' (It is not for that is the rainy season.)

'Phoenix is not far from Chicago.' (I would not like to walk it.)

'Cancún? Ah yes, a nice little Mexican town.' (It's the brassiest, jazziest resort in the country.)

'This airline is by far the best for this destination.' (Not true – it just gives counter clerks a nice little incentive gift at Christmas.)

The one I treasure most of all, however, is as follows: 'It's quite easy to travel from Naples to Tunisia – the train services are excellent. I can send you a timetable if you like.' (I'm still waiting.)

So, as an independent traveller, what can the ordinary travel agent do for you? Not much I am afraid. But he can come in useful provided you already know just what you want when you go and see him and not let him dictate to you. Say, for instance, that you wish to book an airline ticket from San Francisco to Tokyo and then back to London via a certain route (and for this you may wish to read Chapter Three first), walk into your travel agent and ask him, 'Will you please do this' and leave it at that. Nothing more. He will love you for being so positive and helping him to earn a commission with so little work. What it will save you is mainly the footwork and the telephoning to airlines which you might have to do otherwise. The travel agent in this case is a travel agent: he gets you there, even if you have to tell him how you wish to travel.

There are two small silver linings on your horizon with the travel agent. The first is that you should go for size since the large, multiple travel agents are improving all the time. They have more resources, are more with it and can help. They include: Thomas Cook, Pickfords and Hogg Robinson. If your local branch does not have the information you want, insist that they find it, thus making them work for their living. This is especially true in the case of Thomas Cook who sell their own holidays as well as other people's.

The second silver lining is the slow and rather haphazard growth of local travel agents who at least are trying to reverse the trend and go for the particular rather than the pre-digested. They are in fact 'travel counsellors' and already exist in the United States and especially in West Germany. A few of these are beginning to set up in Britain and they are worth patronising. Since no one can truly be a world travel expert, these few pioneers – the emphasis being on the 'few' – tend to be specialists in one area of the world or the other. Mark Allan Travel Ltd are experts on the United States, mostly the western side, and there is little they don't know about the Rockies, dude ranches and great spreads in Arizona or California. If you are going to the Far East, which is a vast and often difficult area, try the one and only Far East Travel Centre Ltd. All their clients are private clients, each one has a proper file and is well looked after. Although they also have straight 'packages' should you wish to buy one, they tailor-make travel to fit the needs of the individual.

Very much to be welcomed is the appearance on the scene of many smaller, more individual travel agents who take better care of their private customers. The trouble is they are hard to find, except by experience. I would recommend such outwardly 'small' people as Sole Bay Travel and Sheringham Travel. Both companies specialise in organising – if that is the word – the kind of travel you want. They sell 'packages' too, of course, but ask them for something different and watch them go to it! Addresses of all the travel agents mentioned can be found on page 212.

Needless to say, such people do not work for nothing. Although they will claim that they are not charging any more, except for the commission they receive from the other end, you don't have to believe it. Your travel arrangements, when they reach you, may cost you more but at least you will have had the satisfaction of dealing with an organisation that knows what it is doing. Another thing, of course, is that to date all these 'travel advisers' concentrate on the 'up-market' in which each client has more to spend. So, I'm afraid, back-packers need not apply.

TOUR OPERATORS

It is when one comes to the second 'moving' part of the travel industry, the tour operators, that one has even less good news. Are there any good tour operators? Well yes, there are some, if you look long and hard and again, inevitably, in the more moneyed, further afield sector. Some tour operators, like Bales Tours, have over the years, built up a fine reputation for sending people up the rivers of Borneo or to the far ends of China without losing any. They specialise in long-haul adventure holidays, which can be enjoyed by people who are not especially adventurous. They cover the world but are best for southern Asia and the south-western Pacific. Old-established companies like Abercrombie & Kent Ltd whose original stamping ground was safari-land in East Africa are now expanding, geographically, into other areas and they too can offer a package that is easily digestible. Smaller, more off-beat but highly intelligent, are the culturally-minded people of Serenissima Travel Ltd who regularly send nicely-balanced, organised parties into some of the more interesting or more remote parts of the world.

Much to be admired is the enterprise of Roland Castro's Time Off company. Mr Castro has wisely specialised and in 1985 one magazine voted him 'the Best Short-Haul Operator'. He concentrates on European cities and now covers 13, from Amsterdam to Zurich and from Geneva to Paris. The company's very expert guides will plan it all out for you and, should you require the service, take you there too. They will also leave you strictly alone if that is what you want.

Most 'intelligent' tour operators have long ago learned that they could only be really good in one, or at most two, countries. Typical of these is The Best of Greece, who have lately marched into Morocco too. Because of costs they do not like dealing with 'oddballs' who want to do their own thing but their brochures offer a steady and good variety of what is best in the countries they cover. Their reputation is high. Again, addresses for all these tour operators can be found on page 212.

And what does one do with the other 99 per cent of tour operators? The ones who offer you eternal sunshine and blue skies, golden beaches (even if they are behind the railway yard) and Spanish dancing imported from Birmingham every Wednesday night? My suggestion is that if you wish to play the independent traveller game, you must avoid them like the proverbial Black Death and walk away. They have nothing for you. By all means, look at their brochures, if possible in semi-darkness and in a private place, just to make sure of the type of holiday you don't want to buy. If they go one way, go in the other direction and you can't be far wrong. By his very nature the tour operator, especially the mass-oriented one, is the fellow who can make the seven wonders of the world look like so many bottles of ketchup.

Not long ago that august body, the Economist Intelligence Unit, took a look at the travel scene and concluded: 'There is now a more demanding tourist. There is a change in the British tourist from being a vacationer to being a traveller. Tourists increasingly look to their holiday to fulfil more than a relaxing time on the beach. Increasing numbers of people expect their holiday to enrich and exhilarate; the consumer wants to learn, to seek adventure and excitement and he wants something designed to his specifications, rather than something taken from the supermarket shelves. There is a growing trend for the more affluent to demand custom-built holidays ... there will be a growth in special interest and activity holidays, self-catering, basic accommodation only, fly drive and flight only arrangements.' This is my gut feeling too.

The nature of the tour operator's business is, contrary to expectations, not to open new windows on the world. It is to make the same window bigger so that he can shoehorn more people into the same place. Looking through brochures year after year and, let it be said, with a few happy exceptions, I am amazed at the lack of inventiveness and enterprise of tour operators. There is hardly ever anything new.

In fact, I should not be surprised. Like most businesses, the tour operators' main preoccupation is to get the maximum return out of the minimum risk. Promoting a new destination is troublesome, costly and not always a good bet. Is there a good air gateway? Are the fares right? Can the hotels be trusted? Will people actually go? If the answer is mixed, the whole thing goes into the file marked 'sometime/never' and consigned to oblivion. Then the tour operator turns to his marketing man and says: 'Last year we sold 2000 holidays to such and such a place. If we could increase that number by one-fifth, our costs would go down and our profits would be up with comparatively little effort. Let's go for it.'

Like the supermarket chain selling breakfast cereals, the operator first of all limits the choice. Then he increases the size of the packet to make you feel that it is good value and then, when you are hooked, the price goes up. Like a sheep, he follows his neighbour for if so and so goes there, so must he because the other one's made a success of it. Instead of initiating, he imitates and, in so doing, he forces the unwary and the uncritical into thinking that this is all there is to travel. You want to go to Sicily? He packs you off to Taormina. Very nice too. 'And every day,' he says in his brochure, 'you will wake up, open your window and gaze at Mount Etna.' Don't look around though because every other tourist in the place is doing exactly the same thing – gazing at Mount Etna.

Has your tour operator never heard of Monreale or Segesta or the luscious beaches of the south coast? No, he has not. If you insist that this is what you wish to see, he might, just might, organise a day trip at so much, including the packed lunch of a cold chicken leg and a hard-boiled egg. Going to Spain with a tour operator is like leaving the fruit and being content with the peel. If it is the fruit you want you are considered odd, or bizarre. I mean, after all, who on earth could possibly want to go to Salamanca, or Mérida? The result is that no tour operator I know offers a comprehensive kind of Spanish travel. We know the problems about southern Italy. The same can be carbon-copied in Tunisia or Morocco, Egypt, the Middle East and indeed further afield. Looking at tour operators' brochures, or 99 per cent of them, one is convinced that there are only two places worth visiting in that beautiful country of Thailand-Bangkok, namely the floating market which stopped floating because of traffic jams and the beach resort of Pattaya, which someone once described to me as the place where every tourist goes with two things, a spare shirt and a ten-dollar bill and does not change either while he is there. Is this really Thailand? I am happy to say that it is not.

Take another aspect of the great rip-off. Sooner or later the tour operator is going to tell you an untruth or worse. You have once been to the Caribbean in January and wonder if there isn't another place like it? The tour operator is at your elbow with a suggestion, the Seychelles. Wonderful. Super. Cheaper too. What he does not tell you is that the seasons are not the same. If you go to the Seychelles in January the rainfall will be about 18 inches (4.6 cm) for the month and you won't be able to leave your room between the down-pours.

Looking at the tour operators' brochures, one could be forgiven for thinking that there are fashions in destinations, that this was all right yesterday but the place to go this year is such and such. Don't believe it because it is all part of a deeply-laid plan by tour operators and national tourist organisations.

Take, for instance, a marvellous, endearing country like Greece. One year, the 'in' place is Chalcidiki, and very good it is too. But it is only 'in' at this particular juncture because this year happens to be the time when the national tourist plans – aided and abetted by the international tour operators – have collaborated to produce a rash of unsightly hotels which must, at all costs, be filled. A few years go by and it is the turn of the north coast of Crete. Having already spoilt Ágios Nikólaos and turned it into a kind of Cretan St Tropez, the blight of mass tourism has now crept along virtually the whole coast. Years ago, by taking the wrong turn on purpose, I discovered a little place called Agia Pelagía, not far from Heraklion. For a few years it was heaven. You left your car at the edge of the beach, waded through the blond sand to the one and only taverna, had your favourite Greek lunch of *barbouni* and salad and went swimming. Then, one year, after only a short absence, I found that a Greek property developer had given birth to a concrete monster of 300 rooms right where my taverna had been. I turned the car around and went the other way towards Fódele, El Greco's birthplace. For all I know they have now got there too.

The basic problem with the kind of tourism tour operators and national tourism bodies promote has to do with num-bers. Numbers are heaven. Some countries count heads. Others count legs too and everybody says, 'Look how clever we are! We have managed to increase our tourist numbers four fold in four years. It's good for everyone.' I am sorry but in my book it is not. It makes too much of the world alike when it should be different. It does not even benefit the local economy all that much. Since tourism must, by nature, be a money-making operation, I would rather make £10 out of one tourist than the same amount out of ten tourists. What really matters deep down is not the number of tourists but the amount of money left in the till at the end of the year. At least one small Mediterranean country is just beginning to discover that though it has four times as many tourists as it had five years ago, the cash profits are smaller. Will the lesson be learned? I am hoping, against hope, that it will be.

Only a short while ago I stayed for a few days in a five-star hotel in Greece. For once, the hotel itself was fine with good style, fine decor and smiling service. On my first night, I went down to the dining room, which is a mistake I should have learned to avoid by now. It turned out to be the size of an underground station and 80 per cent of it was filled with package tourists. The head waiter, busy and off-hand, asked me which tour I was with. I told him that I was not with any tour. Rather surprised, he led me to a perfectly good table in the empty quarter of the restaurant and handed me the menu. I read the first of the main dishes – Escalope Holstein – and called him back.

'Don't you have any Greek food?' I asked. The surprise nearly knocked him sideways. 'You actually want Greek food?' he asked incredulously. 'I'll go and ask the chef.' The result was the arrival of a *stiffado*, consisting of lovingly casseroled beef cubes, with little onions, herbs, young carrots and country rice. 'Are you sure this is what you want?' the head waiter asked. I assured him that it would do fine. Of course, I had a good dinner and the chef actually came out of the kitchen to say that this was not very good but then his mother made a much better *stiffado* than he did. I told him I would have liked to meet his mother.

One tour operator friend (a good one) told me when he knew that I was writing this book, 'You won't win of course but it is a good idea.' Another man, eminent in the airline field, said to me: 'You are converting people to better travel. The most important thing is to convince the independent traveller that what the tour operator offers is not the only thing he can buy.'

ARE DIY HOLIDAYS CHEAPER?

Take the matter of cost. Most people are convinced that the package holiday is always cheaper than the DIY kind. This is not so. It includes less aggravation but it is not necessarily cheaper. The breakdown of, for instance, a £300 package to Mallorca for two weeks is simple. Ten per cent goes to the retail agent. The package and ticket may cost £70, which leaves £200. Roughly £10 goes to the local agent, and 14 nights at the hotel might cost £140. This leaves the tour operator £50, or one-sixth of the total, to cover the cost of his brochure, his advertising and administration costs and profits. When I hesitatingly suggested to one tour operator that his profit margin might be in the region of 20 per cent, he smiled and replied: 'If this was so I would not be in this business,' implying that I had underestimated his profit margin.

It is my firm belief that 90 per cent of all holidays advertised in a brochure could be made cheaper by the independent traveller if he cared to make a few telephone calls. The tour operator friend quoted above recently travelled to India with his family. He told me: 'I looked at all the brochures and did not like what I saw and so I decided to do it myself. In the end, I saved 50 per cent on the brochure price.' I suggested to him that since he was himself a tour operator he had an initial advantage – he knew how to set about things. 'Nonsense,' he replied, 'any reasonably intelligent person can do it if he cares to make a few telephone calls.' This is where we return to the jigsaw puzzle game. If you approach your leisure travel as comprising many interlocking pieces and take one piece at a time, it becomes easy, and even easier once you know the ropes. For instance, when it comes to hotels (please see Chapter Three) the package traveller will almost certainly get a better deal in the middle price range. The independent traveller will win at the top and bottom of the range.

TIMING

Timing, or as one might put it, the travel season of the year, has a great deal to do with the putative luck of the independent traveller. It is obvious that the mass-oriented hotel man in, say, Marbella or Miami, is not going to welcome an independent inquiry at the height of his season since he is already doing well. Ask him at a less favourable time for him and he will probably welcome you with open arms and state a very attractive price. The same goes for airlines.

Timing, of course, is a matter of your own flexibility. If you can manage not to travel in the high season, the odds are with you. The periods known in the travel trade as 'the shoulder months' are usually very attractive whch, in temperate climes, might be April/May/June or late October/ November. In tropical climates, it is equally important to choose the time just before or just after the so-called high season. The Caribbean is a good case. The islands' 'high season' is from 15 December to 15 March. Book your holiday just a few days before or after and the price might come down by as much as 30 per cent. On a recent trip in February and March to Cyprus, when the average temperature was in the mid-sixties Fahrenheit and the bananas were flourishing, I found prices 50 per cent lower than in summer time and the island was a good 80 per cent empty of tourists. The better-known cases are obvious: as everybody is aware, the time for an old age pensioner to have a holiday in Spain is the winter – he will make it within his DHSS pension. You should take great care about big cities, such as Hong Kong or Singapore, San Francisco or Bombay, that are business centres as well as leisure travel destinations. The reason is simple: no sooner have the tourists departed than the local hotel men are welcoming the business conventions organised long in advance. The timing for the independent traveller is obviously wrong. I recall once arriving in San Francisco when the whole of the marvellous city was filled with a convention of lumberjacks from the American north west and prices were sky high. These good people went home on a Wednesday and on the Thursday morning even the price of the breakfast in my hotel had gone down by a quarter!

So one important part of your jigsaw has to do with the foreknowledge of social or business events. This is quite easy to obtain. Just ask your source of information (see Chapter Three) about the things going on at your destination at the time of your visit.

Another consideration about timing is the weather. Obviously, if your time is limited and you want a hot time on a hot beach at the height of the so-called season, you will lose out. Think about weather carefully. Is the weather of prime importance for the kind of holiday you are looking for? Do you really need a temperature in the nineties Fahrenheit for a touring trip in France, or would the middle sixties and low seventies be equally acceptable? Don't take anyone's word for it. Get down to the nitty gritties. Study isotherms, rainfall figures, and wind directions at a particular time. It can be a fascinating business especially when you discover that at a certain time the temperature in Positano is ten degrees higher than in Naples just a few miles away on the other side of the Sorrento peninsula. Go into the business of what weather experts call micro-climates, that is the subtle but often important differences between, say, Athens and the north coast of Crete or Cairo as against Tel Aviv. A long look at detailed weather maps, which you can get from Stanford's in London (page 212), can be a complete education.

My own bible when it comes to weather is the four-volume British Meteorological Office tables for temperature, precipitation and so on, which cover the last 30-odd years in places as far apart as Aarhus and Zamboanga. Over the years I have rarely found it wrong, though there is always the rogue year, but unfortunately it does not always cover the sort of places you want to travel to and regional differences –

micro-climates – can be substantial. When Cairo shows up at 75°F (24°C) it might be 20 degrees Fahrenheit warmer in Hurghada on the Red Sea coast of the same country. Well-known areas like southern France offer the same challenges for the differences between Provence, east of the Rhone, and the Languedoc, west of the Rhone, are often unsuspected. That lovely Dordogne area can be wetter than England and other places like, for instance, the Black Forest in West Germany, are almost always better in mid-autumn than they are in the spring. In Greece I have had January days in the Peloponnese when the temperature went up to 75°F (24°C) at noon while in Thessaloníki, people were wrapped up in heavy coats.

In your jigsaw puzzle, the weather must have one or more pieces all to itself and here I would make a plea for not ignoring what most people would consider unsuitable weather. Some of my finest memories of the Taj Mahal go back to times when I saw it at the height of the Indian monsoon, emerging pale and ghostly from the wet mist like some ethereal dream. I can swear to the fact that the Parthenon, seen on a chance winter morning with patches of blue in the sky and a sharp little Aegean wind blowing the smog off Athens, is infinitely more striking than seeing it covered with Japanese tourists. So yes, try and see famous places at the 'wrong' time of year.

What is more, another piece of the jigsaw might be swapping one famous place that every traveller goes to see for another, less obvious one. Try the Temple of Apollo at Bassae instead of the Parthenon or the Tomb of Itma ad Daulah instead of Fatehpur Sikiri. Could you be your own tour operator? Of course, you could and you have nothing to lose but your inhibitions. It was not always like that. As a nation, the British were the world's first real travellers. Whether they were dandyish lords or penurious art lovers they went everywhere, but everywhere, and there is hardly a part of the world where British footsteps did not go first. Travel memoirs occupy more shelf space in the British Library than those in any other country's national library. An empire founded almost solely on commercial enterprise helped all this. From Chile to Kenya and from the River Plate to the Yangtse, the British worked, grew rich and gained in self confidence and self sufficiency. And still today, statistics show that the British are the world's second most numerous long-distance travellers after the more moneyed Americans.

Nothing stands in your way except reservations about picking up the telephone and making a long-distance call.

Language in this case is unimportant since English is the universal travel language anyway and the reception of a hotel in Khartoum is just as likely as not to answer you in English. Write if you are booking well ahead. Do your homework. Do not go in for the formalised, all-in type of holiday which is the very antithesis of what travel is all about. Obviously, there are things you can do and others which are a little less practical. No matter. Learn what you can accomplish.

The best idea is to buy the right air ticket, book one or two nights in a hotel and then look around for what suits you. You have to be brave sometimes and it may as well be now. Obviously if what you want is Mykonos in August you might have some difficulty in swimming against the trend. But are you sure Mykonos and August are what you want? Would not the end of September be better and somewhere like, say Puerto de Santa Maria, be more attuned to your instinctive needs? Do not follow the herd – ever.

The general tendency is that if you buy a package you tend to stick where you are because, after all, you have paid for everything. For the independent traveller this is instant death. But if you do it the way indicated above, the world is your oyster. Even move localities if you wish. If you go to Skiathos and hate it, it will cost you all of £30 to move on to Crete. People I know even do it with their families and children. They just pack up and move on. Flexibility is absolutely essential. And that goes for local movement too. Millions of people actually never leave their hotel. They are afraid. If only they knew what they are missing around the corner! Car rental, the biggest rip-off in the travel field, is mentioned in Chapter Three and knowing how it works will save you time and money. But, above all, move.

So the message is clear. First, decide on the type of leisure travel you want. Second, get yourself clued up. Third, study each component part at a time. Fourth, go for what you want and don't take no for an answer. Fifth, go after your travel the way you would at home with any transaction – make the best arrangement you can. If you have followed me so far, you are halfway there.

3 Fitting the Pieces Together

AIRLINE TICKETS

Many people outside the travel industry do not realise that an airline seat is about as perishable a commodity as an avocado. Three months ahead of departure, the empty seat is an asset. If it is unsold a week before take-off, it becomes a nagging worry. Once the doors are closed and the aircraft takes off, the unsold seat represents a minus sign on the balance sheet. Once, airlines were run by gentlemen but now that they are run by accountants for the big-time finance boys, this kind of on—off economy won't do at all. One airline friend told me: 'Airlines today are like piranhas that have been given wings. The distant sight of a BOS (Bum on Seat) sends them into a frenzy.'

To its credit, though perhaps rather late in the day, the airline business is one of the few industries that has learned the lessons of poor management, economic tidal waves and lackadaisical marketing. To survive, most airlines have adapted from the lucky (or not so lucky?) few which have a rich government backing them for prestige reasons. Airlines have learned the hard way and if some of the facts of life still elude them this should not detract from their considerable achievements in the past 25 years.

From where the airlines stand, travel is cheap. One can now go to, say, Bangkok, hotel included, for under £500 and going around the world one way or another can be had for under £1000. In America, the land of 'deregulation' ('You charge what you like and if you go bust don't look at us'), they even auction seats five minutes before take off. Because of cartels, so-called gentlemen's agreements etc, European fares are still far too high and credit must surely be given to British Airways and KLM for having at last made a start towards reasonable fares. But, flying is cheap, or at any rate, good value. The cheapest short-haul flight, London to Malaga, is 4.31p a mile and for long haul it is London to Hong Kong at 4.34p and London to New York at 4.33p. While this is going on, London Transport still charges you 8p a mile on the No. 11 bus, down the King's Road.

So far so good. But, my goodness, what travails, what aggravations! Today over 800 million people a year take to the air world wide, 215 million on international flights, but apart from waiting at the departure desk, most can have only an inkling of the tortuous business that has gone on behind the scenes. The tremendous travel explosion of the 1960s was bad enough. Operating and staff costs soared and, just over a decade ago, the oil price increase hit the airlines of the world like a tidal wave. No sooner was this partly absorbed than the cost of equipment went through the roof; it now costs between £120 and £410 million to buy a new Boeing 747 and usually the airline must borrow the money at commercial rates and pay both capital and interest to bankers or governments not known for their sentimentality.

Is all this good or bad for the independent traveller? The answer is a bit of both. Good because there are more opportunities for doing it yourself and bad because the latter has become more difficult. The fares jungle is thicker than ever. *The Airline Passenger Tariff* now has 700 pages and over 2000 separate fares and even experienced airline people agree that one needs a Ph.D. in economics to understand the small print. There are so many discounted fares that you need to be a kind of Hercule Poirot to come to a sensible conclusion and even then you don't always. Recently, I congratulated myself on saving £75 on a ticket to the Middle East. It was only by chance, a few days later, that I found out I could have saved myself yet another £25.

Unfortunately, this is where the travel agent will blind you with science. He thinks he knows the best fare available. He does not necessarily and you should not take what he says for gospel truth for, after all, don't forget that the bigger the fare the bigger is the commission. Airlines don't help much either. As the *Daily Telegraph's Consumer's Guide to Air Travel* (Telegraph Publications) put it recently: 'Airline tickets are reminiscent of doctors' prescriptions. Doctors write them illegibly so that you won't understand them.'

Despite all this it is perfectly possible for the independent traveller to save himself up to 60 per cent on the 'official' fare.

Only a few years ago, unfilled seats on aeroplanes taking off around the world could have accommodated roughly four times the total population of the United Kingdom each year. No business can possibly be run on that basis and international airlines were no exception. On the one side they were caught in the vice-like grip of international agreements administered by IATA, who still thinks that its main job is to protect the weak, and on the other they were faced with dearth of customers, temporary it is true, but nevertheless very upsetting, and the necessity to take Mr A to Amsterdam at a time when he wanted to go and at a price which would make it economical to take him on board.

That was the old bird in the hand and bird in the bush dilemma. How much should the airline allocate to each? Common sense dictated that they should make the most of the bird in the hand, such as tour operators' block bookings, and yet leave some room for the full-fare paying Mr A wanting to go to Amsterdam at two days' notice. Airlines learned some things fast like how to 'flex' the configuration of an airliner so that the number and positions of seats could be quickly altered; nowadays it can be done at any time almost anywhere according to the state of the bookings. The configuration of an airliner going to a purely holiday destination like Faro, for example, could be quite different from one going to Munich or Paris. That purely physical problem was easy enough to solve. Not so easy was the old struggle between maximum profits maybe or quick returns while keeping within the commercial equation.

Every commercial conundrum has its solution. In this case it was provided by what has become known as the 'bucket shop'. Four or five years ago, clever backstreet private entrepreneurs saw the signpost to fortune: if they played their cards right, procured tickets at the right time and sold them on a graduating scale down to panic stations, there could be money in it. There was. Overnight, bucket shop advertising took over entire pages in daily and Sunday newspapers. How much for Malaga on Sunday week? What about Helsinki next Wednesday? Or Sydney the week after? Business grew like wildfire and bucket shop people bought up virtually every air ticket the airline could print. They were quick, adaptable, pushy, sometimes a little fly-by-night, but always ready to oblige. Some stayed open on Sundays and all night too.

So seat occupancy rose as the public realised that it could benefit. Did the airlines benefit too? They didn't at first. Then, on the principle that if you can't beat them you should join them, they began discounting their own seats as gracefully as they could. Every airline had its own General Sales Agent, which is a company expert at dealing with the demand for a certain area. Big airlines had several GSAs, one for each area, and the airlines began feeding unwanted seats into the GSAs' top drawer – unofficially of course. It is against the law for any British airline to sell its seats at less than the advertised price, which no one ever really sees and for good reason, but to date not a single airline has been prosecuted for doing so. Not to be outdone, local retail travel agents got into the act and today it could be said that the only passenger paying the full price for his ticket is the business traveller.

Airlines, agents, whether ABTA members or otherwise, and bucket shops now flourish side by side and no questions are asked. For the independent traveller the benefits of the system are considerable. Below, culled from recent advertisements (1985–86), are examples of fares available. Official fares, with seasonal and validity variations are shown on the left; discounted fares are shown on the right in bold letters:

Official fares with seasonal and validity variations	Discounted fares
Alicante: £190/£456	**£88 /£118**
Athens: £204/£321	**£109 /£140**
Bali: £719/£794	**£513**
Bombay: £570/£562	**£360**
Cairo: £401/£567	**£199 /£229**
Chicago: £490	**£330**
Hong Kong: £510/£900	**£399**
Johannesburg: £452/£1108	**£380**
Los Angeles: £398/£509	**£229**
New York: £229/£389	**£162**
Rio de Janeiro: £670/£1241	**£479**
Rome: £150/£356	**£98 /£110**
Seychelles: £979	**£550**
Tokyo: £745/£778	**£605**

The Airpass There are bargains at every turn, one of the biggest of all being what has become known as the Airpass, which flourishes best in large countries. The Airpass is a roundabout, all-embracing ticket that must be purchased when you buy your main destination ticket to this or that country and which allows you to travel from one destination to another within that country at prices which would make the average airline economist go to his psychiatrist. Major airlines serving the USA all have their Airpasses, some which they operate themselves and some which they delegate to other more regional airlines. For instance, if you flew across the Atlantic with TWA, you could then fly to any one of 16 destinations inside the USA for a maximum of £269! Pan Am (and then other airlines grouped) will offer you 12 stops in the United States for £260. One 'inside America' airline, Republic, will allow you to cross the Atlantic with any carrier (standby only) and offer you an unlimited number of US destinations for £300 – you could be flying for ever! Among other countries offering Airpasses are India, Brazil and Australia. They are well worth looking into.

Gateways Another aspect of air transport which deserves a glance is the recent multiplicity of gateways. It pays nowadays not only to go shopping for an air ticket but for an airport as well. With destinations like New York or Los Angeles becoming increasingly crowded and frustrating for the traveller, many airlines – mostly those to the USA but also to the Far East – now use hub-gateways-airports which were not even on the map a few years ago, like Dallas-Fort Worth, Atlanta, Boston, Minneapolis or Detroit. This makes for both flexibility and accessibility. It all depends on where you are going. Dallas, for instance, handles over 30 million passengers a year, two-thirds of whom have no intention of staying in Dallas and who just use it as a jumping-off point for other places with over 400 flights leaving Dallas a day.

Some Guidelines

So, as an independent traveller, where does this leave you? It is back to the drawing board as they say or, as stated in this book, back to the jigsaw puzzle game. Here are some main points which will help you.

● Buy, beg, borrow or steal a copy of *The Airline Passenger Tariff* or the *ABC Air Travel Guide* (see page 212). These are voluminous and fairly expensive publications but, though there will be changes in fares, you will be using the book or books many times if only to check the conditions attached to most flights and the investment is worth making. Then sit down on a dull winter's evening, with blank pieces of your jigsaw in front of you, and read through the pages devoted to your desired destination – footnotes, symbols, provisos and all. Then read them again. And again. If a piece of information is not clear study it in isolation until you have mastered its intricacies. If some human being could write this mumbo jumbo, another human being should understand it.

● When you are studying your APT or ABC tomes, there are a few things worth remembering. Seasonality is one of them and most important it is too. All airlines have four or five seasonal 'bands', which can make a great difference to the fare level. For instance, when going to Australia, the secret is to go out in the outbound low season and back in the inbound low season. The cheapest flight to Hong Kong, for another example, is in November. But beware. It sometimes happens that an airline low season band coincides with the destination's high season, so you can't expect to win every time.

- Routings can make a lot of difference too. All fares are officially calculated on what is called the 'Maximum Permitted Mileage' (MPM) basis. This is the distance between points of departure and arrival with a little on top. Most members of the public do not realise that within the MPM, they can have a stopover at no extra charge wherever the airline lands for refuelling and so on. This can make a great deal of difference to the independent traveller when planning a flexible itinerary.

- Telephone or call on the airline of your choice and ask for the official fare within each category. Then ask for the name and address of the airline's General Sales Agent. If the counter clerk says that you can't have it, he is talking nonsense and you should telephone the office of the airline's sales manager and ask for it. You will get it. If someone says that his airline does not discount fares, don't believe him.

- Contact the GSA and say simply, 'How much to Milan or wherever on such a date returning on such a date.' He will tell you the 'official' discounted fare and the happy difference will be visible at a glance.

- You may find that the best bet for booking your ticket are the big boys of the retail travel industry – companies like Thomas Cook, Hogg Robinson and Pickfords. They may not be the cheapest but they have the resources.

- Then go down the line and study the bucket shops' advertisements in newspapers like the *Daily and Sunday Telegraph*, *The Times*, *The Sunday Times* and the *Guardian* and the London *Evening Standard*. Bear in mind that quite often the bigger the advertisement, the higher the fare the man will offer you for someone has to pay for the ad. Don't neglect the small, rather breathless classified ads. Find the man of your choice and ring to find out his best available fare for the dates you want to travel.

- Listen to the experts. Several magazines have lately become not only very entertaining but extremely good at giving you their views. My feeling is that the *Business Traveller* is the best of all.

- Although there can be many views on the subject of cheaper fares, I concur with both *Business Traveller* and the already mentioned *Daily Telegraph Consumer Guide* in nominating the following 'discounters' as the most reliable: For the Far East and Australia, the smart and quick-off-the-ground Euro-Asian Travel have been very good in the past. For the Middle East, Wingspan have a good reputation. For Africa and much of Asia try Bestways. In a class by itself is Travel Mart Ltd now with three branches in London and two outside the capital. They have a lot of experience and will quote you a reasonable fare to anywhere in the world. Addresses on page 213.

So, get to work. Set out the pieces of your jigsaw in front of you, mark each one of them with one or more of the points made here and construct your own leisure travel. Troublesome? Of course it is. But what wouldn't you do to save say 60 per cent of the cost of any purchase?

HOTELS

Hotels are a world of their own. Indeed they are. There are roughly 65,000 listed hotels around the world and even the great and mighty American-based *Hotel and Travel Index*, which unfortunately is unavailable to the general public, with more than 700 pages and which is revised every three months, cannot cope with more than a marginal proportion of the hostelries between Kamchatka and Mexico City, Cape Town and New Delhi.

Speaking personally, I love all hotels. I have great respect for the really expert hotel men and over the years I have even grown to respect some of the chains. Great hotels, wherever they are, thrill me. Middling hotels interest me too because of their potential. Bad hotels – and they are the majority – appall me because they show quite clearly that many people have gone into a business activity without knowing anything about it, created bad design, bad food and bad hostmanship.

Hotel life is romantic, fast moving, exciting and almost always larger than life. It is a study in human nature and national characteristics. But, if you are an independent traveller looking for the right place to stay, they can be a nightmare. And don't let all that romance fool you. If I find that César Ritz himself founded this one and then discover that the bath plugs won't fit, I am very quickly deflated.

Be ruthless. Remember that somebody somewhere is trying to sell you a room, or better still a suite or a meal, or all meals. Like everything else for the independent traveller, the choice of a good hotel depends on you, what you like, where you would like to be and, most importantly, what you can afford. And, naturally, you should never take no for an answer. Like an airline seat, an unoccupied hotel room is sudden death to the hotel man. I well remember after the war, pushy German tourists waiting outside hotels in France for the six o'clock deadline while the French proprietor looked at his watch. Before that fateful hour, the empty hotel room is an asset. Who knows who might drop by? Let the clock chime six times and the Germans would be in there like William Tell's arrow, bargaining like hell. All hotels the world over have what is called a 'room rack', which is the tariff they would like to get if they can. But if anyone tells you that hotels don't discount their prices, just smile and go the other way. Of course hotels discount their prices, everywhere and all of the time. What can the independent traveller gain by finding out and arguing?

I would say that you could gain a wide margin of concessions, say between 10 and 40 per cent. It all depends on the time of the year, the state of business, the way you go about it. Once again, at the height of the season, it would be foolish to expect much. Trying to find a discounted hotel room in Marbella in August is like trying to find a decent pitcher of sangria in tourist land. You must also demand to know the answer to all your questions and don't be put off by some vague generality. Ask on the telephone what the current 'room rack' for the room is, inquire how it is classified, what the room includes, how big it is, which way it faces, how far it is to such and such a place that you want to visit.

Once at the hotel, ask to see the room, for, after all, you are paying for it. Try the bathroom fittings. Try every light in the room and the air conditioning or central heating. If it's a warm country, open the windows to see if they work. Are there shutters? Have a good look at the sheets and the mattress. Are they clean and will you be able to sleep on it? Look at the general state of the room. Have the rubbish baskets been emptied? Has the place been properly dusted recently? Is the wardrobe large enough and deep enough to take your clothes comfortably? If you are on your own and are offered a twin-bedded room never use the bed nearest the telephone. That's the one the habitual traveller uses when he makes his telephone calls and the bed dips down into the Rift Valley and rises up to the Himalayas at the ends. The choice of a good hotel depends on a thousand and one factors — mostly quirks — which most of us have. For instance, I like to sleep with the curtains open — to see the new day coming up — and

I do hate brash neon advertising lights flooding into my room all night. You might well have another pet dislike, so go ahead and make sure it is not there. Complain, always complain, though with good cause of course. Except for the really good hotels, room service is generally bad. Make a note of the time you ordered. Give them 20 minutes and then start hollering for your sandwich every 5 minutes. You would be surprised how the grapevine works – this man is a loony. Tip well if you can at the start of your stay, then not at all during your stay and finally leave a small parting present. The grapevine works here too.

Hotel stories are legion and they don't really have a place here. Happily, there are guidelines for choosing a hotel and some of them appear in the many hotel guidebooks now being published. The best of the best, of course, is my own *The 300 Best Hotels in the World* (Macmillan). It appears every two years, contains the kind of hotels I would like to stay in myself and why and it carries no advertising of any kind. It describes itself as the 'most idiosyncratic hotel guide in the world' and from Vancouver to Tokyo, happily, people agree with me. It tends to be an up-market guide containing nothing but the best but don't let that put you off for one of the listed hotels within charges you £12 a night.

Another good and reliable friend is *The Financial Times World Hotel Directory*, which again is published every two years. A good deal less adjectival, it covers 2800 hotels in 150 countries. It is very detailed and accurate and if you have to make a quick dash to Lagos or Caracas, that's the one for you.

Then there are the 'recommendation' guides like *The Good Hotel Guide*, which covers about 1000 hotels in Britain and Western Europe. The only hotels included are those which are recommended by readers and this means there is little or no element of personal editorial choice and therefore no set standard. Naturally, almost every large tourist country produces its own hotel guide and I for one would not dream of travelling in Britain without Egon Ronay's *Lucas Guide* (Egon Ronay Organisation) which appears every year. I have to take my hat off to Mr Ronay who is one of the two or three most knowledgeable hotel experts in the world. I have never known him and his team to make a serious mistake.

If you do not wish to phone direct to the hotel, remember that virtually every hotel chain or hotel complex has its own office, usually in London I am afraid, and a quick call will yield the right booking. Even hotels which are not affiliated to chains are often London-represented and great tomes like the Travel Trade Gazette's *Travel Trade Directory* (see page 213) list them country by country.

One very simple system which is virtually unknown to most members of the general public is the work of the person who is known as a hotel representative. There are now scores of them. They represent the hotel concerned, will know all about it, or can find out, will give you a lot of otherwise difficult to obtain information and in the end make your booking to your satisfaction and charge you nothing for they get commission from their clients. Many of the better hotel reps have now got together in one body, the British Association of Hotel Representatives (BAHREP) (please see page 213) and one telephone call can direct you to the hotel rep who is best suited to the area.

Some shine. For instance, The Leading Hotels in the World are just what they claim to be – the best. They have hotels, usually big and citified, literally all over the world and they don't represent little hostelries around the corner. So if you are looking for a good, not inexpensive hotel in some big city, try them. You could do far worse.

Another good example is Windotel Ltd (page 213). This small, personalised company had specialised in the Caribbean area for many years and there are very few, if any, hotels in the islands that this company does not know about. It can tell you how long the beach is, what the services are, who the general manager is, what the weather can be expected to be at this or that time of year and it can fix up itineraries for you if you wish.

How can you obtain hotel room discounts? There are many ways. The Ritz of the business is Room Centre (page 213). They have been in the business of booking rooms world wide for many years and, though they are strongly business oriented, they can also cope with private inquiries. They are extremely keen, well informed and, though they may not promise you the moon (the average discount is in the region of ten per cent), they will deliver what they promise. Among smaller and often go-ahead firms that can get you discounts ranging from ten to forty per cent on rack prices are companies like Reliance Tours UK Ltd, Value Travel and Trinifold Travel (see page 213). Everybody loves a bargain and saving on a hotel room will allow for more flexibility in your overall expenditure.

TRANSPORT

Travel means movement and the truly independent traveller needs 'wheels'. Speaking personally, I cannot conceive of any intelligent traveller going off to some country or other without the certainty that he is going to be able to move about, see places, think for himself, go or stop as he wishes to do. Anything less is not really travel. However, it is almost impossible to generalise here about rail, bus and sea transport in each country; the reader should consult the relevant country chapters for more specific information.

Hiring a car

Alas, it also happens that car rental is, in my opinion, the biggest rip-off in the travel business. Companies that rent out cars quote all kinds of reasons, high taxes on the purchase of cars, VAT, high oil charges, high maintenance costs, staff and so on and in some instances quite rightly. Nevertheless, I have worked out my own answer with the aid of my trusty calculator. Even in Britain, basically an expensive country, I could buy say a Ford Fiesta, hire it out for nine months of the year and end up with profits roughly equivalent to the cost of the car and enough money to buy the next one! On the other hand, I can recall last winter while staying in Cyprus for a longish period that I was able, though with the help of knowledgeable friends, to hire one of those Japanese tin boxes on wheels, with unlimited mileage, for £6 a day. One can hardly do better than that. I am not going to take up the various explanations or excuses offered by car hirers because there are so many and they are so confusing. I am going to look at it only from the point of view of the independent traveller who needs wheels, needs them fast and cheap, and extrapolate a few points worth remembering.

● The old controversy about whether to rent from a multinational or from the little local fellow is largely immaterial. The multinational can rent you a car anywhere from Wagga Wagga to Timbuktu at any time. The car is likely to be reasonably new, except on islands, well maintained, though not always, and can of course be rented here and dropped there. He offers you convenience when you are at your weakest − without wheels. The local car rental man may well beat the multinational's price and in fact he almost always does. But beware of the age of the car and its mechanical condition. Find out if you can exchange the car in almost any place if the first one does not work. How good is the insurance he offers? Ten to one, he is not keen on accepting your plastic money which the multinational will. That might make a difference to your overall budgeting. The choice is one for you.

• Carefully study the reasons for your hiring a car. Do you just want the car to go to the supermarket and back or are you going to really log up a lot of mileage? That might make a great deal of difference between you demanding unlimited mileage or paying for the mileage. The first might be simpler but it might not be the cheapest way.

• All cars come in 'classes' or groups of similar-sized cars. When you get to your destination you might find that you have been given a bigger or better car. The usual excuse is that your 'class' wasn't available. That's too bad. In this case you have a right to insist on the car you booked or a bigger one at the same cost.

• Go shopping for your car. Do not automatically assume that the best bet is to hire a car from the airport. It is not. Leave your luggage behind as you can always collect it later, catch a bus or a taxi and look around at what is available in city centres and, especially if you can, in suburban booking offices. You could save up to £50 a week.

• If you are renting from a local company ask to see the list of their main offices in the area where you plan to go. Take the list with you.

• In all things connected with car rental, be very, but very suspicious. It's not that car rental people are more dishonest than others in the travel field but simply that they are busy, sometimes offhand and dismissive. But you are in no hurry. The man behind the counter will always say that the car is in perfect condition. But is it? Go around the vehicle. Make certain that the last driver's dents are not added to your bill. Insist on trying the car out. Drive around the car park and test the main items like brakes, lights, state of the tyres and so on. Do as I say and not as I did: I once got stuck in an almost vertical Spanish village with a rented car whose brakes did not work and whose engine stalled in traffic. Think what could happen to you!

• The car rental man will tell you that the insurance is comprehensive. But his idea of what is comprehensive may not be yours. What exactly are you insured against?

• If, somewhere along the way, you must have minor repairs carried out by someone other than the rental company don't forget to ask for a receipt. You will need it – and badly – at the end of the journey.

• From experience, let me suggest that you don't always opt for the car that is smallest and cheapest. It does not pay.

Think of the luggage and number of passengers you are carrying. Think of the indifferent roads you will have to travel on. Think of your poor old back! A car made for a diminutive Japanese geisha girl may not be right for you.

• Make sure that the instruments are accurate. I once rented a car in a country where the fuel tank showed 'F' when it was empty and 'E' when it was full. You get surprises that way.

• Most good car rental companies give you at least one map of the country. Make sure that they do and that you understand it, especially in and around the big cities. And if you are going to spend most of your time in a big city, don't hire a car at all. It won't be worth your while since you will spend most of your holiday looking for a parking space. Make sure you understand all the country's road regulations. I was once rather surprised at being stopped by the police in a largish city in Arizona. It was dusk and coming in from the country, I had put on my sidelights. But the police told me that it was a serious offence to have your lights on within city limits!

• Do not rent a self-drive car in a country where the language has an alphabet you do not understand. Try for instance to find your way in an Arabic speaking country where you can't read the road signs!

• As a general rule, do not hire self-drive cars in distant, exotic countries like, for instance, India (too many sacred cows), Nepal, Brazil and Mexico. This being said there are countries like the United States, Canada, France, Germany, Italy and so on where I have personally found self driving to be a great pleasure and an education. In those countries mentioned above as being unsuitable for self drive, labour is often so cheap that it is worth while having your own driver. But be careful: in India, if he is a Hindi speaker, he will be just as lost as you are in Tamil-land or Karnataka or Kerala! Fortunately, English is the lingua franca.

Lastly, Bon voyage!

TRAVEL INFORMATION

This should really have been the start of this book. Travel information, real travel information is one of the hardest things to fit into your jigsaw puzzle mostly because it is haphazard, good or bad, inaccurate or too detailed. Some people know but won't tell. Some people are keen to tell but know nothing or cannot communicate.

At the risk of appearing to plug my own profession, I would suggest that you first go for the travel writer, the travel journalist, find one whose work you know by experience that you can trust and follow him. Travel writers are professionals. They write about places where people want to go and, sometimes, places they have not even thought of. They have relatively few axes to grind and for them writing about travel and holidays is a job, which most of them do as well as they can. But do try and make a distinction between the man or woman who is the travel correspondent of a newspaper or magazine or the writer whose byline you see constantly all over the media, and the little girl who's just been on holiday in Mykonos and thinks it is 'divine' — she's just paid for her holiday with her article and some editor was misguided enough to believe that she could put it over for a general audience.

This, of course, leads us straight into the business of boning up about the place you fancy. Nothing beats your personal reaction to a piece of evocative or informative writing. Spend your winter evenings reading up because you can never have enough of it and you might even well end up knowing more about your chosen area than the travel agent or tour operator! Yet, it is strange to realise that after four centuries or so of English-speaking people travelling around the world, writing about the world at large is by no means a 'settled' craft.

Guide/Travel Books

There is no perfect travel writer and the demand has been such in this new field of leisure that the output can never match demand. People want too much. Among my own readers I have an English duchess who always wants to know things like the temperature of the seawater along the Tunisian coast in the second half of October. Ten to one, she'll get me into a corner and force me to find out all the ifs and buts. There are people who want to go walking in the Rockies, sailing around the Caribbean, exploring Australia's Northern Territory or visiting what is worth seeing in Chiang Mai, Thailand. There are also people who expect me to fix up a church-gazing itinerary in France, or schlossing up in Germany. Recently I even had a correspondent who asked me to tell him about the Italian Renaissance. Just like that.

Travel writing inevitably leads to books on travel and, indeed, to guidebooks and for once I fully agree with Paul Theroux who recently wrote that there were 'writers who travel and travellers who write'. I am not ashamed to admit that right through my working life, books on travel have fired my enthusiasm enormously and my own day is made when I discover a book about Timor or Zanzibar. Some books have been, in my case, so fantastically emotional and motivational that I have just upped and gone, which probably was not at all what the writer intended. Occasionally, it can even be a footnote or a little digression that sets me going. Among writers who are no longer alive are the obvious names like Joseph Conrad, Somerset Maugham, Ernest Hemingway, Rose Macaulay, Karen Blixen, Nikos Kazantsakis and among those who are, happily, still travelling in this world are people like Jan Morris, Patrick Leigh Fermor, Laurence Durrell, James Michener, Paul Scott, Larry Collins and Dominique Lapierre, Robin Lane Fox and John Keay. And among the younger ones are names like Tim Severin, Gavin Young, Geoffrey Moorhouse and Bamber Gascoigne.

Some books are especially welcome because they strike an immediate chord. After all, what would one do without Charles Allen and his *Plain Tales from the Raj* (Futura). Or Arthur Grimble and his *Pattern of Islands* (John Murray). Some books, which are not basically travel books, have the curious effect of making me want to go there. Among these were Trevor Fishlock's *India File* (John Murray) and James Pope Hennessey's *Verandah* (Century). Other books which are definitely 'travel' are for me such classics that I would not go to the area without reading them again, for instance, Ernle Bradford's books on the Mediterranean and Dana Facaros' *Greek Island Hopping* (Gentry Books). Another good example is Richard Binns' books on France, which are published by Chiltern House Publishing Company. I thought I knew France but it was only when I began reading Binns' sometimes disjointed *vagabondage* in that marvellous country that I realised how little I did know.

What about out-and-out guidebooks? Are they any good in your independent traveller game? Well, yes and no. No one has yet discovered the perfect format or content for the ideal guidebook of the late 1980s. Perhaps it does not exist because people, happily, want different things.

I would suggest that 'proper' guidebooks like the *Blue Guide* series (Ernest Benn Ltd) are well worth the investment if only to show you what you must not miss. Bypassing any sight or monument not graced by at least two stars should condemn you to spending the afternoon in the airport and *Blue Guides* are rarely wrong, though their emphasis is sometimes placed on things that don't interest you.

Although they certainly do not need my endorsement I would thoroughly approve of the *Fodor* series (Hodder & Stoughton). They assume a certain intelligence and awareness on the part of the reader. They are well rounded when it comes to items like history, cuisine or the arts and are generally useful on the main lines of travel in this or that country. Inevitably they have to gloss over certain aspects of travel and are not terribly detailed. But they are honest and good value.

I am also very fond of the *Michelin Green Guides* for the countries which they cover. They are detailed, easy to find your way about in and remarkably informative on things like history, architecture and the arts. They would rate full marks on my shelves. Also interesting are certain guides properly meant for businessmen but surprisingly useful for all in their enormous and detailed knowledge and among them I would list *The South American Handbook* and *The Gulf Handbook*, both of which are published by Trade and Travel Publications. They have never let me down.

Further upfront are guidebooks which have tried to find that elusive and pleasing new format I mentioned above. The French-originated *Today* series now covers about 20 countries and areas, like the Loire Valley or Scandinavia or Morocco and many are available in English translation. They are good looking and intelligent and they too don't assume that you are the village idiot. For the first time too, this series has realised that 'the picture tells the story' and their photographic content is superb. I would recommend them highly. Another admirable series is the *Insight* one (Harrap) which now covers many Asian and North American destinations. They are printed on high quality paper and have well researched, intelligent texts with much expert advice.

How strange it is to recall that it is little more than two decades since those charming flower children began their quest for the Holy Grail all over the world? First they made for Nepal, then they tried Goa and a few went onto Bali. Stranger still is the fact that this was the start of a revolution: the young are on the move and everywhere they are trekking to impossible places which their elders only knew from maps. Hence the tremendous growth over recent years of what one might call the survival guide to this and that, how to go overland to Nepal, how to paddle your own canoe upriver in Borneo, how to cross the Andes at the very spot where no one is supposed to cross.

These books come and go, mostly go, but some remain

and, though I am not stuck on Swiss army knives and double soled boots, I always look – they quite probably know something I don't. Alas, their appeal for me is limited. Being an unrepentant sybarite, I do not believe that travel has to be that tough and I do not believe there is all that much merit in walking to Kathmandu. I have been known to sleep in a doss house in the Sudan and, indeed, to open a tin of cling peaches with a sharp stone and eat the contents with my fingers near the Queen of Sheba's Palace. At the other end of the scale, I draw the line at the American hotel in a lovely city in Pakistan which describes its balconies as 'the perfect way for the foreigner to meet the mysterious East'. Somewhere in the middle lies the beginning of wisdom and reasonable comfort.

I am only too glad to suggest that one of the slightly 'weirdo' guides which is bound to keep on going is the *Travellers' Handbook*, edited by Melissa Shales (Wm Heinemann Ltd). If you are over 40, are curious and have no intention of travelling in a manner which becomes your lifestyle, that's the one for you. It has everything from travelling with a pack animal to how to survive without money. I don't mind at all, if it will get people on the move, it is good enough for me.

National Tourist Offices

What about Government tourist offices? In your efforts to establish yourself as the independent traveller they can be the first or last stop depending on how demanding you are. Generally speaking, the smaller or more distant the country the better the tourist office. In principle they need you as a traveller possibly more than you need them as a destination and will make a greater effort. Some tourist offices are superbly organised. Others are hopeless. All share a revulsion to handing out what I might call the nitty gritties, that is, this hotel is better than that one and so on. The reason is simple. They are government agencies and as such must be very careful not to show favouritism to any specific part of the travel industry. Their counter staff, if natives of the country, are good and if not, don't bother, because you are likely to know more about the subject than they do. Often, by going higher up the civil service ladder, that is to the director, you will get a proper answer.

Occasionally tourist offices are dispensers of ready-made leaflets or brochures, which are bound to answer most of your questions in general and none in detail. Sometimes, government tourist offices are short of money. Sometimes they have too much and spend a great deal of it on smart aleck marketing men who know as much about travel as I do about Eskimo carvings. Mostly they are understaffed and mass oriented. If you are a visiting tour operator, you will receive a great welcome. If you are a private individual who wants to know the name of that church in the village of so-and-so, you will sometimes get a blank stare or a cold shoulder.

London is awash with government tourist offices. They are mostly in the West End, in very expensive locations for prestige and all that, and the home authorities almost always measure their success by the increase in tourists in any one year which may or may not be a good yardstick. Yet some have managed over the years to survive simply by good organisation and good public relations. Some have not even started.

It would be invidious to make particular comments. But then this whole book is invidious so here, for what it's worth, is my own evaluation. It is not, of course, a complete one.

The French Government Tourist Office is almost always good. It has a long tradition of service to Francophile Brits, is well equipped and well staffed. The Spanish Tourist Office is awful. With 30 million tourists a year maybe they don't need anymore? They don't even answer their telephone. The Italian State Tourist Department is wayward and patchy and it rather depends on the person you speak to. The Government of India Tourist Office is, considering its task, very good. It has a lot of information, much of which is not upfront, and is unusually friendly and helpful. The National Tourist Organisation of Greece pays too much attention to tour operators and not enough to the independent traveller. They are, however, quite well informed and well documented.

Worthy of praise are the tourist offices for Cyprus, Morocco, Tunisia, Turkey, Egypt, West Germany, Hong Kong, Jamaica, Malaysia. Indifferent are Kenya, Tanzania, Sri Lanka, Thailand, Japan, Mauritius and the Seychelles. The addresses of all can be found on pages 213–4. Obtaining official tourist information on the West Indian islands can be a headache since only a few have their own tourist offices and there is no one information system for the islands as a whole. Even harder is getting tourist information for the United States. Odd as it may seem, it is virtually impossible and the reason is that in America, tourism is the responsibility of the individual state and not the federal government.

There is a federal tourist information office in London, The United States Travel Service, and, like most federal bodies, it is underpaid and understaffed but it can at least give you some general intelligence and tell you where to write for more if you have the time and the patience. Some American cities are great on tourist information (New York, San Francisco, Dallas, Phoenix, Tucson, etc) and, likely as not, will send you back reams of material including some excellent maps. A few states, such as Florida, California, New York and Texas, are good if you know where to write. Some states have lately grouped together to try and project a regional picture, which is a very good idea. Among them are Arizona, New Mexico, Utah, Colorado and Nevada. Unfortunately, they are not represented in the United Kingdom.

How should the independent traveller make use of the government tourist office? Obviously, in view of the above, you should not expect too much. My advice is to walk airily in when and if you are in the vicinity, pick up those leaflets you require and take them out to study them. Then go back again with a small number of questions, say three, and make them as precise as possible. Your own knowledge and interest will count for a lot and the people behind the counter will be impressed that you should already have done some homework. Don't try to work it all out with telephone enquiries. Most people are not very good at this and a simple, direct letter is often better. For those living outside London, it is probably best to write to the tourist office stating clearly the information you require. Use the government tourist office not just as a source of 'general information' but, by reading between the lines, as a shortcut to the people who might possibly know, such as airlines and hotel groups. Don't expect the national tourist office to make bookings for you. It can't and it won't.

PART TWO

EUROPE

France

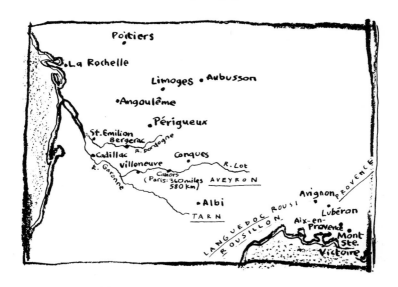

PROFILE

The famous statesman, Mirabeau, who, during the French Revolution, once exclaimed: 'Every man has two countries – his own and France' was not just making a political speech. He was speaking an obvious truth and could well have had the intelligent traveller of the 1980s in mind. At the risk of offending other countries (who need not be), I would suggest that France is almost certainly the best country for the independent traveller.

The largest country in Europe, it has beauty, which no one can doubt, more variety I believe than in any other country, traditions, personality, history and the arts and an everlasting air of being able to survive change. It is a country of extreme individualists who, when you meet them on their home ground, know better than most of us just what is *la*

53

douceur de vivre. It is a country of supreme realists who keep talking of those people in Paris as 'them' and are quite content to see two bakers' shops open up side by side.

Above all, and this is great for the independent traveller, France is the perfect country in which to get lost. Once, having had my car windscreen shattered by a stone not far from Bordeaux and after replacing it with one of those awful plastic 'temporaries', I was dreading the drive back to the Channel ports until I decided, quite wisely as it turned out, to reach them without once driving along a busy main road.

Out came the map, down went the itinerary and off I went, turning off here and there, crossing the 'Routes Nationales' but never using them and for ever chasing the Michelin map's little yellow and white roads. Eventually, I made it to Dieppe and in the process discovered another France which I never knew existed. It was a country of old, mellow bridges spanning half-forgotten rivers, of little country churches with magnificent altars, of incredibly grand chateaux lording it over the countryside, of tempting little hostelries where the 'patron' wiped his hands on his apron before greeting me, and sitting me down to a gargantuan lunch of wild mushrooms, blue trout, a choice of 45 different cheeses and, of course, a drop of something or other to finish up with. I discovered, or rediscovered, a country where almost every village and every little town has its artisan speciality. One makes knives, another brooms or shoes, another swears by its truffles.

In France, you are on your own. You do what you like, when you like and where you like. Nobody minds and nobody interferes. Once, in deepest Auvergne, I met an Englishman who turned out to be a very high-powered marketing man from London. He was sitting on a thousand-year-old bridge, watching the river water flowing past. How had he found this place? 'I took the wrong turning,' he told me, (always a good thing), 'found this village and this river and decided then and there that this was where I wanted to spend my holidays.' He took a room at the local *auberge*, at a mere £4 a night, where the owner's wife fixed him up a picnic every day for lunch. He would sit on the bridge, spend hours in the local church or join a gypsy in his caravan to go to a country fair. He did some fishing, went for long walks in the woods and read bits of François Villon from the book in his knapsack. How long was he going to stay there, I asked him. He looked a bit sheepish, 'I am afraid I have lost track of the time,' he told me. 'I suppose I shall have to ring up the office and find out when they want me back.' Then he brightened up: 'Perhaps they have given me the sack?'

Unlike the man who is supposed to have written the Marseillaise on a grain of rice, don't expect me to describe France in the same way. France needs a book to itself. On this side of the Channel the shelves of the booksellers are filled with books on France – more than on any other country. And so they should be. In every direction the heavenly hexagon is filled with treasures. Have you ever sat out the afternoon in front of the great church at Vézelay? Or watched, from afar, the sun playing around the great steeple of Chartres Cathedral peeping over the wheatfields? Or counted the Romanesque doors in western France? Or learned something about the great Médoc wines, or the 'confit d'oie' of the Périgord? You haven't? Then, believe me, you have missed something.

All I can do in this ridiculously short space, is to point out to you some of the things and places I have loved over many years. And if you don't share my enthusiasm for this or that, don't worry too much: just take the next wrong turning and find your own France.

What is France good for? Just name it. It's all there and it all depends on you because one of the best things about France is that though it likes tourists, and especially intelligent, sensible ones, it does not wear its heart on its sleeve. You take it or you leave it.

BEACHES

With roughly 4000 miles (6440 km) of coastline, there are bound to be some. There are but again the choice depends on you, on what you want and what you expect. From Dieppe to Lorient, the Normandy and Brittany beaches have always been favourites with British small children, generations of whom probably built their first sandcastles there. They still provide good, safe swimming, lots of sand and many things to do for all the family. Apart perhaps from Deauville they may lack sophistication but not general appeal. Try especially the beaches of the Côtes du Nord in Brittany, which are very beautiful.

As for the Atlantic coast, from the Loire to the Pyrenees, it is my belief that it has long been neglected by foreign tourists and it is a great pity for here are some of the finest strands in the whole of France, infinitely spacious, fresh and clean and very invigorating. The bigger resorts like La Baule and Les Sables d'Olonne have always been very 'French', beautifully equipped and most up to date. You just have to plunge into this great Frenchness by the seaside and enjoy it. For the life of me, I cannot understand why more British visitors don't go, for instance, to those miraculous beaches of Oléron Island which, to my way of thinking, are among the finest in the world. One of the great advantages of the western beaches is that you are never short of things to do away from the sand as the whole of the back country is full of sights and tastes. At the back of that heavenly fishy place La Rochelle is the mysterious 'Marais Poitevin' where you might as well forget the time of day or even the date, with its marvellous churches like Aulnay, St Savinien, Pont l'Abbé or the old city of Saintes. Cognac is just down the road and also Marennes, where all self-respecting oysters come from, is in the other direction. Try Brouage. In the time of Richelieu it was an important port for voyages to the New World. But now, all silted up, the great ramparts stand in the middle of the fields. Very romantic too if you care to find it.

South of the Garonne, sand fiends have nothing to worry about as they could walk from here to Spain without once leaving the beach; great dunes of it and relatively unspoilt.

If you are aged between 20 and 40, the Languedoc–Roussillon on the Mediterranean side, from the Spanish border to the Rhône, will be the beach scene for you. Here, on this formerly uninteresting coastline, the French authorities have built some of the best appointed and most modern beach resorts in Europe; places like St Cyprien, Port Barcarès, Port Leucate, Gruissan and Cap d'Agde where every outdoor activity is catered for including sailing, surfing, riding, golf and tennis. There are many hotels but basically this is a sort of do-it-yourself holiday coast, with houses and apartments to rent where you can sail your boat right up to your front door. I like Gruissan best of all.

Cross the mighty delta of the Rhône, the romantic Camargue, and you come to the traditional Côte d'Azur. From Cassis in the west to Menton in the east, it's all here: the palace hotels, the little family places, the camping sites and the famous see-and-be-seen promenades. This is probably the world's most famous seaside strip. It starts tamely enough perhaps, in the resorts of the Var *département* like Bandol, Sanary, Le Lavandou. I have always had a soft spot for the Var. It is unpretentious, gay, family-oriented and the beaches are great. One then graduates to a flurry of bikini tops around the one and only St Tropez, becoming 'proper' again in St Raphael and the resorts of the Estérel coast before ending up in the golden miles of the 'real' Riviera in Cannes, Juan-les-Pins, Antibes, Cap Ferrat and Nice. Here, and in the hills of the back country, the really rich of this world have disported themselves for over a century and, though the beaches may not be so marvellous, it is being there that counts. To date, the queen resort of them all is still Cannes where, incidentally, I was more or less brought up, which makes tremendous efforts to stay on top and manages to do so with consummate skill.

Beaches, did I say? France has one or more for almost every mood and the choice is yours.

COUNTRYSIDE

This, of course, is where France scores as every British motorist knows, being a country so vast, so varied and yet so 'human' in scale that you feel at home almost everywhere. It just depends on how you like to take things. France is so amazingly bountiful, even in its remotest corners, that it never ceases first to amaze and then to charm. I once thought I knew France and yet it was only when I began reading books like Richard Binns' *French Leave* books that I realised how a real enthusiast can find admirable places just by turning left or right.

Every Francophile traveller has his secret address book of favourite places and I willingly share some pages of mine with you. If you want small hotels or auberges try Les Hospitaliers; an eagle's nest of a place a mere 30 minutes east of Montélimar. Or the old-fashioned peace and quiet of the Chateau Le Scipionnet at Les Vans in the Ardèche. Or the almost unknown Chateau Le Violet at Peyriac-Minervois, only 16 miles (26 km) from Carcassonne. Or again the charming and gastronomic Cheval Blanc at Sept Saulx near Rheims. Maybe you would like the lovely, mellow Ste Foy at Conques in the Aveyron where you can almost touch the fantastic Romanesque church steeple by leaning out of the window? There are so many charming places that perhaps you should not stop at all? Just keep going – two days here, three days there. That's what France is marvellous for.

So how does one describe the whole of this heavenly country? One does not. It is not possible. So let us pick, at random, three areas, which are not exactly unknown to intelligent travellers.

Let's begin with the Loire Valley. I once travelled the length of this river of kings starting at its humble birth in the Auvergne. Some 624 miles (1004 km) and 78 bridges later I emerged where the tempestuous Loire meets the Atlantic in a great embrace and I cannot forget those wide, pale blue skies, the honey-coloured houses with their black slate roofs and the long lines of poplars pointing the way. You can still get lost, really lost, in the great forest of Chinon and come to think of it you might do so too in the woods of Chambord where King François I went hunting and which the dramatic imagination of Monsieur Houdin gave birth to that noble idea of 'Son et Lumière' a generation ago.

This is chateau country. There are over 30 magnificent piles between Orleans and Angers, most of them well known like Chambord, Valençay, Loches, Chenonceaux and Azay-le-Rideau. Travelling the Loire Valley is indeed an enchanted journey. One can go and listen and be moved by the Gregorian chant of the Benedictine monks at Solesmes, wonder at the Plantagenet tombs at Fontevraud or listen to romance in the grounds of Ussé, the inspiration for *The Sleeping Beauty.*

My own notebooks recall more than 112 chateaux in the Loire area, many of which are little known and hardly ever visited. Once, at Chambord, I met a young Englishman studying to be an architect. He told me that he was making a point of looking at the lesser known places. I told him about the Chateau of Montpoupon, almost halfway between the river Indre and the Cher. No, it was not on his list and before I could breathe he was off like lightning. Along the magnificent waterways, history and the arts mingle in a truly inebriating cocktail: Balzac and George Sand, Rabelais and Ronsard, almost every king of France, Joan of Arc, of course, and even Descartes. But here too, go off the beaten track, leave the main tourist route and make for this inspiring and sinuous river valleys like the Cher and the Indre, the lazy Vienne and the lesser known Sarthe coming in from the north.

Come now, follow me right across France, to heavenly Provence – no, I don't mean what Côte d'Azure people call Provence but the real thing for which you must base yourself in Aix-en-Provence, not too far from the central fountain and the Cours Mirabeau which I consider the most elegant period street in the whole of France. Visit Cézanne's studio complete with his beret and smock, palette and easel – just as he left them. Then drive slowly, and I mean slowly, along the D17 road to Tholonet. Round about here, the painter sat day after day, month after month, painting his favourite scene; the passing of the sun over the celebrated Mont Ste Victoire. Deep down, I have always fancied that somewhere, sometimes, through good luck or good judgement in some art shop, I would come across one of those forgotten Cézanne Mont Ste Victoire paintings, chequered with light and shade, suffused with the magnificent sunshine which to me remains the artist's ultimate creation.

Then, as you go north bowling along the motorway, don't go too far because you are about to discover one of the really secret places of France, the Lubéron mountain and its valley. Go 30 miles (48 km) due east of Avignon and you are there, a place filled with bright sunshine and the hum of the bumblebee. What really make the Lubéron are the villages for each one is a place where you might choose to end your travels and adopt as your own. There is Oppède-le-Vieux perched like most of its neighbours on a high craggy hill and with house foundations going back to Roman times. There are Ménerbes and Bonnieux, equally beautiful. To the north in a wild and almost enclosed valley, is the glorious Abbey of Sénanques, built by Cistercian monks in the twelfth century, marvellously peaceful and beautiful. Gordes is perhaps the most photogenic village of all, with a lovely square and a Renaissance chateau. Nearby are the curious 'bories'; simple stone huts where medieval man retreated when soldiers, or the plague, appeared on the horizon. The most unusual place is Roussillon which is in the centre of a region that produces natural ochre, with 16 different shades of red. I personally counted even more but then that was after lunching at the Restaurant David and that's another story.

Now we come to the part of France which literally draws me to it every time I cross the Channel. I call it Aquitaine, though the actual Aquitaine is rather larger, comprising a huge chunk of country going from La Rochelle in the west to Vichy in the east, from there to Perpignan and right across to Arcachon. Here indeed is the France I love, filled with marvellous churches and abbeys, little villages of great charm, the potent, yes it is still, atmosphere of the Hundred Years' War, enough of Auvergne to make me breathe deeply this totally unpolluted air and above all those four magnificent river valleys of the Dordogne, the Lot, the Tarn and the Aveyron which I have always considered to embody the real France.

Aunis, Saintonge, Limousin, Poitou, Guyenne, Quercy, Rouergue, Cévennes – so many old provinces, so many areas filled with poignant memories. Between La Rochelle, which is surely the fishiest place in Europe, and the beginnings of the Dordogne country lies a slice of country dominated by proud old cities like Angoulême, Poitiers, Limoges and Périgueux but drive out a few miles and you can go for miles without meeting the crowds. A charming, rather secretive landscape with small fields, rivers that seem to meander to nowhere in particular and, of course, superb eating and drinking too; old and mellow city of Cognac is not far away. The Romans made this one of their centres and at Saintes you can still see the arena.

This part of France, very much the hub of the great pilgrimage centres, reeks with the incense of unchanging religion and it has more of those gorgeous Romanesque churches than any other area. Every village has one, squat and timeworn, which may not appear very distinguished at first until you notice the fantastic carved tympanum of the entrance porch, with its saints and its devils, its allegorical figures and its divinity rising to the heavens. Crafts flourish everywhere. Limoges has been making lovely porcelain and enamel from time immemorial and nearby Aubusson shines with tapestries which have been made there since the seventh century and have become world famous especially since the emergence of the contemporary work of Jean Lurçat.

South of Périgueux, you begin to catch the scent of the Midi. It comes from the gorse of the high plateaux, from the occasional olive tree or from the dense bush that lines the river valleys. Bordeaux country, on both sides of the rivers Dordogne and Garonne, means, of course, wine. Spend a morning on the terrace of the Hostellerie de Plaisance in St Emilion and I defy you not to be intoxicated by the powerful aroma of this fantastically bibulous town which medieval English kings patronised so well. St Emilion produces some 400 wines led by the mighty Château Cheval Blanc and Château Ausone which you visit as you would cathedrals. Purists often go for the Médoc area on the other side of the Garonne and settle in places like Pauillac, just to be near the Margaux and the Lafites of this world. In between lies the delicious Entre-Deux-Mers with marvellous old villages like Cadillac, Branne and La Sauve.

Speaking personally, it is when I reach Bergerac or Villeneuve-sur-Lot that I come into my spiritual inheritance. It is a land of milk and honey and pâté de foie gras too where everything appears to conspire to make me linger a while longer. Cahors with its great banking past and the famous Pont Valentré, which is so often photographed, or Albi with its strange pink brick cathedral and its great Toulouse Lautrec Museum make very good centres and I love them both. Every time I go to this land I fall in love all over again with the countless villages which seem to change colour and character every few miles. There is the famous Rocamadour where pilgrims painstakingly climbed the face of the rock for so many centuries and all those lovely places along the rich Dordogne like Domme, Beynac and La Roque Gageac, or a little to the south, Gourdon. Then come places along the Lot, like the never-to-be-forgotten St Cirq-Lapopie, Cabrerets, Calvignac and Capdenac and the incomparable Conques where Ste Foy still reigns in her reliquary of gold and jewels. Medieval Cordes is worth seeing and oh so many others.

In between are all those marvellously *sympathiques* old country towns like Montpezat-de-Quercy, Villefranche-de-Rouarge, St Antonin-Noble-Val, Montpazier or Castelnau. Many are old *bastides*, cities built by either the French or the English during the unending wars; almost every one still has its noble arcaded square, its ancient houses sometimes reddish or grey and often biscuit-coloured. Even the smallest and humblest ones, such as Puycelci, has a story and here it is of a valiant pig that saved the day and made the English go away. At La Couvertoirade in the Aveyron it is the evocative depiction, in stone, of the Templars and the Knights of St John of Jerusalem that counts.

The four river valleys, Dordogne, Lot, Tarn and Aveyron could not be more different. The Dordogne is rich and lush and meanders through a country of incredible *richesse*. It is well known to British visitors who drive there in their hundreds and sometimes live there. The Lot, my own favourite, is a little rougher, often choppy and sometimes calm and overlooked by incredible farmhouses the colour of champagne, each with its own pigeon loft and its long barn for drying the tobacco crop. It then goes really wild in its upper reaches around Espalion and Entraygues. The Aveyron is secretive, often difficult to find among the hills and the Tarn, which begins so tamely, ends up by being one of the great sights of the whole of France when it reaches the Gorges du Tarn which, if you can see them out of the high tourist season, are quite beautiful and surprisingly unexpected. You might stay in La Malène for one or two nights and go and see the noble river as it twists and turns at right angles along the great cliffs and the gravel beds. For myself, I will go back at any time – convinced as I am that here is nature mansized and infinitely more poignant than someone else's Grand Canyon.

And so, through Robert Louis Stevenson's Cévennes and the tumultuous sources of the Loire (yes, it too has gorges) one is back. Or is one? For France is like that: an almost unending patchwork of superb countryside and memorable villages just made for the man who likes to turn away from the main roads and the more humdrum side of a modern country.

France? Of course, the independent traveller should try it — just to feel how independent he can be. No other country in western Europe gives you such a chance.

CITIES

Like all great cities and possibly even more so, Paris is a story in itself and deserves a book of its own. Since *A Guide for the Independent Traveller*, as already stated, is not a guidebook in the proper sense of the word, I can afford to be a little cheeky and suggest to you, dear reader, that you should paddle your own canoe up the Seine and find out for yourself. *Fodor* (Hodder and Stoughton) have an excellent guide on the French capital and you could do much worse, for beginners, than to take one of Time Off's (see page 212) very flexible packages. Some French provincial capitals shine too and deserve some time, often more, than you think.

I would single out my own favourites: Nancy, for so long the capital of independent Lorraine, is a very beautiful city indeed: see the Place Stanislas and the Arc de Triomphe.

Rennes, also a one-time ducal capital, has a very handsome Palais de Justice and a fine cathedral.

Bordeaux, the wine capital of the world so far as I am concerned, has always had much attraction for its spaciousness, good town planning and quite a few museums.

Avignon, where the Popes settled for 500 years, is eminently worth staying in. The papal palace is unique and so is the famous Pont Bénezet, yes, the Pont d'Avignon, or at least what is left of it.

Grenoble, despite the often chill alpine winds which come down the valley I have always had a soft spot for the very handsome, classical city of Grenoble which, with its huge university, is now one of the intellectual focal points of France.

Montpellier, one of the oldest university towns in France, was once a very Protestant centre. This ancient city is lively and very handsome, especially because of its unique 'prom-enades'.

Yet, to my way of thinking, it is often in the smaller cities that France shines brightest of all and I have long had my own favourites which I would strongly recommend: Blois and Chinon, Chartres, Bourges with its most unusual cathedral, handsome Nevers, Limoges, Cahors, Nîmes of course and also Le Puy, my favourite Aix-en-Provence, the very special Carcassonne and not least of all Dijon. This ducal city of Burgundy which is without a doubt one of the finest art cities in western Europe has so many places and old patrician houses and museums that you will never have enough time to see them all.

GREAT SIGHTS

This is where one tends to become not only lyrical but verbose. One has no sooner finished describing a place or an area than another springs to mind which cannot be left out. Yet, as has been said, this is not a guidebook but a personal companion. So all I can do is reminisce and point you in the right directions for places which I have never forgotten. The rest is up to you.

The Loire When somebody asks me what they should see in this glorious area I have little hesitation: Chenonceaux, Azay-le Rideau, Chambord and Chaumont will probably sum up the French chateaux as well as any and all for different reasons. So don't miss them. But try to spare time for sights like a panorama of the Loire, under pale blue skies, with its sandbanks and its curious grey-blue-brown water. The best spot for this I have found over the years is by the front of the church at Candes, the place where St Martin (he of the cloak) died.

The Dordogne Try and see it from the Promenades des Falaises at Domme, high up over the river and if possible on a day when little white clouds go scudding around the sky.

The Lake of Annecy Short of the little watery pearls of the Vosges and the Black Forest, this is undoubtedly the most beautiful lake in Europe, for which I hope my Italian friends will forgive me. Spend some time on the Talloires side or the Duingt side and you too will be convinced. Go a little further south of the lake along La Combe d'Ire. It is unforgettable.

Northern Burgundy Of the great abbeys and castles of the region, Vézelay takes pride of place. I could spend hours there just looking at this fantastic Romanesque tympanum. But there are also places like Ancy-le-Franc, Tanlay, Fontenay and little villages and small towns such as Semur-en-Auxois and Flavigny-sur-Ozerain.

The Cévennes East of the Gorges du Tarn, this region of incomparable beauty has drawn intelligent, reflective people since long before Robert Louis Stevenson thanks to its lush valleys, secretive byways and quite gorgeous vegetation.

The Velay and the Forez East and north of Le Puy, don't miss this whatever you do. I must admit that once, on my way back to Paris, I discovered it almost by accident; a region of superb wooded hills running down into valleys of intense green like some bucolic symphony. Scenically, this is what France means to me.

Provence Anywhere north or south of the Durance River and along the banks of the Drôme is enchanted country. Plus of course the proximity of Van Gogh's Provence at Arles and St Rémy. Is there more? Naturally, there is but you will have to read more specialised books or, better still, go and see for yourself.

CLIMATE

Don't let the statistics fool you, France is not the land of eternal sunshine, more the land of infinite variety. North of a line from say Strasbourg to Nantes, don't expect miracles because the French weather will be much like your own. South of that line, your chances of fine weather improve but don't count on it. I have been frozen stiff in the Auvergne in May and shivered on the Atlantic coast, chilled to the bone by great gusts of wind. In the Dordogne, for instance, it rains almost as much as in Britain and if you go to Grenoble in the spring take your winter coat with you. It is only when you reach an imaginary line going say Montélimar to Bordeaux that you begin to feel the warmth of the Midi. The roofs of houses become flatter, the old stones much drier and you feel that though it might rain sometimes, which it does, this is a land which is used to the caress of the sun. Study the microclimates – they are very important. It may be useful to know that the French Government Tourist Office does not actually lie about the French climate. It might exaggerate a little but on the whole it is reliable. So, choose your time, from mid- to late-spring, and the whole of autumn are marvellous times to go touring in 'la belle France'.

INTERNAL TRANSPORT

By Road: France has the largest road network of any country in Europe and, though it has its share of motorways (roughly two and a half times as many miles as in the UK), the great thing to remember about touring in France is the enormous overall size of the road network and you get an idea of this by buying any of the 90 or so Michelin yellow maps, which are the regional ones. One cannot conceive of travelling in France without the appropriate map for the areas one is to visit. All 'routes nationales' are marked in red and are numbered. Below these comes the extremely large network of 'route departmentales' which, depending on their quality, can be marked in yellow, or white and are also numbered. Any Michelin road is well worth travelling on for one reason or another. The Michelin 'red' maps are of course for longer journeys and I recommend those that split France into north and south. The famous *Michelin Guide*, a new edition of which is published every Easter, is the bible of any self-respecting independent traveller. Once you have mastered the intricacies of its symbols it is undoubtedly the most complete and best guidebook in the world. Besides noting things that are worth seeing along with hotels and restaurants in ascending or descending order (with up-to-date prices too) the red guide has street maps of the larger cities. The result is quite invaluable. Not to be forgotten among the services rendered to the travelling public are the Michelin Green guides, which cover special regions or areas of particular interest. They are intelligent, detailed and make no attempt to play to the gallery. What they say is always but always right and that's that.

By Rail The French, not being shy, also claim that their trains are the best in the world. Quite possibly. The country has made a fine art of rail travel and quite apart from the headline-making 'TGV' – *trains à grande vitesse*, most trains in France run at between 100 and 125 mph (161 and 201 km/h) and there are 1400 services every day some of which go to the remotest parts of the land. French trains provide food that not even a British tabloid newspaper could find fault with and the system, known to all as SNCF (Société Nationale des Chemins de Fer), also offers cheap rail passes which are well worth inquiring into. French Railways (see page 215) have all of the answers.

By Air Air travel to and in France does not just mean a quick dash to Paris with Air France. The country has two major internal networks, UTA French Airlines and the ubiquitous Air Inter which last year carried 11 million passengers to over 30 destinations within France. There are also a number of smaller, more localised airlines like Air Jet, Air Languedoc, Air Littoral and Air Vendée (page 215).

Hotels France lists over 19,000 hotels, which is more than any other country, ranging from the Ritz on Place Vendôme to the little gîte deep down in the Cantal or the Finistère. The choice is truly enormous and in France hotelkeeping is often very much a family affair where one is welcomed, made to feel wanted and refreshed and fed in the best tradition. In this type of book, it is obviously impossible to list more than a very few and this I have done in the appendix (page 215), noting down only a few of the places I remember best. France is good value. I well recall the Sunday when I stopped in the small southern town of Casteljaloux and was offered a menu at 30 francs which included a choice of five starters both hot or cold, three entrées, four main dishes, 40 odd cheeses and dessert if I wished! And the experience can be repeated in many parts of France. Even in Paris it is perfectly possible to eat a decent lunch for less than 13 francs.

As befits a country where there is such a large choice of accommodation, many groups operate across the Channel. Some are commercial and some are merely groupings of like-minded people offering roughly the same idea. Although there are too many to mention, here are just a few of the best:

Rèlais et Châteaux This organisation, known all over the world and also operating in other countries, is very up-market and expensive. Its members, 150 chateaux hotels and restaurants, are regularly inspected and very strictly classified. Nothing but the best here.

Relais du Silence What a marvellous idea! Here is a group of some 216 places where the jukebox is unknown and there is no piped music. Absolute quiet.

La Vie de Château Here are over 200 small chateaux, manor houses and superior farms where you can stay and be yourself.

Château Accueil If you would like to be a paying guest of Madame la Marquise, here is your chance. Some 36 private owners of historic places will put you up in their marvellous homes and they have the staff to make things work.

Logis and Auberges de France This is the mammoth and well-tested organisation which over the years has collected over 4500 small hotels, simple country places and pleasant little restaurants, again with much surveillance and selection. A logis is almost always within reach.

Gîtes de France Farmhouses galore. Some all inclusive too and you do your own thing. They could not be better.

SPECIALISED HOLIDAYS

Oodles of them. Even if it's a horse you want, France has listed some 40 *Fédérations Equestres* whose organisers will fit you up, point you in the right direction and let you go.

To be highly recommended as agencies specialising in French holidays of all kinds are the following: Billington Travel, Blackheath Travel, Alec Bristow Travel in Chertsey, Celebrity Holidays and French Leave. Please see pages 215–6 for addresses.

France did you say? *On y va!*

Italy

PROFILE

When Dr Johnson wrote: 'The grand object of travelling is to see the shores of the Mediterranean', he was referring to Italy. This boot-shaped country stretching right across 'mare nostrum' has an almost immediate appeal — just as it had in the days of the Grand Tour. In those days, the aristocrats who could afford it, though not always the ones with the best brains, thought that mere proximity to the great names of Rome and the Renaissance might somehow make them more cultured. Sometimes it did. Nowadays, even the holidaymakers who go to the Adriatic beaches to catch a sun that they could catch anywhere go to Italy because they may be vaguely aware that somewhere, in the first chamber of the Uffizi or the back streets of Milan, they are in the presence of something more refined, of that awful word 'culture'.

Italians of today who are so expert at denigrating their country, though not their native city, and so good at not paying their taxes, are not always aware of this. They are convinced that all foreigners are mad. I don't believe we are.

But who is right? In a country where everything is always desperate yet nothing is ever serious, how would one know? Italians are masters of brinkmanship and since this is a pastime I do not personally revel in, I prefer to look at their country as an intellectual and emotional battery-charger. It reminds me that the world is not all rubbish and that here, in this unpromising country, much of what we know as civilisation did start.

So, open your eyes, go with a fresh mind, pick something here and another thing there and you will find that Italy will more than repay you. Don't go by the guidebooks, for there are too many of them and each tries to cover too much and, after all, who is able to spend three weeks in the Uffizi?

What is Italy good for? *Questa Questione.* ... What a question. Italy has mountains, including one side of the Alps, lovely soft plains if you know where to look for them, lots of sporting possibilities, though happily only 70 golf courses, and a long, long coastline, with clusters of intriguing islands just over the horizon.

BEACHES

I wonder why I always feel slightly superior to all these good people who go to Italy for a beach holiday? Why shouldn't they? Why not indeed. Italians themselves are not basically beach or country people. When they see a sandy strip, they want to 'organise' it by putting up rows of little canvas huts and bits of a boardwalk so they don't get their Gucci shoes messed up. An Italian beach is also an intensely convivial place – all those mammas, all those 'bambini'. I must admit that I don't care overmuch for the half-strangled beaches of Liguria but I am well at home as soon as I get along the Tuscany coastline around Viareggio or Marina di Pisa. Castliglioncello is even nicer – at least it has a shape. I do go for Porto Santo Stefano and its neighbour on the Orbetello peninsula, Porto Ercole. They have a certain 'chic' as well as local colour. However, even better, to my mind, is San Felice Circeo, south of Rome, where not all that many foreigners seem to go, and to be near Gaeta and Formia is reward enough.

Anything south of Naples is a different world (see pages 72–3) but going around the southern end of the boot, so to speak, to the east coast I would make a strong plea for the beaches around the Gargano peninsula, the 'spur', which I believe to be among the nicest and least developed of the whole Italian coast – all those around Peschici and Vieste are well worth descending on and so are those around the Testa del Gargano. The road around the midriff of this mysterious land was opened only about 20 years ago. The quality of the beaches improves north of Ancona, which is why so many foreign visitors make for places like Rimini and Cattolica. Venetians for whom La Serenissima is the centre of the world rave about their own Lido, which is just a nasty strip of sand to us – but if you want to be seen in good company that's the place to go. For myself, I'd rather spend the morning at the fish market in Chioggia. For one thing it is not deodorised.

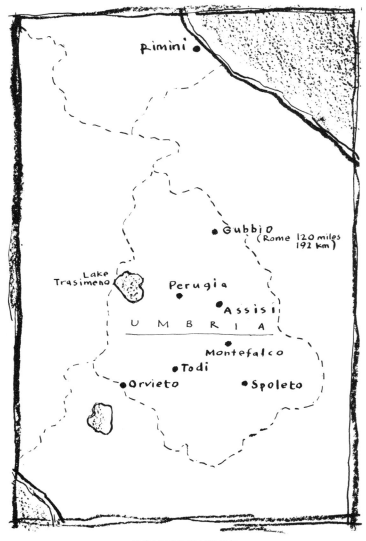

COUNTRYSIDE

Urban man *par excellence*, the average Italian looks down on his country cousins, the sons of the soil, up and down the long country. Not me. In fact, I had quite a job deciding which rural part of Italy to choose for *A Guide for the Independent Traveller*. The Po Valley? Well, yes but. The Venetian Arc? Too strictly tied to the apron strings of Venice. Campania? A bit soft for me. In the end, I cast my vote for two areas, Umbria and what Italians persist in calling the 'Mezzogiorno', which is anything south of the line from Naples to the Gargano.

They call Umbria 'the green heart of Italy'. I must have always visited it at the wrong time of year because when I make it to Umbria, the rich dark earth has always just been titivated by some artistic-minded tractor carefully avoiding all those delicious hedgerows and inviting little round woods. Elsewhere, the fat, dark furrows run up the hills to the horizon past the neat farms with their pigeon lofts and down again into some secretive valley which I never have time to see. Umbria looks for all the world like the background to one of those Italian Primitive paintings – just pre-Renaissance maybe? The sky is light blue, the sun stronger than you think and the whole province seems enveloped in a strange mauve haze. Umbria shares with much of Italy this curious business of being the borderline between the end of the countryside and the beginning of the city's proud walls. There is no in-between, no sprawl.

Perugia, sombre and elegant, has the feel of a self-important capital. Its citizens knew the Greeks and the Etruscans. For the Romans they had nothing but contempt; a kind of 'vieille noblesse' attitude which has weathered the years well. The Corso Vanucci, Perugia's main street, illustrates this: at one end is a lovely thirteenth-century fountain facing the cathedral and the municipal town square. Cobble-stoned and of noble proportions, the Corso Vanucci runs down to more recent and less distinguished buildings. The three famous medieval streets, which remain in toto, are worth seeing for all the tourist propaganda: the Maesta della Volte, the Via dei Priori and the Via Biglioni.

But it is Umbria's smaller cities that stand out most in my mind. Much nearer Rome and the true Renaissance, Spoleto has become world famous since Gian Carlo Menotti began his Festival of Two Worlds a quarter of a century ago.

Montefalco, amid olive groves and vineyards, is charming. Quite besides the wine, Orvieto is both charming and impressive, with one of the finest views in this part of the world and a magnificent, and rare, Italian Gothic cathedral. Todi, Etruscan, Roman and medieval, I have always liked very much and within its three sets of walls, it keeps its great past to itself. As for the precipitous Gubbio, it has always been one of my favourites too because it is noble, eloquent in its relics and a place where sensation-seeking day trippers don't go all that much.

People who know me are well aware that when it comes to southern Italy, I cannot be trusted with adjectives. It probably comes from the fact that for years Italians and others told me not to go there. 'Italy, south of Naples? There is

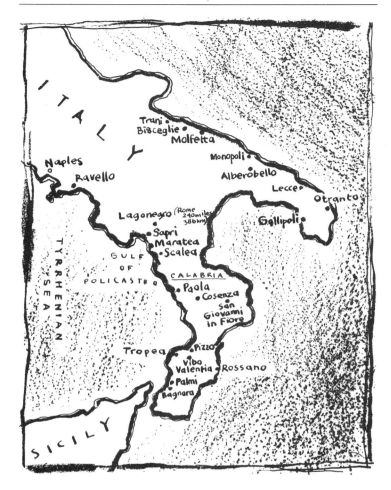

nothing there.' Only some of the finest, unspoilt touring country close to home, Greek temples, Byzantine churches, shorelines that seem to lead straight to heaven and so on. Years ago, I ventured gingerly down the Autostrada del Sole and when I had driven down to an undistinguished place call Lagonegro, I knew that I had found my stamping ground. Mountains piled up as far as my eye could see with villages grimly hanging to their slopes, the air was clear, colours ran from brown and green to mauve. There was no one there, least of all a tourist board official. When I carefully picked my way down to Sapri and my beloved Gulf of Policastro, I knew that this was 'it', a land of ghosts and legends, of brutal bandits and *bella figura*, condottieri, of beaches so fresh and clean that I could swear nobody had been there before me. This wasn't true of course but it was something to think about. I discovered Maratea almost by chance, with its gorgeous inland village and the *porto* with one of the best hotels in the Mediterranean, the Santavenere, which has remained good despite a rather chequered career.

I went careering down that coast, past Scalea and Diamante, up the improbable Paso Crocetta from Paola to Cosenza, down to Pizzo, Vibo Valentia and lovely Tropea. Then I went down again to Palmi and Bagnara where they go for swordfish in boats with enormously tall look-out masts and across to Rossano where, in the now famous San Marco fifth century Byzantine church, behind an open door, I found the Codex Purpureus, which is the second oldest bible in the world and which they have now locked up for safety in the Episcopal Museum. By then I was hooked and I decided that the 'Mezzogiorno' was for me. I have been back many times and have never been disappointed.

I reached San Giovanni in Fiore on one Good Friday afternoon, just in time to see the locals, tired of carrying saints in and out of the churches amid clouds of flowers, just sitting down drinking strong red wine and slicing up strange red onions. From there it was only a stone's throw away from Apulia's Alberobello and its amazing *trulli* conical houses and I discovered yet another face of the south of Italy: the remarkable and rarely visited region of the 'heel' of Italy where the eating is superb and the drinking even better. Someone told me about Lecce which, it appears, once had a Roman theatre right in the middle of the more recent piazza and I found a truly marvellous eighteenth century city, all baroque and curlicued architecture. Then, going north I discovered places like Trani and Molfetta, Otranto and Bisceglie, Monopoli and Gallipoli from where crusaders sailed for the Holy Land. I also found the Castel del Monte, the tremendous fortress built by Frederick II 'Stupor Mundi'.

And everywhere I saw fantastic churches and cathedrals, superb villages perched almost out of reach, marvellous medieval harbours and mountains so vast, and so quiet that if I stopped the car I could hear the tick of the clock. Southern Italy will never be 'packaged'. It's too awkward, too lacking in what the bigwigs of the travel business think the tourist wants. It is ideal for the independent traveller.

CITIES AND SIGHTS

What can I say about Rome and Milan, Florence and Naples that has not been said before? And since this is not a guidebook in the proper meaning of the word, I won't try. Of my beloved Venice even I shall say nothing except that if you have not been there you have missed something which no civilised person should miss. Instead, let me make a plea for some of Italy's smaller cities because I believe that, apart from perhaps France, no European country has such a wealth of delights.

Take Siena for instance. All I need is to get there and I am there, sitting on the Piazza del Campo for a whole afternoon, watching the world go by and leaving the tourists to find their way to Florence. Or take San Gimignano, or Urbino, with its famous Palazzo Ducale and its poignant memories of Raphael. Or Amalfi with its polychromatic duomo, or again the one and only Ravenna and its echoes of Byzantium.

Memories come flooding back. For example, of the time I saw the sun going to bed beyond Capri from the heights of Massa Lubrense. Of the early morning I spent facing the Convent of San Damiano near Assisi and swore that I could see St Francis feeding his birds. Of the warm lazy afternoon in the gardens of the Villa Rufolo in Ravello listening to the hum of the bumblebees. It was a good two hours before an elderly local said to me: 'Did you know that he (that terrible man), who once lived here, actually composed music about bumblebees?' I felt like telling him that the *Flight of the Bumblebee* had little to do with Richard Wagner and then thought better of it — why disappoint the poor man? After all, this was Italy, the land of anything, anywhere, anytime.

CLIMATE

Don't be fooled by statistics. The sun does shine on Italy. Some of the time. Some of the time too the sky comes down, the rain pours like a torrent and one could be in Manchester. Unfortunately, Italian weather is almost as wayward as its British counterpart and there are no rules. Speaking from experience, I can say only that my favourite seasons would be middle to late spring (apart from in the Alpine regions), and mid-autumn. Italy shines then.

INTERNAL TRANSPORT

There is no problem here. Italian trains, which are run by Italian State Railways are among the best in Europe. There are four kinds: 'Rapido', 'Espresso', 'Diretto' and 'Locale'. In addition there are two world-famous trains: the Settebello, which runs from Rome to Milan via Florence and Bologna, and the Adriatico, which runs from Milan to Bari. Some also put the Vesuvio, Milan to Naples, into that category but since it once broke down for three hours while I was a passenger, I will give it notice but with personal reservations.

Internal air travel is easy too. With 26 local airports and at least three domestic airlines that are mostly bookable through Alitalia, it is quite easy to go direct to Milan or Rome and fly onto a regional destination.

So far as I am concerned, Italy may well have invented the motorway. From the Autostrada del Sole to humbler ones such as that between Rome and L'Aquila, Italian motorways are not only superb but they are beautiful too. Nobody but an inspired Italian civil engineer could have straddled the whole of the Mezzogiorno for instance with a motorway which, like a giant's causeway, goes from hill to hill with daring and a dash of genius. Unlike their British equivalents, Italian 'autostrade' are also superb when it comes to resting or eating places. The Italian Automobile Club (ACI) is among the best in Europe. They have dozens of local offices and one call to Rome 4212, at any time of the day or night, will get some action. Driving in Italy is a pleasure once you have learned the ropes. However, don't try and drive in cities like Milan or Rome, and especially not in Naples. It ain't worth it.

HOTELS

There are about 40,000 hotels of one sort or another in Italy but, unlike in France, the good ones are not always in the right places and anyone who has tried Verona, Mantua or Foggia will know what I mean. Italians are not awfully good at country hotels but some, both in cities and in the country, which stick in my mind are mentioned in the Appendix.

SPECIALISED HOLIDAYS

Asking for a decent, intelligent tour operator who knows Italy is not easy. However, you do not need a guiding hand and, even less, a pre-digested holiday. You just need to go. My own way out, when I do not know, is to refer everyone to Citalia Ltd, which is a little unfair since they don't much like dealing with private clients. However, being a ubiquitous Italian company they know everything. Another good bet, especially for art places, is W. F. and R. K. Swan. Page & Moy are also good and knowledgeable specialists as are Serenissima Travel. Villas Italia have a good selection of places to rent for a week or two. The Italian State Tourist Office (Enit) is on the whole quite helpful, if a little patchy.

Please see page 216 for addresses.

Spain

As most people know by now, Spain is really two countries. The first, the 'costas', is roughly 3000 miles (4830 km) long and 10 miles (16 km) wide, filled with beer-on-draught, sausage and mash and German 'bratwurst'. Everybody goes there. In 1984, about 32 million people did. They made a dash for the sun-soaked beaches, turned over and came up all tanned, tried the local disco at night and went home convinced that they had been abroad. The fact that they did not meet a single Spaniard, man-to-man, did not bother them overmuch. Spaniards are just those people whose policemen wear funny hats. Once, not long ago, I attended an expatriate Brit's birthday party in Marbella and it took me a good half hour to realise that there was not a single Spanish guest.

The other Spain is what is left of the country – or 98 per cent of it anyway, which you discover when you cross the border between mass tourism and the real thing. It is grand, often austere, infinitely beautiful, filled to the brim with art and history, culture and good living. It is certainly a place to remember.

It's only a few years ago that I once took a prominent and not at all anti-social Spanish hotelier to a spot about 40 miles (64 km) from Valencia and suggested to him: 'This is where you should build a hotel...!' He looked at me as if I had just escaped from some lunatic asylum and said, most politely: 'Nobody comes here.' Ha again. Spaniards are not entirely to blame. They did not invent mass tourism. Their country was just there, surely big enough, and the sun shone for a good part of the year. On the other side were the tourists, the streets, the jails, the caffs, the instant 'paellas' and the all-night discos. They just put the two together and came up, laughing all the way to the bank. After all, if all that the tourists wanted was what the 'costas' had to offer, why bother about the rest? They, the Spaniards, always had the rest to fall back on. Occasionally, though, they are a bit wistful about it all.

At least two Ministers of Tourism in Madrid lost their job because they tried too hard to 'sell' Cuenca or Valladolid and

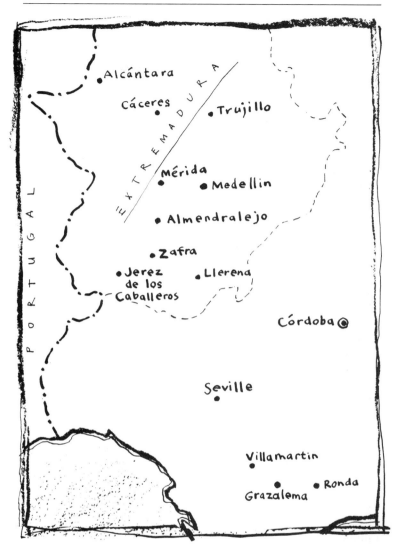

neglected the drains in La Manga de Mar Menor. One of them told me, long afterwards: 'Nobody really cares about the real Spain, the real Spaniards....' It's not entirely true. I care and so does the independent traveller and thank goodness we are left alone to indulge our passion for the offbeat, the evocative and the real. All we can do is get on the road and shout 'Arriba, Espana.' Nobody will thank us of course but it is we who should thank the Spaniards for letting us see their country, which is one of the strangest and most rewarding in the whole of Europe.

Meanwhile, working Spaniards are there, laughing all the way to the bank. International tourism has changed their lives. It has given them battery chickens, wine in plastic containers, traffic jams, smog (have you ever really looked at Madrid at ten o'clock in the morning?) a huge all-European market for the produce they once could not sell, television and video too and all the things we have got back home. I hope they are happy. But still, eternal Spain remains: Goya's *Tres de Mayo* is still in Room LV-A at the Prado Museum, the 'girasols' of Andalucia still turn their face to the sun and the ghost of Don Quixote still tilts a lance near La Mancha. Once, at Illescas, just south of Madrid, a gentleman with a small goatee beard saw me looking at El Greco's *Annunciation* and asked, in good French, 'How did you know it was here?' I told him that my guidebook had inspired me to make the trip. We sat on a wall for an hour and he told me about the great painter as if he had lived yesterday. As we parted, he said: 'I did not know foreigners cared about that sort of thing,' – I assured him that a few of us did.

What is Spain good for? I would say almost everything. From 'costas' to the 'rias' of Galicia and from Santiago de Compostela to Granada, Spain has as much culture, art and history as, for instance, France or Italy, though they are often very different. It has great food – if you care to look for it – and good wines too. It also has landscapes guaranteed to take you out of yourself.

BEACHES

Unless you are the kind of person I mentioned at the start of this chapter (We-only-came-for-the-beer), don't bother. Spanish beaches, once among the finest in the south, have been so littered with rubbish as to be unrecognisable. Only two small bits have escaped so far: the Costa de la Luz between Cadiz and Portugal and the north west, on the Atlantic coast, between, say, Ribadeo and Pontevedra where it rains a lot. It might as well be Brittany or Cornwall. The rest of the Spanish coast has gone, being covered with ghastly hotels whose roofs will cave in tomorrow or just horrible shacks that will be swept away by the tide. You might just be lucky on the Costa Brava, which was once one of the most beautiful stretches of coast anywhere in Europe. The chances are that it will be in the off season and, didn't you know, nobody goes there in the off season. That's what travel agents and tour operators say anyway.

COUNTRYSIDE

Choosing one's favourite place in Spain can be as difficult and as rewarding as in any other country. No, Spain is not at all the same. Apart from the north west, grey-green and very Celtic, and Catalonia, which always seems to belong to the northern Mediterranean, Spain is very much the *sol y umbra* country where pictures should be neat but are not and where the sun has for ever and ever fashioned not only the land-scape but the people too. Provincial differences are many, and so are traditions. It's a big country, chunky and remote, the highest in Europe not so much in terms of mountain peaks or high plateaus.

Nowhere else in the world does the traveller feel less important – a mere ant crawling between earth and sky, from one silent village to another. Churches are massive and magnificent. The monasteries are even more so. Apart from the urban centres where supermarkets have already brought colour, and rubbish, Spanish country people appear sombre-looking, dressed in uniform black and on the surface seem so independent that you might swear they don't care much about anyone. They are themselves. In Spain, art, history and man-made beauty are never far away but dis-tances are great, or appear great and, like, say, northern Mexico or parts of the United States, Spain is a country where the independent traveller can let himself go, be him-self, make his own decisions as the miles go by.

Most travellers, of course, make for the obvious, such as the softness of Andalucia, the harshness of Castile, the intense greenness of Levante. I will go somewhere else, to a country which few tourists ever visit.

Take the western road out of Madrid and when you reach the little town of Oropesa you quickly get the strange feeling that you are in unknown land. To the north are the fastnesses of the Sierra de Gredos. To the south there is nothing, or so it seems. To the west the land rises and falls in great slabs, rather like the Castile you have just left, only more so. Hori-zons are vast, the land is tawny and sometimes green along the river beds and at first glance it could not support a flea. However, that is not so. It is poor all right and in times gone by it was even poorer. You are now in Extremadura – very hard indeed – and it was through men from this unpromis-ing land that Spain became an imperial power. Those men became the *conquistadors*.

So I shall point my car westwards and go and investigate. In the late sixteenth and early seventeenth centuries, men went from here to the ends of the earth and took Spanishness

— Hispanidad if you like — with them. They had little to their name: religion and a burning faith, greed and brutality, singleness of purpose and, above all, that recklessness of those who have very little to lose, nothing to come back to. Trujillo, he who put an end to the glittering Incas, was a pig-keeper. He couldn't read or write. Cortés, the son of a small town teacher, was a little better. Balboa, de Soto and Valdivia were not much better socially. They all were trying to escape the grinding poverty and the lack of opportunity in their native province. Extremadura, bitterly cold in winter, hot as Hades in summer, had nothing to offer. The New World had.

And so you descend, or climb into this remote and virtually unknown province. Personally, I always make first for Alcántara because it seems to be the end of the world, right smack on the Portuguese frontier. It is a small undistinguished town where the Roman Emperor Trajan built a remarkable bridge over the Tagus, which is still in use today. Then I doubleback to Cáceres, surely the queen city of Extremadura. A French traveller once wrote of the 'Barrio Monumental' — the old city — 'Ici tout est noble'. He was right, of course, and he could have added that everything was paid for with silver from the New World. Conquistadors never forgot the native land that had in fact done so little for them. They returned in droves, rich as kings and now hidalgos all, to prove to the rest of Spain that they had made it. In Cáceres and elsewhere they built, and built and built — palaces, monasteries, statues, churches and treasuries. They were the nouveaux riches of the times. One, I think it was Valdivia, even endowed his native city with a sewerage system which is still in use today.

Cáceres itself is a must, especially the Palacio del Commendador, the Casa de Godoy (not that Godoy), the Casa del Sol and many others, all magnificent period buildings with mellowed stone, marvellous windows and an air of patrician beauty. One exception is Medellin which Hernando Cortés did not beautify because he found more in Mexico and stayed there so long. Today it is a sleepy little town, with a modest plaza and an old church with, facing it, a rather odd and latter-day statue of the great man. The castle dominating the town is formidable indeed but Cortés had nothing to do with it. One man with whom I talked on the plaza told me that his name was Cortés. The local grocer was also called Cortés and it would seem that many local people still carry the revered name.

And so, as in a kind of historical trance, you go from one

birthplace to another looking for the man who crossed the
great ocean and made his fortune. In Jerez de los Caballeros
it is Balboa, the first man to see the Pacific Ocean and de
Soto, who discovered Florida. The prize in my opinion is
Trujillo. Because it is much smaller, it shows more and the
city of the pig-keeper has become a place of stirring beauty,
especially with its narrow streets of dressed stone and its
vast Plaza Mayor, the noble facades of the Orellana-Toledo
House, the Vargas-Carvajal Palace and, above all, the house
of the Marquis de la Conquista, which was built by Trujillo's
son-in-law to commemorate the founder of the family for-
tunes. In the middle of the place, stands the old man himself,
a relatively modern bronze statue, larger than life, sword in
hand, pointing the way and appearing to say: 'Go West,
young man. That is where the money is.' You soon forget
Trujillo's brutality and remember only his courage and his
durability. And everywhere there are castles and moats,
bridges and forts, churches and cloisters.

Not far from Trujillo is Mérida, once the Roman capital of
this part of Iberia and still showing off some very impressive
monuments. Extremadura grows on you as you drive along.
One little town succeeds another: Almendralejo, charming
little Zafra, Villa Nueva de la Serena, and the beautiful
Llerena. One place is a must. Due west of Trujillo is the vast
and magnificent monastery of Guadalupe, a name that has
gone around the world wherever Spaniards have travelled
and for centuries one of Spain's greatest pilgrimage destinations. Go and see the great cloisters and the Zurbaran paintings.

By and by, you climb over the Sierra Morena (ignoring
Seville and Córdoba since they belong to another, greater
story) and come to the *girasols* of Andalucia. Go and see
them around Arcos de la Frontera – and one gets to the route
of the white towns, an itinerary hardly ever covered properly since everyone naturally stays in Ronda. Here, in the
parched hills, is a whole series of little treasures, places like
Villamartín and El Bosque and particularly Grazalema and
cliff-bound Setenil, Prado del Rey and Zahara. They all have
little white houses, pottery tiles, flowered windows, little
inns with inviting tables and much good food. You might
end up among the 'decorators' of Marbella (I hope not). It is
much better to drive back to Seville or indeed to
the one and only Córdoba. But try Extremadura now. The
Joneses are not there.

CLIMATE

Don't go to Spain in the winter unless it is along the coasts. You might regret it. For inland Spain, spring and autumn are best but summer is almost unbearable.

INTERNAL TRANSPORT

Spanish roads, which were once notoriously bad, are now quite good and huge 'autopistas' will lead you almost anywhere. 'Carreteras nacionales' are also good although signposts are often a little wayward for the uninitiated. The biggest headache when driving in Spain is the commercial transport, which is among the heaviest in Europe and occasionally very dangerous. So watch out for the big lorries and trucks. Spanish trains, especially the star ones like the Talgo and the Ter, can compete with the finest and with either Iberia or the local Aviaco airline you can get almost anywhere.

HOTELS

When Spaniards boast of their hotels, they are of course speaking of those along the 'costas' so don't be misled. The 'other' Spain is not so well served though occasionally in cities like, for instance, Seville, Santiago, León or Burgos, you will come across a hostelry that you will probably remember to the end of your travelling days. When a Spanish hotel is good, it is good. The best bet by far when travelling 'inside' Spain is the Government-run parador or albergue. There are about 40 of these throughout the country, often housed in some sumptuous period building and they have saved the life of many a weary traveller. One could design an itinerary entirely based on paradores and not go very far wrong. Accommodation and price range from the simple to the extravagant.

SPECIALISED HOLIDAYS

Don't expect too much (in fact don't expect anything) and you won't be disappointed. Spain is bad, very bad at promoting itself and the Spanish National Tourist Office does little to help. After these many years I still have to find the one 'inside' Spain tour operator who will give me what I want. People like Cox & Kings, Sovereign, Mundi Color or Fairways & Swinford come closest of all. The national airline, Iberia, has a programme called 'Freedom of Spain' which, if you can find it, is passable. Otherwise you are on your own.

Please see page 217 for addresses.

Portugal

PROFILE

If there is one thing that is guaranteed to make an otherwise calm Portuguese really angry it is for the visitor to imply that he is, after all, much like the Spaniard next door. That, he certainly is not. The Portuguese are special people, out on their own, Atlantic-oriented, rather romantic and even mawkish (just listen to their *fado* singing). Their language is only a remote cousin of Spanish and is virtually unpronounceable. They have their own often peculiar history and while most other Europeans looked to the rest of Europe and the Mediterranean, the Portuguese looked to the oceans of the world, most of which they conquered through sheer courage and determination to build up a commercial empire which their small country could not possibly sustain.

They developed their own architectural style, the Manueline, which is like rococo gone mad, and used the profits they made out of Brazil, Africa and the East Indies to beautify their own land. Right now, they are only just emerging from the long years of the Salazar dictatorship and, to my way of thinking, they are to be allowed the occasional, and apparently quite mad, foray to the right or the left. They are finding their own way and it is not easy. A friend of mine who, after the revolution, was responsible for the redistribution of land well remembers the day when he gave the deeds to some fields to a Ribatejo peasant. The man took the papers, turned them upside down and asked my friend: 'And now, señhor, what are my orders for the day?' When told that he was now his own boss and that he should make his own rules, the man went away shaking his head and muttering that things had never been like that before. Indeed they had not.

For the independent traveller Portugal is special. Although relatively small, it is really unlike any other country and if you care to go off the beaten track a little you will be rewarded with such sights and sounds that you could be a million miles away from the grey north of Europe. Apart from the budding industrialisation of the Lisbon area and

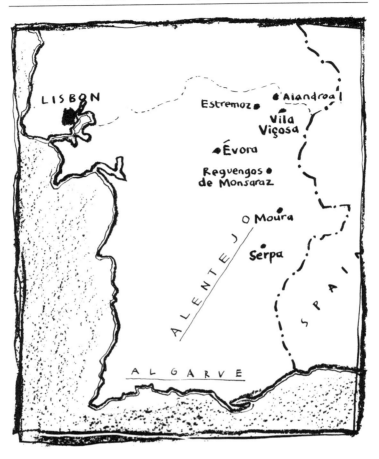

the sometimes phoney genteelness of the Algarve, Portugal is there to be discovered if you are that way inclined.

What is Portugal good for? A complete change which alone is worth the trip: rough mountains in the Trás-os-Montes in the north east, the old provinces of Beira Alkta and Beira Baixa, also mountainous, the three areas of Beira Litoral, Estremadura and Ribatejo that are really the heartland of the country, the vast and little known Alentejo and, of course, the smiling and welcoming Algarve.

BEACHES

Portuguese beaches are Atlantic, always clean and invigorating and, to be frank, sometimes windy. To my way of seeing things, the Portuguese authorities have wrongly divided their country, beach-wise, into a number of 'coasts'. First, from Spain to just south of Oporto, comes the Costa Verde in which Viana do Castelo and Ofir are the most developed resorts. Then comes the Costa de Prata, or Silver Coast, where there are dozens of quite attractive little family resorts with Figueira da Foz being at the top. Next comes the Costa de Lisboa, with such international winners as Estoril and Cascais. And far to the south there is that 150 miles (242 km) of the Algarve where the beaches are often spectacular, sometimes among the best in Europe and with enough hotel styles to please everyone. My own favourite beaches would be Praia de Luz and Armaçao de Pera.

COUNTRYSIDE

This is heavenly almost everywhere but my prize goes to the vast horizons of the Alentejo. The Portuguese don't make much fuss about it. They believe foreigners would find it dull and themselves make a quick dash for their beloved Algarve. But the Alentejo is anything but dull for it is one of the last really virgin areas of Europe where the traveller who is on his own can do what he likes. It has vast carpets of wheatfields, rolling hills, the occasional cluster of cork trees looking for all the world like the final performers of the last big top, gorgeous little white towns and villages and huge farmhouses, known as *montes*, crowning the hillsides.

I must admit that I came to know the Alentejo years ago when, having lost my way, I hit the small town of Alandroal, which few visitors go to, and found it to be a perfect time capsule of mellow stones and ancient walls. There was, of course, much more to the region than that. There was charming Estremoz, the centre of marble quarries and the heart of Portuguese pottery land. At Vila Viçosa, I discovered that generations of Portuguese kings had made this their favourite country seat and embellished it until it is today a real museum piece. Monsaraz, close to the Spanish border, is an old fortress which has virtually not been touched since the seventeenth century. Moura and Mourao I loved too for they are lovely old villages where life does not seem to have changed much. Serpa is a delight to the eye; it is an old town almost hidden on a wooded hilltop where the streets are cobbled and old women still cook the main meal of the day on a charcoal brazier in front of their door.

The best town, of course, is Évora, which is the true capital of this extraordinary land. The Romans built it and they left behind a charming little Temple to Diana, now almost cheek by jowl with the famous Monastery dos Lóios. Évora is a very artistic, very lively little town which certainly must not be missed.

The Portuguese tourist authorities hardly ever say a single word about the long coast line between the Lisbon area and the Algarve and, broadly, anywhere where tour operators don't go, the independent traveller should. Try seaside places like Sines, Vila Nova de Milfontes and Odeseixe in the south. You might be the only tourists there.

CITIES

He who has not seen Lisbon has missed a lot for it is one of the last truly civilised capitals of Europe, well designed, airy, with plenty of trees and avenues where you can actually walk. From the Belém Tower to the new suburbs near the airport, Lisbon seems to exist for only one reason: to face and embrace the wonderful Tagus estuary now so easily crossed by the thin silver ribbon of the Salazar Bridge. This capital is a city of the sea and it lives by the sea. It is the only large city I know, apart possibly from Venice, where one of the main squares, known as the Black Horse, is actually three-sided — the fourth being the sea. Much of Lisbon is eighteenth century, rebuilt after the great earthquake by that much maligned gentleman the Marques de Pombal. Life is to be found in the 'baixa' (pronounced 'baicha') around the Rossio, the beginning of the Avenida da Liberdade, the Rua Augusta and the Rua Garrett.

Fish is what one remembers about Lisbon. Fish and more fish. Go, as I have done so often, down the Rua de Portas de San Antao, which runs parallel to Liberdade, and see first the fabulous antique and junk shops, then make a long stop in one of those marvellous fish restaurants where, it seems, all the denizens of the sea decorate the windows. Afterwards you should end up in the old district of the Alfama, totally medieval, very pretty and home of *fado*.

Portugal's second city, Oporto, I know less well and therefore probably don't appreciate as much, though its frontage on the Douro, the Moorish Hall at the Stock Exchange and, of course, those endless wine lodges are things one remembers.

GREAT SIGHTS

These must include Coimbra, which is one of the oldest university cities in Europe and the place where Arab geographers and Christian monks vied with each other to get the world to rights. I suspect the great monastery of Batalha, north of Lisbon, means more to the Portuguese than it does to foreigners since it was built in the fifteenth century to commemorate a famous battle. Nazaré, very pretty, is for the tourists. Óbidos is one of my great favourites and a place well loved by all serious photographers since its white houses are all bunched together inside the darker ramparts.

Tomar takes everyone's breath away for it is dark, dramatic and bathed in intrigue. It was the seat of the Knights of Christ who took over from the Templars in Portugal in the fourteenth century. The world-famous Manueline window, which everybody goes to photograph, is only one of the visual delights of this fantastic place.

CLIMATE

Except in the Algarve where the sun always seems to shine (average winter temperature is 54°F/12°C), the weather in Portugal can be a matter of luck. I have seen the suburbs of Lisbon looking as grey as Manchester and I have also travelled in March in the north of the country when the weather was what June is sometimes like in Britain. So you take your pick, always remembering that Portugal is an Atlantic country, not a Mediterranean one. With this proviso, travel to Portugal when you feel like it and you will probably not be all that far wrong.

INTERNAL TRANSPORT

Portuguese train services are good and reliable. The roads are all that plus sheer enchantment and beauty, especially when you get away from the big cities and take yourself into the country areas. The Portuguese take a particular pride in the state of their roads and from village to village they still hold competitions every year to find the nicest stretch, the best-kept kilometre, the most flowered bits and all that. One feels that many larger and supposedly more advanced countries could take a lesson or two from little Portugal in making their roads a matter of pride.

HOTELS

There is no need to rough it in Portugal for hotels run from the regal to the simple and prices range from the 'normal' to the very cheap. Certainly the Costa Verde and Oporto, the Lisbon area and the Algarve are not short of international hotels. Like Spain, Portugal also has a network of about 20 pousadas, or places of rest in Portuguese, which are mostly housed in palaces, convents or monasteries.

All are very clean and beautifully run and every one is a prize for the independent traveller who is looking for something out of the ordinary. I remember with delight the pousadas in Óbidos, in Estremoz, Évora and Serpa. There can be no doubt that a resting place like the Pousada dos Loios in Évora is well worth seeking out. The Portuguese Tourist Office can give you the relevant details.

SPECIALIST HOLIDAYS

As I have said, Portugal is an ideal country for touring and especially for those who like to take things easy and stop a few days here and there. In this little country, the owners of many old houses have opened their homes to paying guests and the rewards are infinite. There are about 20 to 30 of these places, depending on the season. Some are authentic ancient castles. Some are manor houses or big farms and several offer special attractions like riding or fishing. I have been left with happy memories each time I have tried this kind of Portuguese sophistication, simplicity or merely hospitality. Again the Portuguese Tourist Office can give you details and one commercial company, Harlen Travel of Staines, has 'packaged' this kind of holiday. A few other Portuguese hotels are mentioned in the appendix.

One sport or pastime that is particularly associated with Portugal is golf. There are 17 principal golf courses in the country, 11 of which are of world championship standard, and many of them are situated on that blessed Algarve coast where the sight of a man with a golf club is the norm rather than the exception. The well-organised Portuguese Tourist Office can also help you there with quite a few intelligent brochures and much good advice.

Please see page 217 for addresses.

Greece

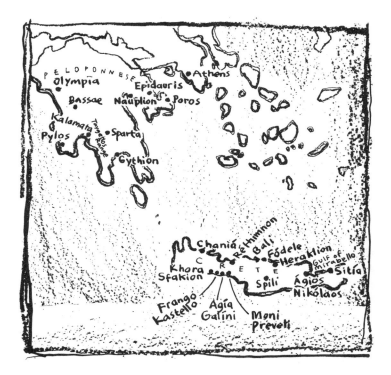

PROFILE

The real trouble with Greece, for me at any rate, is that this comparatively small country has so much more beauty – sheer, simple, inebriating beauty – than I know I will find anywhere else. Don't ask me why. It is all there, so real, so vivid and, in a way, so normal for Greece, that I just go bonkers. I have no sooner raved about the virginal beauty of the Cycladic line – all white and blue – than the light-coloured woods of the Pelion next to the blue sea call me over and seem to say, 'Look we are here too.' I might suddenly go mad about Mystras or Monemvasia and then, out of nothing but utter longing, I recall the poppies dancing in the breeze around the Temple of Apollo in Bassae or simply the incredibly limpid, lustrous Greek morning almost anywhere. How could this little country at the rump end of Europe have this effect on me?

89

It so happens that I like the Greeks too. I know that they are an awkward, cussed lot for ever raising hell about something or other. But have you ever watched a Greek eating a red mullet? He looks at it as if to make its acquaintance, raises two fingers to grasp the fish high above his mouth, grates his teeth, true or artificial, on the fish leaving just the head (and not always that) and only a poor zip fastener of a thing on the side of his plate. He wipes his lips, looks around for an audience and seems to say: 'Didn't I do that well, eh?'. He is an endearing fellow all right, incredibly generous in big things and predatory and mean in the small ones, curious about people and objects, outwardly supremely uninterested in money and yet carefully picking up the five drachma coin he has just dropped. He is passionately proud of his own brand of *philotimo*, which he himself invented. And he claims as his own the fantastic past that he knows will get him anywhere. He is convinced that Sophocles was his great-uncle and Pericles his godfather, carefully forgetting all the Turks and Levantines, Vlachs and Bulgarians, Slavs and Venetians who happened to come in between.

Yes, after that Hellenic column, the sunset over a wine-dark sea (who said that?) and that Greek with a gold-toothed smile I am hooked again once more. He is a Greek god and let us face it, a god-damned Greek too. The combination of that divinely beautiful land which the sea seems to kiss at every turn and the man who lives there, so much more individual that most other Europeans, acts like a sip of nectar.

Of course, tourism has spoilt much of Greece. How could it avoid doing so? Annually there are now two tourists for every three inhabitants and Greece is the world's fastest-growing tourist destination. It is particularly favoured by the British, a million and a half of whom went there in 1984, which represents a nine-fold increase in fifeen years. Yet, the curious thing is that nobody can really, but really, spoil Greece not even the National Tourist Organisation of Greece, bless them. A small country, its coastline is almost as long as that of France and so indented, not to mention the 300 islands, that if you just go around the corner you are quite likely to find a small inlet, a little bay which the dreaded hand of the mass tour operator has not had time to grasp. Good, because it leaves more of Greece for us to discover and that is undoubtedly one of the greatest rewards of this travelling age. All this is so even without the remains from a time when Greece was the centre of the world inventing, among other things, philosophy, democracy, medicine, geometry, much of architecture and finding a new meaning for that much abused word − beauty. Have you ever compared a Greek statue with its Roman counterpart? One is divine form and the other a butcher on holiday. The Romans knew that well and were not at all ashamed of facing up to the superiority of the Greeks.

What is Greece good for? The revelation of earthly beauty and the sudden feeling you have that this is where it all began. A small, quite lovely country which has not yet altogether been spoiled by mass tourism but which is sufficiently well organised most of the time to satisfy the majority of tourists.

BEACHES

Greek beaches range from the divine to the so-so and, unlike most countries where one area might have great beaches and another none at all, beaches in this little country are so spread out that one often needs the skills of a gold prospector − they are hardly ever in the right places.

Years ago, for instance, people described the western coast of the Peloponnese to me as being beach country and, after seeing the immense stretch of coastline all the way from Killini in the north to Gargaliani in the south, I would have agreed. That is until a few months ago when, almost accidentally, just north of Pylos and Nestor's Palace, I found Boidokila, a perfect three-sided beach, of such haunting beauty that it left me breathless. And there wasn't a soul there. That's Greece for you. And the same goes for the eastern coast of the Peloponnese, north and south of the Monemvasia and around Astros and Leonidion, though these are more difficult to reach.

Most Greeks believe that the finest beach in all Greece is Koukounaries, on the island of Skiathos. Quite. It takes a lot of beating but then a lot of other people have discovered it too. Those Greeks forget the nearby islands of Skopelos and Alonnisos. Beaches in the southern half of Rhodes are twice as nice as those in the north for being half as crowded and the humblest Greek isle does boast at least one magnificent strand. I have seen some on Karpathos, Symi, Samos, Naxos and even lonely Kythera that would send tour operators straight to their psychiatrist. And what about Parga in Epirus? Or those woodland fringed beaches of Thasos in the north? Or those on the unfashionable east side of Corfu?

For sheer breathtaking beauty you would have to go far to see better than that island's famed Paleokastritsa which, in my early travelling days, had not yet been invaded. Or what about the Mani and beaches like Fare or Mantenia? Then there is the Pelion, that crooked-finger peninsula in Thessaly where beaches like Milopotamos are only just beginning to get known. Even islands which, like Lemnos, famous nowadays for the Akti Myrina Hotel, one of the three or four best holiday hotels in the whole of the Mediterranean, has more superb beaches than there are days in the month. Because of the shining light, the pale blue water and the blissful marriage of land and sea, Greece is one of the few countries in the world where even a modest pebble beach will send people into raptures. And there is always another one, just around the corner, either sand or pebble or both. Halkidiki in the north has its share of both and some of its beaches are, in my book, among the finest anywhere.

Beaches did I say? Go to Greece to see the original. I guarantee that you won't be disappointed.

COUNTRYSIDE AND SIGHTS

Writing about Greece is difficult. How many books have we got? One, two or maybe three? What, just one small chapter? And when it came to choosing my own favourite bits I got into real trouble because memories of marvellous places came flooding in. Perhaps I should write about Halkidiki, that heavenly trident of the gods in the north and its three prongs of Kassandra, Sithonia and Mount Athos? The Pelion appeals too because of the curious combination of sylvan beauty and the sea. Or perhaps it should be the northern part of Greece, all the way from Delphi? But how could I do it better than Patrick Leigh Fermor in his famous book *Roumeli* (Penguin Books)? And what about all those almost countless islands? The alternate softness and ruggedness of the Dodecanese, the riches of the east, with landfalls like Samos or Chios or even the almost unreachable Samothraki, the matchless Cyclades?

In the end, a choice had to be made and I settled on two areas. The first is the lesser-known face of Crete and let us hope that it does not become too well known too quickly so that the independent traveller still has somewhere to go in this most intriguing of all Greek islands.

Much of Crete is routine, of course. Zorba the Greek and all that. The northern coast, apart from a few places like Bali and Fódele, which is the birthplace of El Greco, has long been got at by tour operators who, since the airport is at Heraklion, find it so much more easy to funnel tourists east and west and leave it at that. Nor is Crete to be sneered at: the magnificent Venetian cities of Chania and Réthimnon and, in the east, the miraculous beauty of the Gulf of Mirabello where little Agiós Nikólaos has long ago been transformed into a kind of Cretan St Tropez and the more quality-conscious purlieus of Elounda. Further east there is enchanting Sitía, that famous beach at Vai where a few out-of-breath palms carefully nurtured by the National Tourist Organisation of Greece seem to grow right on the water's edge.

But you have not seen anything yet because the interior of Zorba's island is more than worth the trip. The southern road – if you can call it that – around Khóra Sfakíon and Frango Kastello offers the wildest and most romantic coastline in Europe. You emerge from the tortuous Imbros Gorge and there, suddenly in front of you, is the Libyan Sea, the only barrier between Africa and you. Like a great stone tiara the craggy mountains crown Zeus's island. Khóra Sfakíon, once a famous Venetian stronghold, is quite well known now but it is neither spoilt nor crowded. Tiny Venetian houses, often with lovely doorways, surround the little stone-girt harbour. Two places on the southern coast which have always disappointed me, Matalla and Palaiohora, are both still plagued by back-packing hippies whose way of life, I'm afraid, is incomprehensible to me.

However, of all the Minoan sites in Crete I much prefer the lordly Phaistos to the better-known Knossos. Further east in the lee of the massive and legendary Venetian castle of Frango Kastello I have, in the off-season, often shared a lunch with no more than about 25 travellers scattered in 3 tavernas. Further east again towards Sellia and that village called Peach-Rhodakinon, I have travelled and met no one. In village after village there are white houses with blue doors, fig trees cascading down over white walls and domed ovens producing in turn delicious lamb and bread and the inevitable vine-covered tavernas where locals, in baggy black trousers and white blouses, turn around and smile shyly, absolutely amazed that any one should have got there at all. Often too, I climb to the famous monastery of Moni Preveli, one of the last strongholds of Cretan-British resistance during the War, and meander down to that enchanting and only slowly changing village of Agia Galini – Holy Serenity – which has always for me lived up to its name.

A word of warning about driving in Crete: maps are delightful pictures rather than works of reference. Signposts point whimsically up riverbeds and the road, which began as a wide, asphalted highway, has a way of petering out into a goat track. The only exception to the general rule is the highway which now lines the northern shore of the island. It is indeed a very good road but is it Crete? Yet, almost everywhere along it, places like Spili, Sifnari, Kefali or Sougia bring back warm memories of Cretan friendships. You have to know Crete to realise that the world is not all the same.

My second choice for a place to visit in Greece must be the Peloponnese. Many of my Greek friends in London are convinced that I am the secret public relations man for that curious appendage. I wish I were. It might have won me a few extra red mullets. It is simply that over the years I have become inordinately fond of the place. It is a tough, grand and bony sort of country, rather like Crete except that it is tied to the mainland by the umbilical cord of the Corinth Isthmus.

Like most Greek geography, the Peloponnese is totally and wilfully contrary. It is uninteresting in the north, flat and green in the west, as mountainous as Hades in the centre and almost inaccessible in the east. Those who doubt the penultimate statement should be sentenced to drive, in mid-winter, along the new road from Kalamata to Sparta over and around the tortuous contours of the Taygettos range. The highest point, Profiti Elias, is 7500 feet (2286 m) high and looms around every bend like a second-hand ice cream cone with ice stalactites hanging in the caves and rushing torrents greeting you at every turn. It's no place for weaklings and that is why the ancient Spartans used to leave their young on the summit for a night or two. If they surrendered their souls to Zeus that was that. If they survived they were the kind of chaps who could stop the Persians at Thermopylae when outnumbered two hundred to one. Rather like an English public school really.

The rocky summits of Taygettos extend for ever southwards where they come to make up the legendary Mani. South west and you descend to the Laconian Plain (yes, some Greeks were laconic in those days) amid the orange and lemon trees ending up in Gythion, the ancient port of Sparta and, later, of the Byzantine Mystras, where the first tourist hotels were built only a few years ago. Seen from the east, Gythion is very pretty indeed, draping its once-Venetian houses between Taygettos and a seafront cluttered with fishing nets. Just offshore, with a causeway leading you on, is the tiny island of Marathonisi, once called Kranae and very famous. It was there that Paris of Troy, having eloped with Helen, took his prize and spent the first night of a honeymoon which eventually led to the Trojan War. He chose a pretty spot.

From here, it is a mere few miles – if you are a crow – to the other side of the Mani and the first sight of Kalamata, which you may not wish to see twice. Across the wide Messenian plain lies the westernmost finger of the Peloponnese where wise King Nestor once ruled near Pylos and one of history's most famous naval battles later took place – at Navarino.

Travel north and you reach Elis and the aptly-named Arcadia, a smiling land of green fields, orchards and cypresses where you fully expect to meet the flute-playing Pan in some sylvan glade. Instead you find the noble Temple of Apollo at Bassae and, of course, the lovely Olympia which, somehow, keeps coming back into my dreams. If you travel east you are soon in that other enchanted land, the Argolis, the right direction for the charming Nauplion, the first capital of Greece, the truly unforgettable Epidaurus and the Mycenae of Agamemnon. If you really want to know about that marriage of the sea and the land, follow my advice: take the wrong road, past Korphos, past Ano Phanarion, past the lively and beautiful Poros and try Kilas where they still build boats with an adze and drive to Epidaurus by the road over the Didymon mountains.

To the south, another great mountain range, the Parnon, creates the bony structure for the third and easternmost finger of the Peloponnese. The coast is so inaccessible that it is the only part of the whole peninsula that does not have any road at all around it. Its little ports look to the outside world and its people were and still are the best sea traders in the business. Their story is best summed up by the singular profile of Monemvasia, the so-called Gibraltar of Greece. Few places are so impressive as this huge rock just out to sea that has belonged to the Franks and the Venetians but mostly to the Byzantines. Today, over 100 ruined churches each still with burning candles decorate the great rock.

All this plus more mountains, rich plains, pretty villages and numberless little coves and beaches. That is the physical part of the Peloponnese story. The rest is another matter because for all those who are enthralled or even mildly intrigued by the past, the Peloponnese is heaven itself. Its magnificent historical panorama is stuffed with the curious and almost legendary stories of the Myceaneans, the Spartans, the Corinthians, plus Macedonians, Romans, Byzantines, Frankish lords, Venetians and Genoese, Turks and even Egyptians, without mentioning the hilarious deeds of some of those great *klephts* or bandit captains of the Mani. It was here that the story of Greece rose like a swell and flowed into the present. In modern times, it was the birthplace of the Greek nation. In the Peloponnese there are over 2000 Hellenic sites, quite apart from Frankish or Venetian castles, echoes of the Crusades and 3000 years of civilisation. That's one part of the story. For the rest, you will have to go and ferret for yourself because the Peloponnese does not easily give up its secrets.

CLIMATE

This is ideal – some of the time. I once landed in Athens to be greeted by a snowstorm and on another occasion, an early March day, the outside temperature next to my glass of ouzo in a Kalamata taverna was 74°F (23°C) at noon. Northern Greece can't be relied upon early or late with Thrace and Macedonia often being snowbound as are the mountains around Olympus and the higher summits in the Peloponnese and Crete. Epirus and the west of northern Greece can be chilly but, almost everywhere, fruit trees bloom early and the valleys are temperate to warm, with the coastline offering some of the finest and clearest winter weather in the Mediterranean.

There are always exceptions. In August, for instance, the famous *meltemi* blows down the Aegean and makes things uncomfortable. With so many nooks and crannies, Greece has many micro-climates worth watching for. In general, bad weather comes from the north east and any spot which is protected from this direction is almost bound to be good.

INTERNAL TRANSPORT

On the whole, this is good. There are 29 official airports in Greece and Olympic Airways gets you to all of them swiftly and comfortably, including 20 island destinations some of which are seasonal. Apart from some islands and remote mainland places Greek roads are good but there is only one true motorway, which runs from Thessaloniki to Athens, Corinth and Patras. Some main roads, notably in the east and west Peloponnese, into Epirus and the north west and along the northern coast of Crete are as good as any in Europe. With limited resources, Greek engineers have done their best and some roads are spectacular. Gradually the whole country is being opened up. Signposting, in both Greek and English, is fine and very visible, though it can be a little wayward in remote areas. Car hire tends to be more expensive than in the rest of Europe, especially in the islands and, at the time of writing, petrol is 20 per cent dearer than elsewhere.

Ferries are, of course, ubiquitous. If there is somewhere to go a Greek ferry will get there even if it is no more than a glorified caique. Both passenger and car ferries operate from Venice, Ancona and Brindisi as well as to and from Cyprus, Egypt, Israel and Yugoslavia. Coastal and inter-island services are frequent and good, some of them operated by hydrofoils and schedules are tailor-made for tourists. Fares are cheap and ferries sail more or less all the time, especially during the so-called summer season. Despite its geographical diversity, Greece is not an isolated country. The independent traveller's biggest headache will be choice. Many shipping companies naturally run Aegean cruises on a regular basis though they tend to favour the obvious destinations.

HOTELS

With the growth of international tourism Greece is no longer short of hotels, and large white edifices face almost every popular beach sometimes not in the happiest taste. Greek hotels are classified in De Luxe, A, B and C classes and though the last category is modest, if a location does not have a hotel of a higher class, you often find the C class places are more than adequate. In the high season, properly classified Greek hotels tend to be reluctant when it comes to the independent traveller who is just looking for room only or bed and breakfast. The Greek idea of luxury is relative since it is not a country swimming in the shimmering trinkets of others and so Greek hotels are often informal with much emphasis being put on the outdoor life; barbecues, gardens, etc.

Two aspects of the roof-over-your-head business in Greece should be noted. One is the proliferation of genuine or not so genuine tavernas that now take room guests. Some of them are very good value and very cheerful. Another phenomenon, especially in the islands, is the abundance of 'rooms for rent'. The arrival of any ferry or plane will produce an army of ladies advertising their vacancies on great cardboard placards. So many drachmas a night and so on. On the whole they are a good bet and you are sure of becoming a friend of the family.

One large lady waiting on the quayside at Kalymnos, I think she was called Thea, introduced me to a magnificently clean whitewashed room in her house, opening onto a courtyard which also provided access to the family quarters and had chairs and benches in the centre plus a marvellous tree. My room had a balcony and, though the hot water plumbing was not of the best, everything from transport to food was always available if you asked. The Greek Easter meal I was invited to on that occasion will long remain in my memory. It lasted from noon to 5 p.m. Generally, unless you wish to be, you will never be short of accommodation on a Greek island as someone will take you in and quote you generous prices. It's by far the best way to get to know the country and the people. The National Tourist Organisation of Greece will readily supply you with a list of hotels and tavernas.

SPECIALISED HOLIDAYS

All Greece is special and British tour operators have not been slow in making hay though on the whole they go for numbers rather than quality. The opposite is true of special- ised companies like The Best of Greece Ltd, which has managed to corner the field in upmarket hotels and among others, sells the famous Akti Myrina Hotel on Lemnos. If it is quality you are after, you might do far worse than contact them and though they are not overly keen on making special arrangements, their brochure contains many pearls.

Almost every operator offers 'the Greek islands', which means two or three. One who offers you a choice of 25 destinations, and a few more if you should insist, is Wan- derways Holidays, who are real island experts.

Even the National Tourist Organisation of Greece suggest that package holidays to Greece are for first- and maybe second-timers. Afterwards it becomes a matter of individual choice and I certainly would agree with that. One of the fastest growing types of holidays to Greece is yacht charter- ing and you can either do it yourself or let professionals run the show for you or even go in for the newer and often quite exciting 'Flotilla-sailing'. And if you think this would be out of your reach financially, think again. Competition is so tough that, provided there are several of you, rates might compare very favourably with those of a stay-put upmarket hotel. There are upwards of 50 yacht brokers in Greece and several also operate from London. The National Tourist Organisation of Greece will be able to direct you to the most appropriate to your needs.

Greece awaits you.

Please see page 218 for addresses.

Cyprus

PROFILE

So many near-at-hand countries, especially the small ones, have been got at by the grimy fingers of mass tourism that one hesitates to recommend them. To my way of thinking, Cyprus is a happy exception. Not that mass tourism isn't there – it is – and at the risk of finding that many of my Cypriot friends won't talk to me anymore I would suggest that if the independent traveller stays away from the island east of a line, say from Kolossi Castle to Nicosia, he will not be missing too much! Limassol has become, alas, what Beirut was only yesterday and the famous beaches to the east, such as Ayia Napa and Protaras, have become the almost exclusive preserve of northern European sun-fiends, which is good for business but bad for the island's personality. The once well-loved Famagusta and especially Kyrenia in the north are in Turkish hands and so out of bounds. So what is there left for the independent traveller?

Frankly, more than one would think. I know a crossroad on the western outskirts of Limassol where, in my view, hamburgerland stops and the real Cyprus begins. The whole of the western half of this island, whch is the third biggest in the Mediterranean but barely the size of Kent, Surrey, Sussex and Hampshire put together, is where the readers of this book will still find rewards. Paphos, the 'capital' of this area, is a small resort which would like to be big but which wisely realises that the day it reaches international standards will also be the day when its habitual visitors will look elsewhere. Despite the apartment buildings and the hotels on the seafront (never more than two storeys high), Paphos, and especially the old hill town of Ktima, happily remains itself – quiet, slightly disorganised, nicely Cypriot and not at all pushy. If you are careful to avoid the hot summer months when the hordes arrive, you might find that western Cyprus is still one of the better places of this world.

One reason, of course, is the weather. Most people seem to dismiss Mediterranean islands for the winter season and yet this is when, in my belief, Cyprus shines – as a retreat from the cold and wet, with clear skies, February/March temperatures in the mid-sixties Fahrenheit (18–19° Centigrade), but naturally with occasional high winds and a little rain. If that is winter, let's have it.

Another reason is that Cyprus is Cyprus and, if that sounds odd, let me explain. It would be very wrong to think of this island as a kind of eastern appendage of Greece for it is nothing like it. Although the people speak Greek, the island, in that far eastern corner of the Mediterranean, is almost Levantine with an aura of gentle lassitude and a kind of happy-go-lucky view when it comes to the aggravations of this world. Many traditions, many histories have embraced her, including Greek, Frankish, Venetian and Turkish and, even if the red tape occasionally sends you screaming for help, British. If Cypriots don't look like Zorba the Greek, they have their own attitudes; they are more pliant, more accommodating, more worldly-wise and they also know good plumbing when they see it.

Cyprus is less inebriating than Greece. But it is easier to live with, more cosmopolitan and in many cases more acceptable, except when it tries to pass itself off as something it is not. Cypriot food, with all those Levantine touches is, on the whole, better than the Greek equivalent. Wine is cheap and reasonably drinkable and so is brandy. Having spent some time on the island recently I came to the conclusion that among the things I would probably miss if I lived there were the following: *The Times*, my favourite West End bookshop, continental cheese and large dollops of genuine Scotch whisky, which is available but dear. When it comes to the final analysis all these can be remedied.

What is Cyprus good for? Complete relaxation, especially in the off season, peace and quiet, a good climate, fresh produce and, at least in the western part of the island, an almost total absence of false glitter.

BEACHES

Alas, some of the nicest ones, north of the Pentadactylos range are now, pro tem, occupied by the troops of another nation. Some of the finest Cypriot beaches at Paralimni, Ayia Napa and Protaras are now occupied, in the summer period, by northern European madmen and madwomen who turn over on the sand with the passing of the sun.

Out west, you find your own beach. There are a few good sandy stretches around Limassol, if you like that sort of place, more along the southern coast past Curium and while Coral Bay, north of Paphos, has been reasonably intelligently developed, there are literally miles of 'undiscovered' ones around Ayios Yiorgeos, Lara and all the way to the so-called Baths of Aphrodite.

COUNTRYSIDE

This is quite delicious. The back country of the western part of Cyprus is made for the independent traveller who, with a small, well-sprung car, likes to go off-the-beaten track. For sheer physical beauty I recommend the road from Palea Paphos to Archimandrita or even the shorter one from Paphos itself to Episkopi where great blue-green hills, well-tended vineyards, olive groves and scented trees alternate with gravelly river beds and give one that feeling of unrestricted freedom which is so precious. Villages abound, often half populated, and all boast a taverna or two, an oven for the renowned *klephtiko*, which is one of the finest lamb dishes in the world, and lots of people who have been everywhere and come back to their roots in Cyprus.

Away from the tourist eye, traditions flourish. In Phiti, they make marvellous embroidery, as indeed they do in Lefkara which is far better known. In Phini, they make pottery as their ancestors did two or three thousand years ago. In Anarita they make a Cyprus cheese called *halloumi* and in Lathi, they go fishing and get the fish on your plate as quickly as they can. Many villages still have extraordinarily beautiful and very old Byzantine churches. Try those at Emba or Khlorakas and monasteries like Stavrovouni, Ayia Moni and Khrysorroyiatissa and, of course, the famous Kykko on the Troodos mountains.

The mountains, of which the highest is over 6000 feet (1830 m), is where every sensible person ends when the weather becomes too hot on the coasts. Up here, sunshine dapples through the great forests of cedars and oak, the temperature is an easy 65°F (18°C) in the summer and everybody relaxes, breathes in and pauses in hill resorts like Troodos and especially Platres before setting down in front of a lunch table that gradually gets filled up with, say, 26 different kinds of *medzedes*.

CITIES

Since Lebanese millionaires made Limassol their bolthole, it is just like any so-called resort between Miami Beach and Torremolinos, except for the old city which still has some character. Many independent travellers will want to stay away. Larnaca is going the same way. Nicosia, corseted by its great and ancient walls but unfortunately divided between Greeks and Turks, still has a certain something – a *mélange* of the old-fashioned Middle Eastern charm with the so-called modern. Paphos, for the reasons given above, is a better bet, especially now that it has what I believe to be the finest hotel in Cyprus, the Annabelle, which combines comfort and good looks without the razzmatazz.

GREAT SIGHTS

Apart from the above-mentioned monasteries, you should look in at Kolossi Castle and that splendid sea-facing Graeco-Roman amphitheatre at Curium. In Paphos itself are the landmarks of the medieval castle high on the harbour, the famous House of Dyonisos with its celebrated mosaics and the early Christian basilica.

CLIMATE

Here I would make a strong plea for the independent traveller to go to western Cyprus when other people, that is tourists, are not there and that means anytime between November and May – even the local bananas like it so it can't be that bad. Although local records appear to be slightly imaginative, the lowest temperature ever recorded is 51°F (11°C), which is not exactly bad. The post-January average may be in the region of 65°F (18°C) and can go over 70°F (21°C). There are occasional fairly violent storms and some rain, especially in February and March.

INTERNAL TRANSPORT

Although it now has two very good international airports, Larnaca and Paphos, Cyprus has no railways. The main roads are good and the side roads usually acceptable though bumpy, sinuous and sometimes unfinished at the edges. Taxis are cheap. Cyprus, like some Middle East countries, has an excellent shared taxi service which is frequent and comfortable in huge Mercedes cars that the traveller shares with whoever else is going that way. It is excellent for intercity transport.

HOTELS

Many Cyprus hotels are new, having been built since the Turkish war and are classified from one to five stars. Many cater only for summer visitors.

SPECIALIST HOLIDAYS

The Cyprus Tourism Organisation is helpful and sympathetic towards the independent traveller. The best local guidebook is undoubtedly the Cyprus *Blue Guide*. Two tour operators who seem to care more than most for the one-off client are Cyprair Holidays, a subsidiary of the national airline Cyprus Airways, and Sunvil Holidays. Both are of the caring kind.

Please see page 218 for addresses.

Turkey

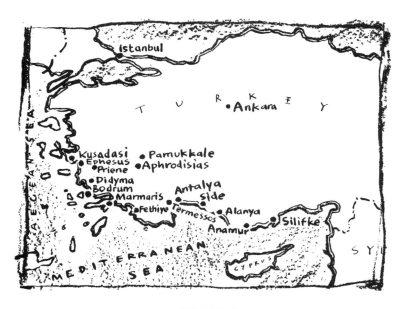

PROFILE

For those who watch the tourism business these days, for it is a business, one of the biggest question marks of all is why Turkey has taken so long to become popular. This vast country, which is three times larger than Britain, has everything that makes for success: it is often as beautiful and varied as France, its coastline, at least in the west and south, rivals anything available in the Mediterranean. Its ruins, Hellenistic or otherwise, are often better kept that those of Greece and its food and wine, and particularly the fruit, are better than expected. Its influence on much of the southern world has been second to none. Yet, until recently, tourists were still going there in a trickle rather than a flood.

Why? Some of it has to do with planning. Turkey is a latecomer in the tourist stakes and I personally do not believe that the proud Turks have yet made up their minds about the kind of tourism they want. They are torn between the 'costas' syndrome and the preservation of antiquity. Although they are generous and surprisingly honest, probably the most honest people in the whole of the Mediterranean area, they make excellent waiters and bad hotel managers. They are held back by a burdensome and often antiquated bureaucracy and it is only now, with the return of so many Turkish workers from West Germany and Switzerland, that the Turks as a whole are beginning to appreciate both the demands and the emptiness of Western life.

They are, however, still amazingly deficient in the much abused craft of public relations. They seem to say, 'Here we are, you take us or leave us.' Well, of course, many people take them and the following year they make a quick return to Greece, or France or Italy. This being said, I still have to meet a single traveller who, having been to Turkey, did not like it apart from the usual grumbles about plumbing, the state of the roads and so on. But no tourist gets ripped off in Turkey. No tourist gets murdered or coshed. Even in cosmopolitan Istanbul, which has all the world's most attractive vices rolled into one, life for the traveller is safe.

So what is the problem? I know from many of my confrères that they feel as I do: they search in vain for an answer. Possibly, one of the reasons for Turkey's comparative lack of success is its size. It is massive and, once again, one is either a holiday maker or a traveller. If you drew a line from Istanbul to Ankara and then south east to, say, Mersin, anything west and south of the line would be Turkey-for-the-tourist. Anything else, two-thirds of the country, is for the brave soul, the real traveller and, at the present time, these are thin on the ground.

Yet, at the back of my mind, the question remains. Why? And the only idea I can come up with is the Turkish personality. Turks are straight-up-and-down-people, often simple and unsophisticated, rather dour. They are not nature lovers. They were the ones who introduced the tulip to the world but who's made the most of it and has gone all soppy and very successful with it? Those clever Dutch of course. Show a Turk a most incredible panorama in his own country and he will try to calculate how many onions he can grow there. He often gets paralytic or paranoiac when he thinks of the Greeks, which is a feeling that is stridently reciprocated.

Above all, and this may be only a surface impression, the average Turk gives the appearance of being a dull fellow who does not think lightly of life in general and does not know how to enjoy himself. I am sure I am wrong but I often wish the Turk would put himself out little more. It took me two long trips to Turkey before I actually found one Turk, a young man, sitting under a tree and strumming some stringed instrument just because he fancied it. I remember it was in Aphrodisias. Turks do sing and dance and very well too but without the spontaneity of the Greek, the Italian or even the Spaniard. It sometimes seems that the average Turk walks about with a little dark cloud hanging over his head. Tourists and travellers don't like that. They like to see everybody happy. Life after all is a bowl of cherries, is it not? Maybe not in the case of the Turk. Shall we just say that the Greek might laugh too much and the Turk not enough.

In a way, this is all to the good for the independent traveller who can travel in Turkey without being too aware of the human element and merely enjoy the unique feeling of being out loose in this very lovely country. Perhaps if he went out of his way a little? Maybe. But don't ask the Turk to make the first move. For one thing, communications are difficult. The Turkish language is fractured and virtually unintelligible to the visitor, but then so is Serbo-Croat or Greek for some and they don't have that problem. I get the feeling it is time the Turks went to a tourist 'shrink' – if there is one.

What is Turkey good for? One of the conundrums of this age – why don't more people go to Turkey? It is a vast country which offers landscapes, a superb coastline, antiquities galore and is inhabited by a people who, on the whole, have not yet learned to take advantage of the traveller.

BEACHES

Of course, not being a Turkish expert, I have not counted them but judging by the size of the country and those I have seen I would guess that Turkey has more and better beaches than almost any Mediterranean country. Those around Bodrum or Marmaris or Alanya are like the antechamber or paradise for all those who can't resist the poetic meeting of the land and the sea. Some, like Side, don't give you only the sandy strip but the antiquities as well. What more could one want?

COUNTRYSIDE

Having already conceded that I am no expert on Turkey, I don't have to apologise for the choice of 'Tourist' Turkey as against the rest. Let those who long to see the 'Big Heads' of Nemrut Dagi or the strange churches and eroded mountain tops of Goreme or indeed the distant shore of Lake Van go and see them at the cost of slipped discs and other discomforts. Me, I am a softie and I will keep to better-known tracks. Besides which, the whole Aegean and Mediterranean coasts of Turkey have so much to offer the tourist – and the traveller too – that not going further is no sin. Besides which, if one can avoid the blossoming bikinis in August in Kusadasi, the coast and its hinterland make a perfectly intelligent stamping ground. Transport is essential. Personal transport at that and by this I mean a rented car, some background reading and a good, if flexible, itinerary.

This particular itinerary starts with historical pyrotechnics, by which of course I mean Ephesus, one of the most important and largest cities in antiquity. Two hundred years before Christ, Ephesus already had half-a-million inhabitants and was a world centre of trade and the arts. By the time St Paul got there, it was virtually the capital of the Middle East, devoted to the many-breasted goddess Artemis. What remains of it today is sensational – one of the most striking and evocative Hellenistic cities in that part of the Mediterranean, with two world-famous streets, the Marble Road with its elegant Library of Celsius and the Street of Curetes, with the Baths of Scholastica, the well-preserved Temple of Hadrian and the Trajan Fountain. Personally, I can think of few more fantastic experiences than to spend the day in this marvellous city, with red, pink and yellow spring flowers growing among the ruins.

Kusadasi calls too with its cafés and excellent restaurants. Only a few years ago, hardly anyone went there. Today it is Turkey's Marbella and St Tropez rolled into one and one cannot ignore it. But I would make a plea for a foray up the famous Meander valley, lush and shining with the good things of the earth and, in some ways, quite reminiscent of France at its best. Up there, on a hilltop dominating the whole country down to the coast is one of my own favourite ancient cities, little Priene, with its magnificent theatre and its Temple of Athena. Never very important politically, Priene nevertheless had pride of place in the ancient world for it was a centre of culture and philosophy.

The whole area is redolent of past splendours. There is Didyma with its enormously high columns and its head of Medusa, little Aphrodisias with superbly elegant fluted columns and porticoes and, of course, the spectacular limestone water plateau of Pamukkale with its dazzling white pools.

Back on the coast, Bodrum appeals very much too, for the former Halicarnassus has much beauty and charm. The whole area here of Bodrum and Marmaris are in tourist land since bays and beaches are second to none but, especially in the off season, this hardly detracts from the sheer beauty of the sites. Along the Lycian coast come more wonders: Fethiye and Demre which, propaganda would have it, is supposed to have been the home of St Nicholas, the original Father Christmas. Antalya, the biggest city in this part of the world, is not to be dismissed lightly either. Although it tends to be rather touristy in the summer, it has great charm, some excellent beaches not far away and a good deal of local life, plus of course the truly magnificent and most impressive ruins of ancient Termessos. Yet, when it comes to leftovers of antiquity, this coast has more to offer, like lovely Aspendos with its great theatre and, of course, Side. One of the most important Hellenistic cities of all, Side has always had a very special effect on me. At one end is the little peninsula, almost entirely walled in, with a very well-preserved theatre, two colonnaded streets and vast agora. On the other is Side's beach, now slightly touristicated but still very acceptable, and the nearness of the two makes the going very pleasant. One of the most extraordinary aspects of this coast is the excellence of the museums that the Turks have arranged so nicely. The one in Side, which is half in the open, is extremely evocative. There are others at Didyma and Aphrodisias.

As for Alanya, it too repays the time given to it, for in my opinion it is one of the most interesting cities on the coast and the first coastal foothold of the conquering Seljuk Turks who, with the forbidding walls and the famous Red Tower, made it one of the most impregnable cities in this part of the world. Life is pleasant here. One can sit at a café terrace and drink in the scene at leisure. Still worthy of a small detour are the fantastic former Armenian castle of Anamur and the charming little town of Silifke further on.

For myself this journey, while it is by no means Turkey itself, pure and simple and rather wild, is one that nobody should miss – its physical beauty cannot be in doubt and both past and present blend in happy togetherness. Just as Istanbul, Bursa and the east cannot be missed in the long run, the west and south of Turkey are easy on the eye, easy to negotiate for the traveller and certainly not without rewards. In the eyes of the initiated it may be obvious but, for the first-time visitor especially, it wins on points.

CLIMATE

This can be tricky, with sudden changes and horrid winds coming down from the southern Russian steppes and weatherwise Turkey is not one of those countries where one can go at the drop of a hat at any time of the year. The country is huge and shows marked regional differences. Istanbul may be an average of 43°F (6°C) in wintertime and Antalya about 52°F (11°C) but central and eastern Anatolia can go down as low as 26°F (-3°C). So be warned.

INTERNAL TRANSPORT

Here and there. Turkish main roads are good though the language (roadsigns and people) can be a little offputting. Smaller roads are often tortuous and not particularly well finished and it is also my personal experience that, apart from the coasts, roads never seem to go where you want to make for. Bus travel in country districts is the best way to go if you don't mind sharing a seat with the livestock. They are amazingly cheap by our standards. Most Turks in the country areas are polite and very helpful to foreigners.

In the summer both Istanbul and Izmir offer some interesting cruises, mostly on the Aegean and Mediterranean coasts which are very useful for the first-time visitor. The bigger and more official Turkish Maritime Lines operate large ships, usually crowded but cheap and they are London-represented. Turkish Airlines fly to and from western Europe of course and to many places inside Turkey via Istanbul or Ankara.

SPECIALISED HOLIDAYS

Since the country is only just entering the world of big-time tourism, there are relatively few real experts on Turkey. I am happy to report, however, that the London Turkish Tourism and Information Centre is particularly helpful and willing to help in even the smallest matters. Among experts I would list Aegean Turkish Holidays Ltd, Cricketer Holidays and Fairways & Swinford Travel Ltd.

The rest is up to you.

Please see pages 218–9 for addresses.

NORTH AFRICA

Morocco

PROFILE

If you should be driving on the high road from Fez to Marrakech and turn off at El-Ksiba, which is not what package tourists do, I can guarantee one of the great sights of your travelling life. Up and up you go into the tortured, rocky fastnesses of the high Atlas Mountains, a grand, austere landscape which has few equals. When you reach the top, stop and climb a small knoll on the left-hand side of the road, open your eyes and look. Turn north and west and, as far as the eye can see, is the whole of smiling, fertile, civilised Morocco – all so green with fruit and crops that you could be somewhere in France. Turn east and south and, from your Atlas perch, you discover another totally unexpected world – down there, in the bluish-white haze, is the fringe of the Sahara Desert, an immensity of sand you can hardly comprehend. As it stretches past the green ribbons of the Ziz and Dades valleys, there is nothing between West Africa and you except sand. And more sand. You are standing on the edge of nowhere.

I have long believed that, scenically, Morocco is the most beautiful of the three countries of the Maghreb. I might even go so far as to say the most beautiful of all Arab countries, and yet it is only three hours from London. Ancient cities, fabulous mosques, splendid mountains, gorgeous little country souks, nice, smiling people and, of all things, good food and wine. It is a country with so many aspects that one could go there every year for ten years and not see the whole of it. Yet 90 per cent of those who buy a package holiday to Morocco stay on the admittedly fine beaches of Agadir in the south or Restinga and Al-Hoceima in the north. Maybe eight per cent visit Marrakech. The last two per cent go off the beaten track and are rewarded accordingly.

This is what Morocco really has to offer: a refreshing change, a total *depaysement*, a place to get you out of yourself. That's what I would go for anyway. Morocco is also slightly upsetting for the Where am I? tourist. Is this the East, the mysterious East? Well, yes, except that here East is

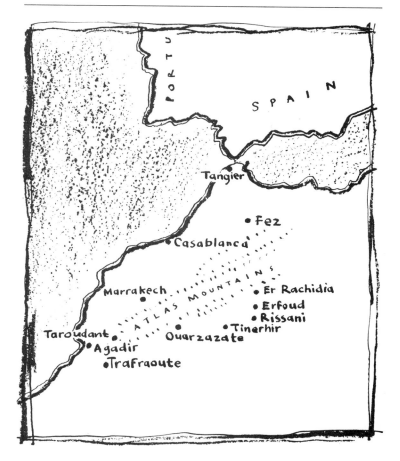

South. Is it Africa? Of course, all the way to the Cape of Good Hope, except that Europe is a good deal nearer, just over the few miles of water which Tarik crossed to land in Gibraltar (Jebel Tariq) and conquer Andalusia. Is this the land of Islam? Without a doubt. It was in AD 682 that the great conqueror Uqba Ben Nafi planted the banner of the Prophet in the Atlantic sands and proclaimed: 'I have conquered the world from end to end.' But Morocco is also Phoenician, Carthaginian, Numidian and Roman, with Christian and Jewish touches at the edges. Is it an Arab land? To be sure, but as Moroccans themselves say: 'Two people, one nation' – the other people being those dour, enduring, brachycephalic Berbers, often blue-eyed, who have been there since before history began. So Morocco is also a Berber nation dressed in Arab clothes.

If one discounts such stalwarts as Juba and Jugurtha, the real founder of the country was Idriss I, a refugee nobleman from Baghdad who married a Berber woman and founded Fez in the year 920. He, and Morocco, never looked back towards the rising sun and this curious land was inexorably committed to looking westwards. It developed its own culture, its own arts, its own dynasties and when the gold caravans began reaching Fez from the Sudan, it became rich, powerful and proud.

What is Morocco good for? The easiest and the nearest way for people to taste the delights of the mysterious East without roughing it too much. Very beautiful in parts, Morocco has much to offer and, art-wise, it is the true birthplace of so much we know as 'Moorish'.

BEACHES

The Mediterranean variety can be found around resorts like Restinga and Smir on the Rif coast. Then, past Tangier, with its echoes of European melodrama, the Atlantic rollers come crashing against the African continent and hundreds of miles of golden sand appear as if by magic, all the way from cosmopolitan Mohammedia to cosmopolitan Agadir, where the bikinis occasionally get wet.

CITIES AND GREAT SIGHTS

There is a kind of inevitability about my own visits to Morocco since they always begin in Fez, or more properly Fes as Moroccans spell it. It is an astonishingly beautiful city, both secretive and welcoming, a maze of tiny streets and endless rows of shops where people make things and all so white that the French, once in occupation, called it 'Fez la Blanche'. But there are really two cities. Fez el Jedid or New Fez (only 700 years old) contains some particularly ornate and beautiful gateways (Bab in Arabic) like Bab Smarine, Bab Segma, the Royal Palace and the lovely Lalla Mina gardens. Facing it across the ravine is Fez El Bali or Old Fez, whose origins go back to the Arab conquest of the Maghreb in the seventh century. There is also the modern city on the other side but to all intents and purposes you can forget this one.

Almost everything that is worth seeing is in Fez El Bali; it is a walled city with hardly any transport except your two feet or the occasional donkey if your spine can stand it and it is within these walls that everything we know as 'Moorish' originated. The craftsmen who built so much of Cordoba and Granada and Seville came from here and you can still see their direct descendants working away at some intricate brass or leather pattern or at a coffee table inlaid with mother of pearl or at a gorgeous saddle fit for a prince or a rich American.

The industrious life of old Fez is amazing; 40,000 people still work with their hands creating beauty, day in and day out, just as they did hundreds of years ago. You can walk down the main street, Rue du Grand Talaa, quite easily despite its tortuous appearance but to turn left or right you need a guide with you, assuming that is if you want to get out again. Within minutes you are in a different world of ancient fountains, massive gates roofed in green, courtyards walled with magnificent yellow or blue tiles or a 10 foot (3 m) pile of oranges next to some priceless silver and gem jewellery.

In Fez, the two great architectural jewels are the famous Medrassa (school) el-Attarine where ancient Arab calligraphy mixes happily with some superb tile work and the much older Qrawyn Mosque, or Karawin if you prefer, which was built as the centre of a university complex some 300 years before Oxford. From the Medrassa roof you get the best overall view of the old city but from the mosque you get a mere glimpse since it is strictly out of bounds for non-Muslims though you can happily snatch a picture from the gateways — as if you did not have enough elsewhere.

Of the other larger cities of Morocco, Tangier is, in my opinion, highly missable and something of a tourist trap, as is Casablanca — a cross between Marseilles and Le Havre. Rabat, the capital, and its little neighbour Salé are worth visiting and so is Meknes with its enormous walls and gates. Little places are far more interesting like Tetouan and darling little Chaouen (or Chechaouen) in the Rif, Arcila on the Atlantic and, further south, Safi and Essaouira.

Only one other large city shares the real honours with Fez; the inevitable Marrakech, so well loved by people looking for travel posters. Unlike Fez, Marrakech is slightly obvious. Fez is a high-born lady while Marrakech is showbusiness, African style. But don't let that put you off. Walled in ochre splendour, replete with great sights and a general atmosphere which Hollywood could not invent, this capital of the south is an absolute must for all intelligent visitors. Marrakech, where one could say northern Africa stops and darker Africa takes over, is almost 'the greatest show on earth' especially if you spend a day on the now famous Djemaa el-Fna — triangular and roughly six times the size of the Place de la Concorde. It is the place where, depending on the time of day, the city comes to life with kerbside restaurants, sandal sellers, fortune tellers, mad dancers from the villages, snake charmers, hawkers, barbers and story tellers who long ago translated the story of Hamlet into Arabic. It's all there, superbly colourful and a quite unsurpassed human spectacle.

Then go and see the Koutoubia, the 200 foot (61 m) high minaret and a direct ancestor of Seville's Giralda, the Saadian tombs where 60 sultans and members of their families lie at rest under great slabs of Carrara marble and, of course, the gardens – both in and out of Marrakech and all fed by underground springs first tapped a thousand years ago. Finally, and to get the overall view, take a horse carriage to do the drive right around the city's great pink-ochre walls. If you can, save your money before a Marrakech visit and stay at the Mamounia, the most celebrated, and justly so, hotel in Northern Africa. If you can afford the Winston Churchill Suite, so much the better.

COUNTRYSIDE

Now I must go back on one of my original loves and suggest that if you call yourself a traveller rather than a tourist, you must, simply must, do what is called the 'Kasbah Road' or, more properly, the road of the ksars as Moroccans call it. In Morocco a ksar is a fortified village which can range from just a few mud houses to veritable cities of pink walls rising behind a date palm grove. I like to reach it from bleak Midelt in the Atlas and get to Rachidia where the two desert valleys I mentioned earlier and their rivers meet – the Wadi Ziz and the Wadi Dades – the first going south and the second going west.

Further west still there is the outstanding valley of the Draa, which is Morocco's longest river. This is guaranteed fairyland, entirely natural, very beautiful and quite unique because of its Saharan architecture. You could stay in Erfoud and drive on to Rissani with its lively marketplace lined with arches and even down to Merzouga where you are actually standing at the very edge of the Sahara, with a 600 foot (183 m) sand dune ahead of you. Then, back along the Dades, the kasbahs begin; there are dozens of them and I especially love Tinerhir, Boumalne, Taourirt and, further north, Telouet and, finally, Ouarzazate (pronounced Warzazat) the long-time headquarters of the famed El Glaoui, Pasha of Marrakech.

Everywhere – apart from the children who know a tourist with a fat wallet when they see one – you can wander at peace through these fortified villages with their towers and their arches, their tiny windows and the vast, hot court-yards. There is also the freshness of the oasis with its palms and its gurgling streams; each is like a technicolour, multi-faced Chicago, miniaturised and set amid sweet greenery. Possibly for the traveller the oddest thing about this Kasbah Road is the excellence of its hotels. Almost everywhere the Moroccan chain 'Diafa' has a small, clean, modern and essentially practical hotel. The best are in Erfoud, Tinerhir, Ouarzazate and Zagora. Drinks are long and cool, the food surprisingly good and people are glad to see you.

Two outstanding pearls remain. One is Trafraoute, a kasbah of almost shocking pink set amid fruit trees which when seen in the spring, are a feast for the eyes. The other is lovely little Taroudant, which is an almost entirely medieval town hiding behind massive 20 foot (6 m) walls. Here too is a legendary hotel, the Gazelle d'Or, where you can have your own musicians and superb cuisine to liven up your evenings.

CLIMATE

One good friend once described Morocco to me as 'a cold country with the sun turned on'. He was right. Apart from the roasting beach in midsummer Agadir and some inland spots, don't expect extreme heat. Don't expect extreme cold either, unless you want to go skiing in, say, Ifrane and the high valleys of the Atlas in the winter. Morocco has an Atlantic climate rather than a Mediterranean one which one can quite easily enjoy all year round depending on the location. Marrakech for instance will be 65°F (18°C) in January. But it can go up to 100°F (38°C) in July and August. Heavy rain can come at any time and especially in the Atlas with its dangerous flash floods. In general, I would say that wintertime is best for the oases close to the Sahara and spring and early summer for the coast.

INTERNAL TRANSPORT

Royal Air Maroc and its subsidiaries will fly you to most of the main cities and the hub is definitely Casablanca. There are fairly good railways too. But by far the best way to see Morocco is by road. Roads are, on the whole, good and sometimes quite impressive and signposting is adequate in the principal tourist areas, most of it being in French as well as Arabic. In the mountains and the country districts there is often a shortage of stopping places to have a drink or a snack so it is sensible to inquire before you set out. It is a good idea to have a car with a driver, who will know the best places, but I for one would have no compunction about driving myself.

HOTELS

Not all Moroccan hotels are as legendary as, say, the Mamounia in Marrakech or the Palais Jamai in Fez, but the standard varies from very good to adequate and it is a relief to find that even in remote places like the 'route des ksars' there is always a decent place to stay. The Moroccan Government and Moroccan Railways are responsible for running hotel chains in places which may not otherwise be economical, but unfortunately, they have a tendency to change their name which can be upsetting. Reservations in the smaller and less frequented places can be a little haphazard so, if you can, ask the concierge of your previous hotel to telephone through and confirm.

SPECIALISED HOLIDAYS

One is glad to report that the Moroccan National Tourist Office in London is better than most. People are knowledgeable and helpful and can answer specific questions. Among the best tour operators are Twickers World and Fairways & Swinford. Among the newer companies operating here is The Best of Morocco Ltd. They have a good, comprehensive and fairly upmarket brochure and are generally willing and helpful.

Please see page 219 for addresses.

Tunisia

Some tourist countries are in a way lucky – they know what they stand for. France, for instance. Or Greece, or Italy or India. Others are less fortunate. They are still looking for a tourist identity which is going to make their product different from others and thus gain them the market lead. Don't misunderstand me, as long as a country makes real money out of tourism, that's fine because tourism is a business and it should benefit the inhabitants. So when I see, for instance, that little Tunisia, with a mere six and a half million inhabitants, managed to attract two and a half million tourists last year, I am glad for it. It deserves to succeed.

The next question is somewhat more difficult. Is Tunisia doing well enough? Is it getting the sort of tourists it deserves? To the first question, I would plead ignorance since I simply do not know enough about the aims of tourist authorities. To the second question, my own answer, formed over many years, must be 'no'. I am always amazed at the millions of people who, year after year, fly thousands of miles and stake a six foot by three spot on the beach without knowing anything about the country to which they are going. Amazed, but not surprised, for this is where holidaymakers get sorted out from travellers and vice versa. My only regret is that there is little I can do for the beach-fiend, for if that is what he wants, he has every right to get it. The trouble is that he might find it in Spain or elsewhere. So why go to Tunisia? If a country is small – and Tunisia is relatively so – it does not have a chance to compete with the big boys and you might say that such a country is selling its birthright for an acre of sand in the sun.

An insistence on a beach holiday only is a mistake and that much is being learned now. Tunisian beaches are among the finest in the whole of the Mediterranean and, early or late, you cannot go wrong since the weather is on your side. Hotels, many born yesterday, cater admirably for you whether you come from Doncaster or Essen. There are even camels on the beach in Djerba and every resort has its evening of folklore. This is 'holiday'. It is not 'travel' and

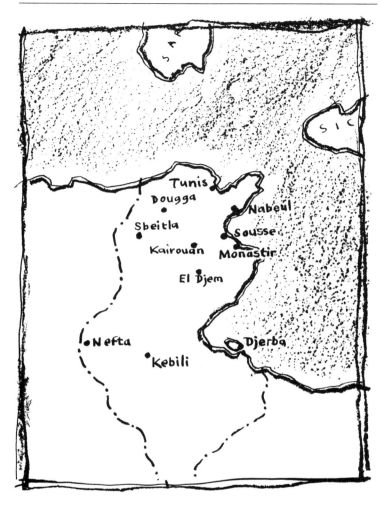

people such as the independent traveller must look hard to find the gems that are there. It is not impossible in Tunisia. But it is not easy.

I can see changes on the horizon. The country is beginning, in earnest, to look at its African, its Arabic and, above all, its Saharan heritage. The vast reaches of the south are now accessible, though the dreaded shadow of the western tour operator is still too much in evidence. One hotel manager who runs a superb hotel in Nefta and whom I telephoned for a reservation one May told me that unfortunately he could not help since his entire hotel – 60 rooms – had been booked by an Anglo-German-Swiss tour operator for that period. I told him, rather rudely perhaps, that if that was the case I would not want to meet his clients anyway. Conversely, a gentleman I telephoned in Hammamet was rather surprised to hear from me. Why didn't I go to one of so many tour operators in London that specialised in his resort? After all, this is what most British visitors did. I put the phone down on him. I can quite understand that he could not survive in his very competitive business on oddballs like me who may, or may not, come. But he should not attempt to shunt me onto somebody's charter flight. It is fortunate for us that holiday buyers are not the same people as travellers.

What is Tunisia good for? Mediterranean? African? Arabic? A little of all three perhaps. A very *simpatico* country where living is easy. Nice people, easy geography and many antiquities that are little known but worth seeing. There are also good local crafts.

BEACHES

Here Tunisia shines. From Hammamet and Nabeul right down to Sousse, Zarzis and the unmatched Djerba (off season please ...), Tunisian beaches cannot be bettered in terms of quality. So whatever the time of year you can count on their being better than at home.

COUNTRYSIDE

Me, I am off to the hills for other sensations – the feeling above all that here, in a country roughly the size of England and Wales, I can find the past and a show of colour and shape that would be hard to match. Tunisia was right in the middle of the ancient world – Carthaginian, Roman, Arab, Turkish and, later, French. One can see what little of Carthage there is left after Cato had finished with it and, next door, a government office that looks like a French *sous-préfecture*. Down the road are the winter quarters of the Roman legions and on the coast the bastions of the early Arab conquerors. Climb a bit, say towards Kasserine, and the whole of Tunisia lies below you, from the fertile fields of the Sahel to the orange groves of the coast.

Go south, past the great salt lakes, and the next vista is the Sahara itself – immense, blond under the clear blue sky and so mysterious that you are simply dying to get lost and cry out, 'My kingdom, my kingdom for a Jeep.' Camels are fine but they are a bit hard on the anatomy. There are ancient theatres, great triumphal arches such as only Roman Emperors knew how to build and minuscule white mosques.

Tunisia is intensely, but intensely, visual. Images are neat and clear, shapes don't get lost in mists and colours are right out of the divine tube and in a way the beauty of it is that you can have it all by just being yourself – Tunisia is a small country with good roads and adequate to good hotels. Where you go first depends on your mood.

My own first port of call is usually Dougga, which the Carthaginians called Thugga. As so often in the rustic landscape of this country, you come upon it suddenly, across the wheatfields and the olive groves. Once, the great Massinissa resided here and now it is one of North Africa's best-preserved Roman cities, with several temples including the famous Caeliestis and the beautiful Capitol, one of the nicest and most intimate I have ever seen anywhere. One just needs the passing of the sun and the occasional Berber shepherd meandering through to feel that the gap of ages has been breached. It is most evocative.

Further south is Sbeitla (Sufetula). Like all Tunisian ruins it has for the visitor the great advantage of being totally untouristicated and non-institutionalised. You just turn off the road and you are there, the superb columns of Diocletian's arch and three small temples where official inscriptions go cheek by jowl with the graffiti left by Roman soldiers or the cursive scripts of the first Arabs. If you are antiquity mad, as I am, the country has enough Roman leftovers to keep you going for some time. Try Bulla Regia, Mades or Utica. There are also many Carthaginian or Byzantine sites but, to my way of thinking, the number-one antiquity site in Tunisia is the magnificent Roman amphitheatre of El Djem (ancient Thysdrus) which rises like a huge time capsule right from the central plain. Almost as large as the Colosseum in Rome, it could accommodate more than 30,000 visitors to the games and much of it is beautifully preserved. As one professor of Tunis University once told me: 'It was built so solidly that none of the passing nomads could do it much harm.'

You expect to hear the roar of lions any minute and, as a more romantic sound memory, there is the death cry of Kathina, the great Berber heroine who threw herself off the top of the tiers rather than submit to the invading Arabs. But the theatre is apparently only the top of the pile. Somewhere in the sand out there is another theatre, Roman baths and villas and paved streets going off in all directions. The African sand is the best preservative.

Arab Tunisia has a great past as well and two monuments have always impressed me. One is the city of Kairouan, which became 'caravan' in our language, and was for a long time the final stop of the great Sahara gold and ivory caravans. Its Great Mosque is one of Islam's most revered and most beautiful religious shrines – it was founded a mere 50 years after Mohammed's death when Uqba Ben Nafi conquered Tunisia. It is made of plain, handmade brick, cedar wood, gilded ceramic work, magnificent rugs and chandeliers plus, of course, great size. The minaret is 100 feet (30.5 m) high and the courtyard immense. Kairouan is an all-Arabic city that does not have too much time for tourists, except for the making of its celebrated carpets.

Another great Arabic landmark, and there are many others up and down the coast, is the great *ribat* of Monastir. Defining what is a *ribat* can be difficult. It was both a monastery and a fortress, held by brotherhoods of dedicated warriors whom one can only compare to the Hospitallers or the Knights of St John. They fought Christian attackers, held services and left behind some extremely emotive prayers like, 'Let us remain together until dawn, my brethren, and let us think of Allah's glory . . . In the paradise to which we shall be going, the waters of the flowing rivers murmur the name of God, the roses spread the name of God and when the good soldier reaches heaven, eight gates open moaning the name of Allah . . .'

South west now and the mood changes because this is pre-Saharan Tunisia and one should not miss its wide horizons where the sand meets the sky punctuated only by the shining salt lakes and the vivid green of the oases. One of the easiest to reach is the great Nefzaoua. It is beginning to attract some tourists and no wonder since it must be the prototype of all oases; millions of palms, soft dunes, little white villages and weekly markets in the arcaded squares. Try and see especially those of Douz or Kebili where they will sell you anything from a string of camels to a silver dagger.

Possibly the greatest of all spots near the Sahara is Nefta where, if you stand on the edge of what is known as 'la corbeille', you face 300,000 date palms, 150 warm springs, countless villages half buried under the green and, beyond, the immensity of the Sahara. Here you are lucky too, for another reason: Nefta is the site of the Sahara Palace, one of the two or three most splendid hotels in the whole of Northern Africa. It's worth the trip.

If you can travel to Tunisia at a time when the package hordes aren't there, don't miss Djerba, despite the disparaging wails. Djerba is heaven and it's been on the travel posters ever since Ulysses first described it as the Land of the Lotus-Eaters. This very flat bit of real estate, so near the mainland, is the kind of place where time means nothing and now is the time to do nothing. Hire a bicycle and go meandering through the two million palms to look at the lovely, white menzel houses, the very old and primitive mosques and fishing villages like Ajjim or El Kantara. You could also go to the two Jewish villages of Hara Kebir and Hara Sriba whose inhabitants have lived there peacefully since they escaped from Nebuchadnezzar.

But your Tunisian journey is not over yet. If you have the time, go and see the cave dwellers of Matmata, the tuna fishermen of Cape Bon in the north or those marvellous potters of Nabeul. In Tunisia, a small country as I said, you will run out of time long before you run out of places worth seeing. Besides, it would be a mistake not to visit great resorts like Hammamet and Sousse, to say nothing of the new, and very up-market, Port el Kantaoui. After all, they are part of the travel picture too.

CLIMATE

Fear not. Tunisia is an all-year-round country. The average winter temperature is listed as being 52°F (11°C) but I remember experiencing 74°F (23°C) at noon in lovely Nabeul and in the south, especially in semi-desert places like Kebili or Douz, it can go much higher. Don't go to Tunisia in the summer, for that's package tour time.

HOTELS

On the whole the hotels are remarkably good, especially if you can get in ahead of the mob or in less frequented places.

SPECIALISED HOLIDAYS

Apart from vague attempts at sand yachting and desert treks by Land Rover, there aren't any but it gets better as you get nearer because Tunisia has an enviable number of intelligent travel agents (mostly in the big cities) who will size you up quickly. The Tunisian National Tourist Office in London is better than most and its helpers are very charming. The same can be said for the national airline, Tunis Air. Most big British tour operators are well ensconced in Tunisia so there should be no trouble in finding the right brochure. Worthy of special marks are Cadogan Travel, the Hove Travel Agency and Sussex Travel. The last two are willing, so they tell me, to deal with 'individuals' and they have a good reputation.

Please see pages 219–20 for addresses.

Egypt

PROFILE

It seems only yesterday that I was sitting in the Cairo office of an old friend who was then Director of Tourism for Egypt. 'Which boat are you going on this time?' he asked. I told him, however, that this was one time when I did not want to go by boat up, or down, the Nile. He nearly fell off his chair in surprise. Eventually, he pressed a buzzer and a wave of advisers entered the room. 'Here,' he said to them, 'is one loony travel journalist who does not want to go on a Nile boat.'

Everybody looked at me, Fahmy this and Ahmed that and, for all I knew, the Egyptian equivalent of Uncle Tom Cobley. I was beginning to feel vaguely uncomfortable. Not wanting to be disrespectful, I told them that indeed I was full of admiration for the country's fantastic past. It was just, I explained, that after quite a few visits, I had pharaohs coming out of my ears. Wasn't there another kind of Egypt one could write about?

There was indeed, and in no time at all we had settled my itinerary. The trouble with Egypt, if you can call it trouble, is that everybody has a preconceived idea of the country. Everybody wants to go up, or down, the Nile and become his own instant Egyptologist. Like France, Italy or Greece, Egypt for the tourist has been typecast for so long that everybody wants to do the same thing. This is fine, of course, not just for Egypt, but for the Nile boat operators, the tour guides, the baksheesh merchant and yes, even the tame camels. It is fantastic for first-timers. Everybody should do it at least once in a lifetime because what is left of that unique civilisation is unique.

The drawback is that it has a déjà-vu feel. After all, who hasn't heard of the great Rameses, or Queen Hatshepsut or, even worse, a girl called Cleopatra? So the mental picture is always the same – there is a pyramid somewhere, or a tomb, a guide and a village youngster who looks underfed but who actually has his own bank account. And the caption under the picture reads: 'There is a column, a mythical beast and the guide has grown a moustache. So it must be Tuesday and it is Karnak.'

Of such stuff are tourists' dreams made. And who am I to cast the first stone that is going to shatter the glass of illusion? Of course, I won't do it, and if I had one chance of seeing Egypt what would I do? You can guess. Go up, or down, the Nile. I am merely trying to show that there is more to Egypt than this stereotype eye can see and this is where the independent traveller comes in. There is Tobruk, and Siwa and Fayoum. There is the fantastic green ribbon on the Nile Bank, the great deserts and the almost untouched Red Sea coast, where there will no doubt be another Torremolinos one day. There is also Cairo, the largest city in Africa and the biggest Arabic city anywhere. Egypt is big, young and vibrant. It is on the move and has many faces.

What is Egypt good for? The complete culture shock. The realisation that not only is Egypt very, very old but also very new and young. It is a country of sudden and sometimes disturbing contrasts and shines with gentleness, politeness and good companionship. Apart from Israel – which they are content to keep at arm's length — Egyptians, especially young people, have no 'side'.

BEACHES

These are probably the most promising and best in the Middle East and are neglected only because of Egypt's other attractions. The whole of the Mediterranean coast west of Alexandria is a potential Costa del Sol but right now Sidi Abd er-Rhaman alone, which is near El Alamein, is sufficiently organised to attract visitors from abroad. But it was only when my driver streaked out of Cairo early one morning to avoid the worst of the traffic, which he did not, and pointed the car towards the ugly suburbs of Suez, which now has a million inhabitants, and turned south along the Red Sea coast that I realised the full potential of this fantastic coastline for travellers.

Egypt has over 700 miles (1127 km) of Red Sea shore. It hardly ever rains. The climate fluctuates between hot and hottest all year round and for western and northern Europeans it will be the Promised Land. That there is a lot of sand goes without saying. On one side are the reddish crags of the eastern desert with its great vales of blond sand and on the other is the world's warmest sea. It is roughly the temperature of a cup of tea, which has been left standing for a little whiie. From the old would-be resort of Ain Sokhna to Marsa Alam in the far south I counted at least 40 sites suitable for beach lizards and it was only later from an Egyptian Government report that I discovered the Red Sea coast had upwards of 70 areas where tourism could be developed.

For the present time, the best is Hurghada. You can either drive there from Cairo, taking the best part of a day, or fly direct to the little airport in about one hour. A not terribly beautiful hotel, the Hurghada, is the focal point. It is built for some reason like a drum and faces a beach of incomparable beauty. The sea is of unlimited pale blue and there are 11 small islands offshore, with some of the finest coral for hundreds of miles around and with magnificent beaches where you can be alone if you try. I have no doubt that Hurghada will make it in the big league. Further south, around the oil port of Bur Safaga and the very old Muslim city of Qusair are more beaches, so far almost untouched which tour operators would give their last pound coin for. Fortunately, they don't know about them. Even further south, if you can get there because the road is a bit rough, is Marsa al-Alam, once known as Berenice and a famous trading port from which the ships of Cleopatra sailed in search of exotic ointments. Even further south, Egyptian friends tell me that the beaches around Ras Banas are sensational. I can well believe it.

This drive along Egypt's Red Sea coast has long remained in my memory as one of the high points of my travelling life and not just because of the beaches. In the Galala country I visited one of the two true birthplaces of Christian monasticism, the Monastery of St Paul (the other, more remote is the Monastery of St Anthony). It dates from about AD 350 and the huddle of white buildings is about the only thing around. I rang the bell. A young novice appeared who spoke some English, turned the huge key and admitted me to a long vaulted hospitality room, whitewashed and lined with homespun carpets and rugs. 'What do you do here?' I asked him. He looked at me as if I had indeed asked him a silly question, which I had. 'We just are,' he replied. 'We help the poor, pray, look after ourselves and bury our dead over there in the little garden within the walls.' Muslims had never persecuted them. On Sundays a few local Copts usually dropped in for their devotions and twice a year there was a big pilgrimage. The last Westerner he had seen, a German student, had left, he counted on his fingers, about seven months ago.

Together we toured the quiet, sun-filled courtyards, visited cells and looked in on the four chapels, two of which are underground and so old that the ancient wall frescoes have long ago been blackened by the fumes of the candles. The library, which is not open to tourists, still contained about 700 volumes, many of them quite priceless and historians sometimes come from as far away as Chicago or Moscow to study them. As we parted, I asked him if there was anything I could do. He looked as if the question should have been phrased the other way around. 'You can leave some money in the box out there,' he said smiling. 'We use it to help the sick.' In return, he gave me a rich gift in this strange, eerie desert: a fresh lemon the smell of which travelled with me all the way down the coast. From Hurghada, you drive to Bur Safaga and onto a splendid tarred road, which leads straight as an arrow across the eastern desert, the second best thing surely to trying outer-space. You reach the Nile at Qena just north of the tourist megalopolis of Luxor and you are in another world.

COUNTRYSIDE AND SIGHTS

As I have said so often before this is not a guidebook. Egypt needs one or maybe two or even three to do it justice. But, in this vast country four times the size of Great Britain, certain things and places remain in my memory.

One is the amazing, breathtaking sight of the green ribbon of the Nile Banks, never more than 12 miles (19 km) wide, snaking across between the tawny desert on either side. Here, the country shines with good produce, intense cultivation and much hard work by the *fellahin* who, day in and day out, work their famous *sakieh* water wheels. Here too, under the palm and the great trees are the country's 4000 villages where, every now and then, one comes across the house of a man who has taken the *hajj* to Mecca and has commissioned some local artist to depict his great journey on the outside walls. It might show a camel caravan, though more often than not a train or an airplane, a shop selling Egyptian film posters in Cairo, the minaret of a mosque in Arabia or even the glasses of green tea he had on the way. Not all that different after all from the daily life depicted on the walls of the Tombs of the Nobles. And every morning, and every night, processions of statuesque women go down to the great river with water pots balanced on their heads.

Another is Pharaonic Egypt, which is of course an unbelievable open air museum of a really great civilisation. With pleasure and a sense of awe, I recall Giza and Saqqara, the Al-Amarna of Akhenaton, Abydos and Komombo and Edfu. The Hellenistic grace of Philae. The grandeur of the reconstructed Abu Simbel and, last but not least of all, the great hypostyle hall of Karnak, whose 122 pillars each of 60 feet (18.3 m) high give a feeling of strength, of lasting faith, of undiluted pride.

The oases of the Western Desert too, places like Kharga, to which one can now fly, Dakhla, Farafra and the remote and meaningful Siwa, which is a world of its own in the middle of the unchanging sands. Then there is the great depression of the Fayum, 43 yards (39 m) below sea level, and more than 30 miles (48 km) across. Then there is the great green land of the Wadi Natrun so long the principal home of Christianity in Egypt.

Cairo is not to be missed if you can stand the pace, the noise, the bustle and the demonic drivers trying to erupt first from the 13 lines of traffic into Tahrir Square. For, when you look hard, Cairo has much more than that: for example, the evocative Mameluke 'City of the Dead' with its magnificent cupolas, the likes of which you are unlikely to see this side of Samarkand; great and ancient mosques like Ibn Tulun; Saladin's citadel; and even a synagogue or two; the lovely bazaar of Khan el Khalili, which is now so much more interesting than Istanbul's and as you meander around the narrow streets of the Muski district, you will see the people who create real art out of recycled Coke bottles. Plus this. Plus that. Don't miss it. Go to Egypt now.

CLIMATE

The best time to visit Egypt is between November and May. The warmest place is Aswan and the breeziest Alexandria.

INTERNAL TRANSPORT

The main roads are good. The one from Cairo to Aswan, for instance, is excellent over most of its 600-odd miles (966 km). So are those from Cairo to Suez and Cairo to Alexandria. Smaller places are naturally less well served and in the villages (especially in the delta) roads can be hazardous and bumpy. Taxis are cheap by Western standards and hired cars are not out of reach moneywise provided you make your own arrangements through a reliable local travel agency. The driver is far more likely than you are to know his way around.

Egyptian trains are remarkably good and punctual though sometimes a little uncomfortable. EgyptAir can now take you to about ten principal domestic destinations. Then, of course, there are those boats on the Nile but be careful: most of them should be inspected if there is time and reservations made quite a long time ahead. The Egyptian Tourist Office service is variable. It is sometimes extremely efficient and occasionally deplorable so the independent traveller must do a good deal of reading beforehand.

SPECIALISED HOLIDAYS

These will depend on just what it is you wish to do and how much you are prepared to spend. There is no shortage of good tour operators and among them I would recommend Abercrombie & Kent, Hayes & Jarvis, Bales Tours, Fairways & Swinford and Twickers World. All are people who have some solid experience in Egypt. Nawas Tourist Agency, an Egyptian concern, can help a lot when it comes to private arrangements. But don't expect too much flexibility from anyone.

Please see page 220 for addresses.

EAST AFRICA
Tanzania and Kenya

PROFILE

No doubt some of my friends in Nairobi and Dar-es-Salaam will never forgive me for lumping their countries together since, after all, they are independent of each other. But for me they mean just one thing, Africa. There are a few interesting differences, however. Kenya is magnificent, grand, varied and very beautiful, also very prosperous and well organised. Tanzania is magnificent, grand, varied and very beautiful, but not so prosperous and highly disorganised. Never mind. In my early days the frontier was often a small pile of stones in the middle of nowhere and you could cross from one to the other just by stretching your leg forward.

East Africa is the place to go for safaris. But no one these days, apart from the Chicago ladies who appear at the long bar of the Mount Kenya Safari Club dressed like Ernest Hemingway, talks of big game any more; it might offend some sensibilities. Quite. You speak instead of photographic safaris. These consist of 'shoehorning' you into some unspeakable minibus until you look like one of many sticks of rhubarb sticking out of the top. Unless you are Japanese, of course, when you might look like a slightly yellowed umbrella stick, carefully poised on an orange box for height and festooned with so many cameras that no one can see your face. So it's click for a lion, click-click-click for a leopard. You should be so lucky. I personally hate those minibuses. They are smelly, uncomfortable and noisy. Besides, I once saw one minibus, fortunately empty, on which an elephant had elected to sit and there was not much of the bus left. Come to think of it, I don't like elephants much either: they are frightening, unpredictable creatures, given to fits of rage and uncivilised behaviour.

So what do I go to East Africa for? One might well ask. It is for the discovery, often totally unexpected, of what the world used to be like; virginal, cruel and kind, miraculously beautiful and unforgettable. And this is where Africa can best be seen. Putting aside cruises, it is sad to relate that no travel currency has been devalued and debased more than the safari. Nowadays, if you are not careful, it is all done by numbers, by computers and by guides whose loud-hailers

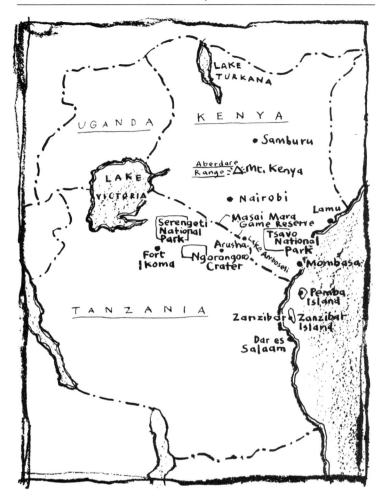

should have been strangled during manufacture. All the more chances for the independent traveller to do his own thing. Is it possible? Read on.

I did at any rate, only a couple of decades ago, when the ghosts of Theodore Roosevelt, Hemingway and all those story-telling white hunters still strode across the bush. It all started in a bar at some hotel in Arusha where we were introduced to some eccentric Polish photographer – eccentric being a euphemism for mad. He was called Stefan Unpronounceable so, to his great distaste, we called him 'Steff'. Now a mad Englishman is easy enough: he just goes out in the midday sun. A mad Russian is slightly more dangerous: he might go to bed with his own bottle of vodka, wake up in the middle of the night and set fire to everything in sight. But a mad Pole? Oeee. He might look like Robert Redford one minute, with warts of course, and act like Frankenstein himself the next. There is no telling.

Do you have transport, I asked Steff. He had. 'How early can you be ready?' he asked. 'Five a.m. tomorrow?' Well, yes, we could, just.

At the appointed hour the transport was drawn up outside the hotel; it comprised the most disreputable, bashed-about, cannibalised Land Rover you could imagine. It was now on its fourth born-again engine and the milometer read 213,000 miles (342,930 km), which was probably an understatement. One spring had gone AWOL somewhere and the sides of Steff's car were completely covered with crusty canvas sheets, pots and pans, 'biscuit'-type mattresses, water barrels, torn sheets and, oh yes, a Union Jack. 'Hop in,' said Steff. 'We are all ready.' 'We' presumably included the African driver whom Steff called 'Bongo' whatever his real name was.

We had not gone more than a couple of miles along the tarmac road out of Arusha when Steff abruptly turned right, off from the road. We went bumping along from hillock to hillock, keeping clear of the metal parts of the *African Queen* as we had already dubbed the Land Rover. 'Roads are a pain in the ...,' explained Steff. 'The real Africa is out there.'

It was too. We drove for hours on end, painfully and noisily. Gradually, the whole country opened up in front of us the way those old lantern slides must have done. Look now, don't look now. Once we came across some zebra grazing and I told Steff what marvellous pictures they made. So he drove right into them, and I mean right into them, until we were engulfed in a sea of stripes and 'Bongo' had a job keeping them from munching the tarpaulins. 'They make very good steaks,' said Steff, adding without the trace of a smile, 'Mind you, the white stripes are always more tender ...'

We set up camp, though goodness knows where. Dinner came, consisting of a stew for which only 'Bongo' had the recipe and we suggested that he should keep it. He could make a fortune as a chef on a health farm for slimmers. Then, out of the blue, came French pâté de foie gras on one side of the plate and tinned peaches on the other, plus a nice bottle of St Emilion. Life, after all, could be good. We dropped off under our lean-to tarpaulins only to find that the whole of Africa was just out there, doing its best to keep us awake through sheer terror.

131

The next day we drove and drove, up and down and often sideways, from dawn till well after dark. Finally, Steff said that we should camp here – wherever that was. We were so tired that in the light of kerosene lamps we could manage only a few biscuits and a mug of skimmed milk tea. At around 5 a.m., which was obviously Steff's favourite time, he woke us up by throwing a bucket of water on our tarpaulin and saying: 'OK, get up. This is it. Come out and look.' We did and promptly forgot breakfast. Camp had been struck roughly 10 feet (3 m) from the edge of a great escarpment several hundred feet high, festooned with those artistic African umbrella-shaped thorn trees. The sun rose behind us, rolling up the night clouds in front of us and there, through the trees, we could see the finest, most immense and mysterious land we had ever seen. 'What the hell is that?' I asked Steff. 'That is the Serengeti,' he said quietly. The sun glinted on streams, suffused hillocks which turned out to be giraffes, snaked around to follow a long string of gnus who were going to where they go when they form a club. Gradually, the whole fantastic landscape erupted into pale pink, then red, then gold and blue and green until it was the creation of the world all over again.

We drove down the escarpment, more by luck than by good judgement. There were tracks but Steff persistently disregarded them. Anything that looked difficult, with the *African Queen* poised, tarpaulins flapping, at a 45 degree angle, appealed to him. We met wildebeest and zebra, lions and elephants. At certain times, though mostly in May, Steff told us the great Serengeti migration takes place, wildebeest and zebras will get up one morning, as many as 200,000 of them, and cross the Serengeti in line at the speed of an express train. Unstoppable.

We zigged and zagged and that night reached the Seronera Lodge, which is a very nice bush hostelry with all the comforts of the white man's world. Plus the fully-grown lion that walked calmly through the open-air bar while all the palefaces took refuge behind the upturned tables and the barman quietly went on polishing his glasses. We stayed two nights there.

Serengeti is roughly the size of three English counties and I think Steff took us to all the best parts, including those where one was not supposed to go. Then, unaccountably, he doubled back to get us to the famous Ngorongoro Crater, the largest caldera in the world, 1800 feet (549 m) deep and roughly 15 miles (24 km) across, which is not only one of the natural wonders of the world but the home of hundreds of thousands of wild animals who, like their human counterparts, never climb the walls of the crater to escape and so they are born there, live there and die there. It is a kind of microcosm of the world, untouched, unsullied and mightily protected from all encroachments. The sight of clouds of pink flamingoes rising from the lake, or an old suspicious bull elephant peering out from behind some huge tree or a massive herd of wildebeest heading down to the food are things that cannot be equalled anywhere at any time.

Then, equally unaccountably, Steff drove full speed ahead to the west and stopped at Fort Ikoma, halfway to Lake Victoria, where a clever English couple have recreated the atmosphere of an old German fort (Tanzania, then Tanganyika, was a German colony until 1918). Trimly-dressed askaris greet you at the door and the dinner table is graced with bottles of Château Lafite. Your thatched-roof rondavel hut holds other surprises, such as a spider the size of a saucer making free with your fresh sheets. We rang for service and a boy came with an instrument looking a bit like a bedwarming pan and scooped up the unmentionable. Bashing it with a wooden mallet would have made an awful mess on the sheets. Besides, one is not supposed to kill anything. Eventually, and I mean eventually, we made it back to Arusha and bade a fond farewell to Steff, 'Bongo' and the *African Queen*. Safaris, did I say? You too can plan your own, though with some difficulty.

What is East Africa good for? A complete change, the realisation that fortunately the world is not all the same. The unique chance to see wild animals in their own God-given habitat and not in a zoo. Plus, of course, an opportunity of lazing a few days away on some of the world's finest beaches.

BEACHES

These are superb and among the best in the world. Kenya has a coastline of 350 miles (564 km) and Tanzania over 500 miles (805 km) and most of it is beach, which is wide with particularly soft sand, lined with palms and with a pale blue sea that is a pleasure to watch. The food is great, and especially the seafood. Kenya is, naturally, more advanced regarding beaches. It has been at it longer and, they say, it is only 12 miles (19 km) to paradise, from Mombasa via the Nyali Bridge to the spots former colonists loved. I would myself make for the Diani beach or Jadini on the south side. I don't care much for Kilifi, which is too clublike, or Malindi or Watamu, which have too many discotheques. One of my very favourite destinations would be remote Lamu, the old Swahili seaport close to the Somalia frontier. Lamu, a time capsule of the great days of Arab dhows and Swahili navigators, is a place to see for it is very historical, filled with mosques and tiny corkscrew streets and fantastic Zanzibar-type doors. One is in another world. My own favourite place is the now famed Peponi's Hotel. The beach next to the hotel is a mere 8 miles (12.9 km) long.

Tanzania's beaches are great too, though far less developed, which is perhaps a good thing. Those at Kunduchi and Bahari near Dar-es-Salaam probably fit the bill best for most people. There are also some good ones on Zanzibar and Pemba Islands; they are not easy to get to but worth while, especially for the deep sea fishing there. Other good beaches are at Pangani and Tanga and I would suggest one place that must not be missed is Bagamoyo. Like Lamu, it is one of the oldest settlements on the East African coast. It was long the transshipment place for the slave trade and it was there that the embalmed body of Dr Livingstone was brought back by his faithful and courageous servants. It is very evocative.

COUNTRYSIDE

This means game reserves, national parks and wildlife sanctuaries of which the two East African countries have more than 40. Some are a mere two square miles and some are enormous, like Tanzania's Selous in the south, which is roughly the size of Wales. In Tanzania the most famous are Serengeti, Ngorongoro and Lake Manyara while in Kenya the better-known ones are Amboseli, the Tsavo (east and west) and the Masai-Mara Game Reserve, which is perhaps the best bet of all for game viewing unless you wish to go off the beaten track. I personally remember with affection the Samburu National Park, just north of Mount Kenya, not least because of the Samburu people, distant cousins of the famous Masai, who hold some very special dances which are still very traditional and not just for your camera. At night, you sit on the terrace of Samburu Lodge grasping your sundowner and watch with a now blasé feeling the barrage of crocodiles across the river. Occasionally, and in remarkable unison, the great jaws open and shut on some prey or other.

If you are just that little bit more adventurous, there is no better suggestion than the vast Lake Turkana, the 'Jade Sea' in northern Kenya, a place which is totally apart from the rest of the country. It is populated by gigantic crocodiles (but they don't eat tourists), the famous Nile perch, easy to catch and up to 400 pounds (181 kg) in weight, and strange semi-nomadic people like the Turkana and the Boran. Yet, now that one can fly to Turkana, things are not quite the same.

I see that I have missed out the famed Rift Valley, the Aberdare Mountains, the drier-than-dry lands of the north east and indeed the shores of Lake Victoria. But how much time do you have?

CLIMATE

Hot or hotter, though it can be damp too. In the two countries the long rains come from the end of March to mid-June (but don't count on it) and the short rains from late October to early December. The high season, which is more expensive for tourists but easier for travel, is from December to March.

INTERNAL TRANSPORT

No fewer than 13 international airlines have regular services to Nairobi and two of them, British Airways and Kenya Airways, fly there every day from London. Tanzanians are trying hard to make Arusha their own air gateway and have built an impressive airport there. And, of course, Dar-es-Salaam is also fairly well served.

Once you arrive in Tanzania you will find that transport services are rare and uncomfortable except in the area around Dar-es-Salaam and the Arusha/Moshi tourist-beat. In Kenya things are far better organised: you can have a seat on a minibus, a private car or even a private plane (Wilson Airport in Nairobi is Africa's busiest place for small planes). You can even see Africa from a balloon if you like things that way. Kenya has a magnificent, and very evocative, train service which runs from Nairobi to Mombasa and vice versa every night and it also continues all the way to Lake Victoria.

HOTELS

As a traveller you will never be short of resting places in East Africa unless you are a duffer at planning. Hotels run from five-star international ones in Nairobi to gorgeous tented camps in the bush.

SPECIALISED HOLIDAYS

This is obviously where the independent traveller gets separated from the horde. There is absolutely no trouble, I repeat no trouble, in booking yourself a safari holiday from existing brochures, though some of them have too much in common with a day trip around the Isle of Dogs. The two 'kings' of East African travel are old friends: Abercrombie & Kent (Europe) Ltd – up-market – and UTC/United Touring Company – middle market – and they have, fortunately, not forgotten what a real safari was like. I know of one titled English lady who insisted with one of these two companies, and I won't tell you which one, on seeing virtually the whole of Kenya from a white Mercedes, with a guide who had letters after his name and behind it all a truck filled with servants and all the goodies they could pack in for each night's stay. It cost her too, I bet. One night she apparently complained that her Perrier water was not fresh and they had some flown in. These two companies know all there is to know about East Africa and they have dealt, successfully, with most types of offbeat travellers. They will be able to help you but don't hope to do it on the cheap.

One can still do things on one's own. Anyone hanging around the famous Thorn Tree Café of Nairobi's New Stanley Hotel will, sooner or later, meet a man who says that he can 'deliver' the greatest safari of all time. You may or may not believe him. London-based Flamingo Tours are also very well represented locally as are Nilestar Tours and, of course, the august Wexas International. Holiday Planners promise they will look after any independent traveller and I am inclined to believe them.

In the end, though, it is personal experience that counts especially if you have done your homework as this book suggests and here I would make a special plea to buy the newest Kenya *Insight* guide (Harrap). Then go to Nairobi, Arusha, Mombasa or Dar-es-Salaam and ask questions. The Kenya Tourist Office and the Tanzania Tourist Office might also be worth contacting for specifics. Go on. Decide what you want and try it now.

Please see pages 220–1 for addresses.

THE EAST
Israel

PROFILE

When beginning to write this chapter, I asked myself one question. What would make me go back to Israel? I did not have to search my memory very far because soon scenes came back at the speed of a lantern slide show run by a madman. Quicker, quicker, ever quicker. An early evening in Acre (Akko). The 'Shabbath' in Jerusalem. The utter and unbelievable peace of the Sea of Galilee. An early morning on the Masada Rock. And so on. There is about this little country a kind of nostalgic, cultural déjà vu that never fails to grab the visitor and force him to say to himself: 'I have been here before'.

In the end, I came to the conclusion that I would just love to go back to Israel for a good argument. There is no better place for one anywhere. The basic Jewish ethos, surrounded by what is supposed to be Israeli intolerance but which is in fact simple pride, produces a love of argument which is unbeatable. I recall sitting on a stone in Jerusalem for a whole afternoon with a learned and most interesting Jewish friend quarrelling about the precise location of the cave where Joseph of Arimathea had laid the body of Jesus. My friend said that it was there, just in front of us. I said no, it was somewhere else and here were my reasons. The arguments went back and forth like a tennis rally, though he, of course, scored somewhat better than I did. We quoted every possible quotation at each other. Time went by. In the end I said: 'Yacov, you win! We would still be here tomorrow morning if I didn't give in.' He looked at me as if he were almost hurt. 'But we have only just begun!' he exclaimed. That is what I would go back to Israel for: the fizz, the excitement, the sheer extravagance of the talk. It's like a tonic and if you can take it, believe me, Israel will be good for you. Besides which, the country is very beautiful and special. So when I land at Lod, I roll up my sleeves, figuratively, and fight.

Of course, if what you want is a complete rest I would not suggest Israel at all, with the possible exception of one or two places maybe. But if you like being taken out of yourself,

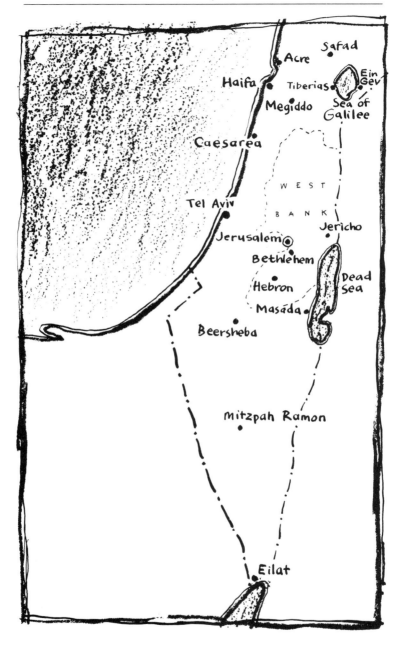

shaken up and down until you rattle and coming out with a different view of things, Israel is the place for you.

No country of comparable size can compete because within its narrow borders, Israel really has everything: history, religion and politics. One can do more, see more in Israel than almost anywhere else in such a short time. As a famous writer once said: 'Going to Israel is like walking through a minefield.' So watch how you go. One morning you might be talking Weber with a member of the Israel Philharmonic Orchestra, one of the world's greatest group of musicians, and in the afternoon exchanging physics equations with an engineer in Arad. You might see Israeli girls dancing the hora behind every bush (they always seem to be dancing) or again the poignancy of Masada might make you speechless. One thing is certain: you will never be the same person again and, after all, that is what travel is all about.

What is Israel good for? It is almost everybody's second home – a small country so filled with man's past that going there is almost always like a second visit. The people are tough and ingenious. A success story against all odds.

BEACHES

I was reminded once again not very long ago that Israelis do have a sense of humour! I actually met a man in Tel Aviv who told me he thought that Eilat was beautiful. Since I would have classified this one and only Israeli Red Sea coast resort as a building site by the sea I was more than a little surprised. Apart from the weather, which is hot to hottest, Eilat is an acquired taste. Israelis are in love with concrete and with building for the sake of building with the result that, to my mind, the resort is massive, ugly and much lacking in grace.

Israel being a small country with a lot of people, it is hard to see how one could take it seriously as a beach destination. Although the beaches are clean and well organised they tend to be crowded with people from the cities. All the way from the Lebanese frontier to the Gaza strip, the Mediterranean coast is lined with with beaches and places like Akhziv or Caesarea, which are perfectly acceptable. Nahariya, Netanya and Herzliya are very crowded. My own favourite by far would be little Dor Beach, between Haifa and Caesarea, where the sandy shore has a shape and a perspective. The climate everywhere is superb and that is a great attraction but then there are many other attractions in this little country.

COUNTRYSIDE AND GREAT SIGHTS

With three and a half million people living in this exiguous land, one would imagine that there is not much room left for real countryside – but it would be a mistake. In fact, Israel is proud of its national parks and sanctuaries and nature reserves, of which there are 40. There are places of incredible beauty such as the springs of Ein Gedi or the pillars of Solomon down in the far south. Also there is the sand-coloured immensity of the Mountains of Moab seen from the western side of the Dead Sea.

Three specific places will always remain in my memory. One is of the day when, feeling more energetic than usual, I climbed the famous hill of Megiddo, where Solomon kept his chariot horses among other things and, on the far side, discovered the great sight of the plain of Jezreel, tawny and green, blue and gold, stretching as far as the eye could see and one of the most beautiful places I had ever seen.

Then, one afternoon, I went to the Mount of Beatitudes close to the Sea of Galilee and there, in the woods surrounding the not-so-beautiful Italianate church on the hill, I caught tantalising glimpses of the Sea. Vast flocks of birds rose from the waters, wheeled over to reach the Golan Heights side only to return on some special errand to the Tiberias side. The air hummed with the sound of the bumble bees, a slight breeze ruffled the normally calm waters and I swear I could, in my mind's eye, see Jesus handing out the loaves and the fishes. There, down below on the lake, was Peter quietly fishing for the famed Peter fish, now sold so efficiently by the lorryload on the opposite shore of the Sea of Galilee, in the kibbutz of Ein Gev.

The third was when many years ago, I drove nonchalantly through the little town of Mitzpah Ramon in the Negev on my way to Eilat only to find that it was built right on the edge of one of the world's biggest volcanic craters. The surprise forced me to sit down, right then and there, to find that the harsh sun of the desert made the vast natural arena into a piece of sculpture unequalled anywhere – not even in the United States' Grand Canyon. The walls of the great depression turned from tawny blond to mauve, from mauve to a strange red ochre and back again. In the space of an hour, the landscape changed beyond recognition and I was not even a bit surprised when one Israeli workman crept up behind me and said, *sotto voce* 'And they say this country is small.' They do indeed but they are wrong. Beyond lay the great tortured Negev, the desert which, in places, now blooms with biblical pomegranates, lemons, avocados and oranges.

In many ways the trouble with Israel is that there is too much to see, too many sensations. Prophets spring up behind every stone. Kings ride, fully armed, to meet Ammonites or Philistines. The miracles of Jesus took place just about everywhere, at Cana, at Jerusalem and the Mount of Olives, hard by this fountain or that stream. It's like a cornucopia of history and faith, all mixed up and ready for the lucky dip. You put your hand inside the bag and only chance knows what you will come up with. It's all been written about scores of times, of course, and much better than I could do it. In a way, personal impressions, which depend on your mood, the time of day and who you are travelling with, are much better. Since you cannot bring order to this maelstrom, just look, remember and fasten on to the things and sights that strike you at the time. Acre (Akko) for instance, the fortress of for ever and ever, has seen 17 major sieges and the ghosts of Richard the Lionheart and Saladin still clatter down its streets.

There is also the white-walled Safed, home of the 'Kabala' and famed Hazor, one of the most fought-over places in the Middle East. I like Caesarea too, the one-time Roman captial with wild flowers growing over the ruins by the sea and indeed Jericho, the great oasis in the Jordan valley, which brings one straight back to Joshua and the trumpets of the Lord or even Avdat where those clever Nabateans did so much to teach us about desert agriculture. Only one of three Nabatean places have so far been excavated inside Israel, the other two being Shivta and Mamshit.

And what about Hebron? One of the four Holy Cities with its memories of Isaac and Jacob and the great mosque which came so much later? By far the most impressive place is Masada, overlooking the Dead Sea where, after a three years' siege, the Jewish Zealots threw themselves off the rock rather than surrender to the Romans. Like all places of great tragedy, it also has a haunting beauty. Then there is always Jerusalem, which one goes to see at any time for a great number of reasons. Or Bethlehem, apart from Christmas time when it is too commercialised or even Nazareth which some people seem to like.

For me, I am so inebriated after all this that I am almost glad to be going back to places like Ein Hod, the artists' village south of Haifa or even old Jaffa (Yafo), which blooms on and on with great art and good food.

CLIMATE

In Israel, wearing a collar and tie is almost an offence to good taste. Judaean winters up in the hills can be cold but the rest of the country has one of the best climates in the world. Something in the region of 70°F (21°C) in Eilat in January can't be bad.

INTERNAL TRANSPORT

This is among the best in the world. It is beautifully organised and very reliable. Buses go everywhere and, for tourists, Egged Buses is one of the better companies. Arkia, the local airline, will take you to half-a-dozen destinations in reasonable comfort. Taxis are plentiful and are of three kinds: the ordinary city taxi which is cheap and convenient, the marvellous *sherut* taxis which can be shared by several people obviously wanting to go in the same direction. The third is the chauffeur-driven taxis which are not allowed to operate unless they have the Israeli tourist emblem on the door. In Israel someone is always going somewhere and Israelis are inveterate hitchhikers. In a country that clocks up only 212 miles (341 km) from Tel Aviv to Eilat, all this comes in very useful.

HOTELS

Israeli hotels are on the whole good and efficient. A few are great. But even the most rabid pro-Israel people would hesitate to glory in the gastronomy which is not great, except in a few cities like Jaffa, Tel Aviv and Haifa. There are also upwards of 2000 rooms available in kibbutzim up and down the country. Some of them are fairly simple and others have come a long way since the early days in terms of comfort and facilities. The Israel Government Tourist Office can give you further information. So can Kibbutz Representatives.

SPECIALISED HOLIDAYS

Israel is the land of the do-it-yourself and quite ideal for the independent traveller who can stay where he wants at the drop of a shekel. Over 30 Christian hospices run by various orders also offer rooms of varying standards which are very good value. The Israel Government Tourist Office can inform you about these. Some self-catering apartments and villas are available in Israel. Contact Homtel Ltd. Many British tour operators offer a wide variety of packaged holidays in Israel and among them I would strongly recommend Peltours, W. F. & R. K. Swan (Hellenic) Ltd and Bales Tours as being people who know what they are selling.

There are several variations on the desert safari tour and most of them are operated by agencies in Eilat. One interesting option for younger people is the amusing and novel trail-riding in Galilee (Vered Hagalil), which provides you with a horse, a guide and basic accommodation and lets you loose on that beautiful northern part of the country. The Israel Government Tourist Office in London again will tell you how to contact them. In Israel itself, two tour companies shine by their ingenuity and sense of adventure. One is the ubiquitous Egged Tours whose handsome air conditioned buses are known all over the land. Their head office is in Tel Aviv and almost every day of the week they provide something like 100 tours all over the country and very good value they are too. The other company is the Jerusalem-based Galilee Tours, which also operate from almost every centre and can take you to Egypt, Cyprus, Greece and Turkey too. Finally, let me say this: Israeli people are extremely hospitable and they are so pleased at seeing you looking at their country that almost every person you meet will give you the information you require, a contact, an address and so on. So go now.

Please see page 221 for addresses.

India

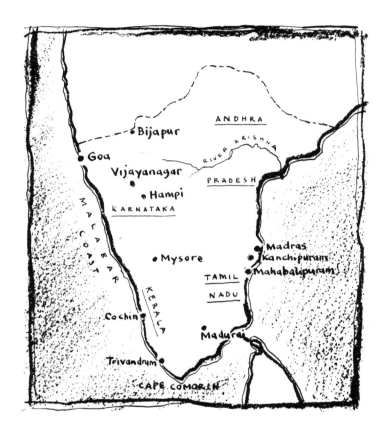

PROFILE

In the early morning haze which precedes the overpowering heat of the day, I watched a man mowing the immense grass verges along the sides of the Rajpath, that vast Champs Elysees of India built by Lutyens to link the India Gate and the Hollywood-style government buildings. Then I looked again. The motor of the man's mower had given up the ghost, if indeed it had ever had a motor, and so he did the only possible Indian thing: he harnessed his enormous bullock to the lawn-mower and the slow, ponderous animal pulled the little machine up and down, cutting clean swathes in the green carpet. That same morning, I read in the paper that Insat, India's own space satellite, had finally given hundreds of millions of farmers the green light to sow the new crop. A technological gap? No, just India.

My neighbour at a party, a well-known accountant, was telling me about the marvellous results of his vasectomy and kept saying: 'The duty of every Indian is not to procreate...' I fear that at first I hardly listened. I was fascinated by the sight of a lovely Indian girl in a gauzy, pale blue sari. She had put four Indian-grown cherries in her Indian-made dry Martini, and gobbled each cherry as if it were the ultimate sin.

As a new Brit (more British than the Brits), I have long inhaled India like a drug, all the way from Thomas Coryate to Emily Eden and from Rudyard Kipling to Paul Scott. There have also been something like a dozen visits. When people ask me that dreaded but inevitable question which of my 104 countries I like best, the answer is always the same: apart from formative France and adopted Britain, two countries always come to the surface, Greece and India. One is small, ravishing and poetically beautiful and so close to both heart and mind; the other is enormous, totally mysterious and unfailingly appealing. I feel I ought to learn something from India, if only I knew what it was. India is gorgeous and infuriating, exotic and yet as familiar as Stoke-on-Trent, maddeningly elusive and visually compelling. I, for one, am never quite the same after another visit to India. Somehow it changes me and the experience is something I cannot forget. I have always maintained that the world is made up of two kinds of people: those who have never been to India and have no intention of going there, and those who have been and can't wait to get back.

Of course, India is 'difficult', especially if you are looking for more than a mere surface impression. For one thing, its size militates against 'instant' tourism. For another, India is not at all the kind of country one thinks it should be. Between the Himalayan snows and Cape Comorin live 700 million Indians, speaking 14 major languages, some of which are more widespread than European tongues, and more than 250 dialects. Some Indians are rich mahogany in colour, others are as fair as Europeans. A few are rich and powerful, most are poor but the land is so fertile that its wealth consistently defies the birthrate. India produces everything from cashew nuts to railway engines and nuclear energy and, when India's star was rising, most Europeans still lived in caves. India is magnificent, breathtaking, utterly exhausting and quite unforgettable.

You should approach India with your mind cleared of all prejudices and preconceived notions. Leave these behind and before you can say anything India will embrace you, look at you, evaluate you, turn you inside out and it is my guess that you will never be the same person again. Don't try to understand India. It would take two lifetimes to do that. Just let India flow over you. In India everything is a contradiction, apparent confusion, noise and secretiveness mixed with an almost total lack of privacy. How can you be private with those teeming millions all around you? What matters is being there.

What is India good for? India does not change, but you do, for it turns you inside out and makes you think. Sometimes uncomfortable but hardly ever forgotten, India is a world of its own and in many ways India has a great deal to teach the Westerner. Don't be too ambitious – take it bit by bit.

BEACHES

Of course. After all, you are on holiday and India can provide you with beaches though most people would not immediately associate India with the idea of a beach holiday. Beaches in Orissa, south and south west of Calcutta, are superb and they have the additional attraction of being very rarely visited by European tourists. Indians themselves go to places like Gobalpur (ugh) but the rest is for anyone who cares to go. The nearer you get to Madras the better, and better equipped, the beaches are.

It is when you turn around the corner so to speak and get to Kerala and Karnataka that the best are to be found but more of this later. Further north, virtually the whole of the coast of a great state like Maharastra is one long beach with soft sand, waving palms, boats pulled up on the beach and so on. As for Goa, well, it stands alone and of this more later too.

COUNTRYSIDE AND GREAT SIGHTS

I am always quietly amused when people tell me they are going to 'do' India and I have even known some who will bravely go to Kashmir in winter thinking that since India is a winter country anyway, this will do just as well and they can take in Kashmir as well as Rajasthan. Brr. For me, the choice of an alternative India is very difficult indeed. First-timers, guided by tour operators, who are great masters of the obvious, all make for the photogenic Mogul India that sends you jumping along from Bombay to Delhi, Agra, Jaipur and Udaipur. I won't deny the benefits of this introduction for, after all, on this route you'll see the Taj Mahal which, in my opinion, is one of the two most beautiful monuments in the world, the other one being the Parthenon. But it ignores the almost unbelievable beauty of Kashmir, Benares (now Varanasi), the Ganges and Calcutta. More seriously, it ignores the south. Which south? Geographically, Andhra Pradesh, the old state of Hyderabad, ought to be included, and yet, along with some of the upper reaches of Karnataka, formerly Mysore, it has more in common with the north.

At the risk of catching some well-aimed brickbats from Bihar or the Punjab, I would suggest that southern India is the real India. This is where the music and the dance come from, and much of the cuisine; where the real Hindu architecture can be found in a part of the subcontinent hardly touched by the magnificent but alien brushstrokes of the Moguls. This was the land of the great and lasting Indian empires, the shores from which Indian conquest and influence reached out as far as China's back door and the Indonesian islands, while, on the other side, the Malabar Coast turned its face towards the west.

So, if you have already done the Mogul grand tour, do try the south, namely the states of Tamil Nadu, Kerala and Karnataka. You won't be alone because intelligent travellers who have begun to appreciate India are now making for the south, but the rush is not yet on and the rewards of personal discovery will be yours. Down there you will find the finest beaches, the greatest temples, the most beautiful silk, the finest hill country, the greenest greenery. You will find people who will not understand even two of your few words of Hindi, people who are shorter and darker. Fortunately, the south is the one part of India where English is the universal second language. The Englishness began in Madras long before Bombay or Calcutta and flourished in such romantic hill stations as Ootacamund ('Snooty Ooty') and Kodaikanal.

Madras, in the state of Tamil Nadu, is vast but, fortunately, not as frenetic as other Indian cities and has avenues so wide that you have to cross them in stages, great vistas, a superb frontage on the Bay of Bengal and, even today, an air of easy-going gentility. Thomas the Apostle, losing his way one feels, somehow got here and is buried on St Thomas Mount and has a cathedral named after him. Here, too, is Fort St George, the raj's first permanent stronghold in India; Clive's House and St Mary's Church, where so many of the early colonials found a premature resting place. Although I have a low boredom threshold when it comes to museums, I would not miss the Madras one. It contains fine examples of India's greatest art-form, bronze statuary, much of which came from the nearby town of Chingleput.

However, Madras is only the front hall to southern India. What matters lies outside. For me the most emotional place of all is Mahabalipuram, 50 miles (80 km) to the south (the name flows off the tongue once you get used to it). This is the famed temple city by the shore, the great seaport of the Pallavas kings 1200 years ago. On my first visit, I arrived at Mahabalipuram ignorant of all local customs, and, it being the night of the full-moon pilgrimage, was greeted by the spectacle of 40,000 pilgrims sitting the night out by their campfires washing clothes, eating, listening to story tellers, watching snake charmers and magicians, and playing charades and other ancient games. In the morning bleary-eyed but excited, I discovered the rest of this amazing place when the whole crowd, as if moved by some magic wand, began its ritual processions. There are five *rathas*, stone temples dedicated to the memory of long-forgotten rulers, intricately carved, small, easy to see and very beautiful. They are guarded by the life-size figures of an elephant, a lion and a bull. Then there is the pyramidal Shore Temple, which is brushed by the surf and strikingly beautiful against the bronze background of an incandescent sea. But Mahabalipuram's greatest glory is an entire rock face, 80 feet (24 m) long and 20 feet (6.1 m) wide, carved into a thousand sculptures of gods, kings, courtesans, elephants and bulls and long processions of attendants. It is the largest rock carving in the world, an awesome and mystifying monument to India's ancient religion.

Nor can you afford to miss Kanchipuram, the Pallas capital inland 100 miles (161 km) to the west and one of India's greatest pilgrimage centres with no fewer than 124 shrines. It is also the home of Kanchipuram silk, the multi-coloured gossamer of breathtaking beauty. Yet there is no doubt that the greatest sight in Tamil Nadu is Madurai further south, the foremost temple city of Indian India. It is monumental, vast and, like everything Indian, intensely complicated. Here, Indian architecture reaches its greatest heights, in ten fantastic *gopurams*, truncated pyramidal towers covered from base to summit with writhing humanity and mythical beasts.

From daybreak, long crocodiles of pilgrims wind their way into the largest temple in India, the Meenakshi, with its hall of 1000 columns (actually there are 997); a marvel of engineering. Outside, there are the musical pillars which tinkle when you touch them, the sacred tank and the grand Indo-Saracenic palace of Tirumala Nayak. Tamil Nadu has other sights too. At sleepy Pondicherry, once the capital of French India, is a statue of Joan of Arc facing another one of Mahatma Gandhi, smells of French bread, French street names and other reminders of past colonialism. In a different context, on the borders of Tamil Nadu and Kerala, are the divinely fresh and beautiful Nilgiri Hills, blue, green and gold, on which are found the fading Victorian glories of Ootacamund and Kodaikanal. There is another great temple in the far south at Tameswaram, facing out to sea towards Sri Lanka and in the north of the state, the fort of Tiruchirappalli (Trichy to all), which was so well known to Clive & co.

When you round Cape Comorin and enter the state of Kerala running along the south-west coast you realise the diversity of India. Despite its lack of great temples, Kerala is one of my favourite Indian destinations. It is like nowhere else; a strip of tropical land of incredible beauty. It has long, golden beaches, of which the best is at Kovallam near Trivandrum, where handmade catamarans wait for the tide while fishermen sit under coconut palms singing Malayalam songs. Kerala is beaches, coconuts, palms and lagoons of shining tranquility. You can drift for days in a slow boat to recover from the exhaustion induced by Tamil Nadu. Kerala people fit well into the landscape too for they are handsome, smiling and remarkably sophisticated as their education system is the best in India. Kerala was once known as the Malabar Coast and is India's most cosmopolitan region for right through the ages anyone who was anyone on the high seas came to Malabar. The first visitors were Jews, the celebrated white Jews of India, who came to Kerala to escape Nebuchadnezzar and were joined by others in a second Diaspora after the fall of Jerusalem in AD 70.

Apart from Trivandrum, with its proximity to the beaches, the most interesting city by far in Kerala is Cochin, a kind of Indian San Francisco, with islands dotted around a marvellous harbour, history and remarkable crafts. For the tourist, Kerala is for drifting about in, without haste, and without making too much effort to understand its mysteries.

The third of my south Indian states is Mysore, now known by its former ancient name Karnataka, and it should on no account be missed. This handsome plateau, with waterfalls and superb views, is grand and orderly. One might call it the south's contribution to princely India. Here flourished the greatest Hindu empire of all, Vijayanagar, which, in its heyday during the fourteenth to the sixteenth centuries, ruled the whole of the Deccan with a vigour which had no equal. The Mysore region was the fountain-head of the Hindu art form, but it knew how to borrow from elsewhere. Take, for instance, Mysore's rocambolesque Maharajah's Palace (circa 1897), which is a gorgeous mixture of Mogul formality, Indian whimsicality and a touch of Maples. Only a few miles away the Maharajahs also borrowed from the Mogul tradition when they laid out the splendid gardens of Krishnahasagar where Eastern nature is disciplined into superb physical poetry. Mysore itself is beautiful – even the post offices, the schools and the railway station look fit for princes.

To Indians, the three temple cities of the thirteenth-century Hoysala Empire, Somnathpur, Belur and Halebid, mean rather more, because they represent the classical apogee of Indian architecture. I must admit that I found these complicated, star-shaped temples rather hard to grasp because their intricacies defeated me.

For me, the most poignant place of all was Hampi, the 10 square-mile (2590-ha) capital of the Vijayanagar Empire era, a kind of Indian Pompeii, half buried in the jungle and still redolent of a great past. Like Akbar's Fatehpur Sikhri, Hampi has enormous nostalgia, great beauty and, one might almost say, a secret in every stone. Even older are the three ancestors of Indian architecture and art, Badami, Pattakdal and Aihole (circa AD 600). To understand all Indian-ness one should really begin here and travel forward in time.

As you travel north in this state, you are increasingly aware of another influence. The Moguls were here and it shows. Fifteen years ago I first discovered Bijapur and, unknowing and unprepared, saw Gol Gumbaz, the mausoleum of a long-forgotten, Persian-Turkish client king of the Muslim emperors, Mohammed Adil Shah. It was a relevation, indeed a shock, for here, hardly mentioned in the guidebooks, was the world's second largest dome – only 15 feet (4.6 m) smaller in diameter than St Peter's in Rome. Although not quite as poetic as the Taj – all sorts of influences were at work – Gol Gumbaz is nevertheless a must, as is the rest of Bijapur, with its magnificent tomb of Ibrahim Rauza and the enormous Jama Masjid mosque, one of the largest anywhere in the world. Bijapur indeed is a treasure house, with over 50 mosques and a score of tombs and palaces.

All this makes an indelible impression, particularly since it is relatively little known. India south of the River Krishna is for the traveller who is not satisfied with the obvious. If you are such a one, your journey will be unforgettable.

Goa is, admittedly, a place apart. This is, or rather was, Portuguese India for 400 years and one is faced with gorgeous Portuguese churches and monasteries where Albuquerque probably worshipped and a landscape that is decidedly Indian. Goa's fortune these days lies in its beaches, which are, it must be said, among the best in the business. The famous Taj Group have built hotels there now and at the end or the beginning of any India tour as you are going back or coming from Bombay, they are well worth sampling. This is westernised India at its best.

CLIMATE

This is monsoon country, of course, but don't let it fool you; some of my fondest memories of India are of travelling in the subcontinent during what is officially monsoon season: you get wet, very wet, occasionally but you dry off, quickly. Bombay and Calcutta are almost always humid while Delhi can be cold at night. In general, the big monsoon comes around the end of May or early June and reaches Delhi in July. Kashmir, Simla and places like 'Ooty' are best in the summer months. In case you are interested, Assam holds the world record for rainfall. Just to break it down a little, here is the line-up:
- Rajasthan is dry. It is very hot in the summer months and coldish in the winter.
- Punjab and Delhi too are mixed, sometimes dry, sometimes humid but on the whole they are bearable at any time.
- Unless you are hellbent on wintersports, Kashmir and the Himalayan valleys are definitely late spring and summer places.
- The valley of the Ganges, Bengal, Assam and Orissa are, to my knowledge, always hot and sultry.
- India central—south (the Deccan) I have always found pleasant almost all the year round.
- Tamil Nadu (Madras) gets its rain late in the year, October to December. Summer is hot and dry.
- From Kerala almost to Bombay, you might describe the weather as 'tropical'.

INTERNAL TRANSPORT

By road: For such a large country this is remarkably good and these days you can reach almost any part of India with a little determination. But Indian roads are not to be trusted. Trunk roads are generally quite good but wearisome. Other roads are bumpy, irregular and winding. India is one of the few countries where self-drive is not encouraged and for good reasons: the signposting is deficient, Indian towns (even small ones) are filled with people who jaywalk and of course there are all those holy cows. The standard car is the notorious 'Ambassador', still made on the blueprint of a Morris Oxford of the 1950s, which is just bearable in the cities (as taxis etc) and totally unbearable for long-distance driving. To me, they always appear to have been upholstered with discarded apricot stones. Better ones, we are told, are on the way. We shall see.

When you rent a car in India, it is with a built-in driver and let's hope he knows the way! If you are going far afield, make sure that your driver has what is called 'an all-India Licence' which, in theory, enables him to drive anywhere. That is, if he can speak the local language and ten to one if he is in Madras he won't be able to speak Tamil and the Tamils will make a point of not speaking Hindi. Once, a mere 50 miles (80 km) out of Goa, I came to an abrupt stop because my driver could not even read the roadsigns. On the whole, Sikhs make the best drivers – slightly self conscious but safe. Broadly speaking, all Indian drivers take what appear to us to be terrible risks. Car rental is cheap in India but if you are prepared to pay a little more you could just be lucky and end up with what is called an 'American car', that is, any car not made in India. With this you would be safe and reasonably comfortable. If you are going off the beaten track, don't forget to take refreshments with you, such as fruit juice or fruit. India is not known for the excellence of its few roadside eateries.

By rail: Because of the indifferent roads – and the vast distances – India's trains are on the whole excellent. All trains in India are steam ones apart from a few commuter diesels near the big cities like Bombay and Calcutta. India, which has plenty of coal, is famous for its steam trains and the country has become a mecca for train buffs from everywhere. Some of the fast subcontinent expresses are among the last of the 'big' trains left in the world and they are worth taking just for the experience but you must check and doublecheck facilities, classes, comfort and so on since these change often and easily and always without telling the would-be passenger.

India has made a feature of its trains and some 'softie' trains can help you see much of Rajasthan for instance. As for Delhi–Agra, don't do it except by rail, there and back in one day if you must. The Indian Government Tourist Office is well informed on this score and can help you. Also able to help, for a fee, are some of the bigger Indian travel agencies, of which there are many. The best by far is the biggest which is Mercury Travel who have branches everywhere in India and can help smooth a difficult path.

By air: Like all large countries, India excels in its air services, which are among the best in the world. Apart from the trunk routes flown by Air India, the be-all and end-all of everything is Indian Airlines who even use the Airbus! They will get you everywhere (again check and recheck) and they usually start so early in the morning, for business customers, that most tourists are still having their early morning breakfast. Ah well. Rajiv Gandhi used to be an Indian Airlines' pilot before he became Prime Minister.

HOTELS

Some Indian hotels rank among the finest in the world. Some are perfectly acceptable for a short stay and some are acceptable because there is nowhere else. Great progress is being made in hotel building and the picture changes all the time so it is worth making enquiries.

SPECIALISED HOLIDAYS

As befits a country with such a heavy overlay of the British raj, India is well covered when it comes to tour operators. Pride of place here must go to Cox & Kings – the oldest travel agents to India – they have been at it for 200 years and smoothed the way for many a subaltern, junior administrator and the like. Holiday Planners were the only agent not to be fooled by some trick questions I tried while researching this book.

Alas, apart from those two, the chances are that you will get everybody's India. Every tour operator takes the view that all we wish to see is the Taj Mahal, Rajasthan, Delhi, with a dash here or there. As in so many cases the independent traveller must first of all choose his area, do a good deal of homework and finally go to it and ask the right questions. This can be tedious but is always worth while in the end.

Please see pages 221–2 for addresses.

Thailand

For people like me — fairly long in years and with more mileage behind than in front — a country like Thailand is a mixed blessing: you remember what it was like and you know that it will never be quite the same again. Somebody called Thailand, 'Old Values and New Temptations', which is just about right too. Yet, this large country cannot be ignored: it is today supposed to be the British traveller's favourite long-haul leisure destination and if he feels like that after seeing only the obvious, there is hope yet. Why should one put him off? I have a feeling myself that the worst thing that ever happened to Thailand was the Vietnam War, not only because it suffered so much but because, overnight, Bangkok became the number one relaxation centre for GIs from the war. And, overnight, national innocence became frayed at the edges. Gone was the Thailand of *The King and I* and in its place was the instant Orient, and serene Buddhist temples had to exist cheek by jowl with massage parlours.

But this slightly bitter feeling should not be overdone. Thailand is still worth seeing, still worth tasting. For one thing, the Thais are without a doubt the most beautiful people in the world, both men and women, copper coloured, lissome and facially unique. Then there is the Orient. Ah, the Orient. It blooms in Thailand probably more readily than anywhere else and simply erupts in a dazzling display of gold and precious stones that sends you reeling back in disbelief. Then there is the shopping and, believe me, your bank account will never be the same again. Finally, there is the awed realisation that in a country the size of France, religion and customs still remain largely untouched by the hand of foreign masters. May they long remain so.

What is Thailand good for? Anything you like because Thailand has got most of it, providing you can stand the pace since it is not the most restful of countries. Obviously, you go there for exotica, for all the things you have always associated with the Orient and on the whole you will not be disappointed.

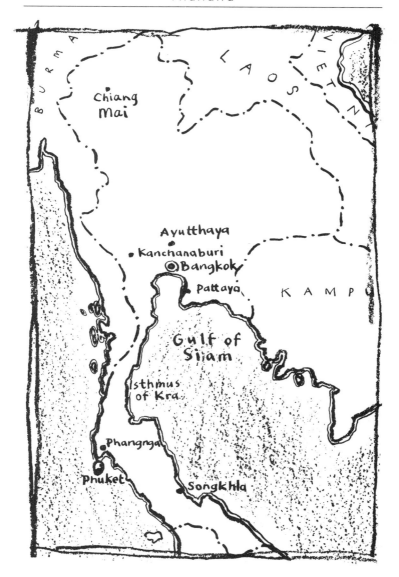

BEACHES

These are among the best in the world – bar none. The whole of the south east and the south west of Bangkok is one long beach and if you are lucky, and firm with your mentor, you can be yourself and live the life of the lotus-eater. On the soft sands of the Gulf of Siam everything comes to you if you crook your little finger: good company, fresh fruit, fresh fish and entertainment. The eyebrow-raising phenomenon in these parts is, of course, Pattaya. Twenty years ago it literally did not exist. Now its 4 miles (6 km) of sand are lined with almost 100 hotels of all kinds, all shapes (alas) and all budgets, Breton crepes at 2 a.m., roaring Yamahas at any time, instant folklore, discos and lots, but lots, of nightlife. I hope this is not what you want but one cannot ignore it.

Definitely one up from Pattaya is Phuket, which is way down along Thailand's serpentine peninsula. I personally like Phuket very much indeed because it has oddities, nice people, so far little commercialism and an air of the South Seas that is worth millions of *bahts*. Phuket and its environs are not just one beach but dozens of them, with names like Karon, Patong, and Nai Yang, all separate, all good for one particular thing which you soon learn. Those beaches facing east towards the Gulf of Siam are inevitably the more accessible and the most crowded. Those facing the other way towards the great Bay of Bengal are, in my book, next door to heaven, with one outcrop of rock dividing one beach from the next and making for privacy. There are, of course, modern hotels but there are also cheap and cheerful little lean-tos of palm and bamboo where you can forget the world. For the time being, Phuket is the word.

Yet, the best-kept secret in this part of the world, though probably not for long, is Songkhla where age-old Chinese, Arabic and Cambodian traditions flourish along a truly pristine stretch of sand, with fish restaurants and sunshades, an odd temple here and a fleet of fishing boats there. Songkhla is heaven and although some tour operators go there, it is really too isolated for the massed piranhas of the travel trade.

COUNTRYSIDE

People often ask me where the real Thailand can be found. Some question. Where is the real France? West of Bangkok I quite like the country around Kanchanaburi and the infamous Bridge on the River Kwai. A detour would bring you to Damnern Daduak where the floating market is ten times more interesting than Bangkok's. I like the north too, despite the tourist hordes taking the morning flight to Chiang Mai (see page 158). This is cool hill country, part of the infamous 'Golden Triangle' and the homeland of many of the country's non-Thai tribesmen like the Yeo, Meo, Lisu and Karens. Some don't like visitors much and who can blame them?

Central Thailand, the great ricebowl, is probably fairly typical of this extraordinary country and, fortunately, few tourists ever go there. It's a country of flat paddies where the vivid green is almost too much for your camera. There is a lot of water in the paddies too, as I know to my cost having fallen in so often while my guides tripped the light fantastic along the little causeways of mud. Here and there, some rustic temple, a statue or two and, if you are lucky, the sight of an entire village sitting down for the midday meal.

But in my memory book, it is the south of Thailand that is most often represented. After three visits, and more to come I hope, I can't have enough of this long sinewy, unexpected strip of territory which goes all the way down to the Malaysian border. My own first sight of the unpronounceable Phangnga Bay years ago was enough to convince me that this was the Promised Land. You go off on a not too safe-looking Thai fishing boat into the thinly-misted, mysterious, calm water of this amazing bay to find, on all sides, the extraordinary shapes of limestone outcrops rising sheerly out of the water. Fish jump out too and you can almost catch them with your hand. There are no tourists, because there are no hotels, only 'Chinesey' establishments that would like to be the new local Hilton but can't quite make it. It does not really matter where you sleep, and neither does it where you eat because your days are filled with wonder and you know that tomorrow will bring more discoveries.

There are about 80 islands on the east and west coasts of the Isthmus of Kra and you can take your choice for they are as yet unherded, untouristicated and unpackaged. There is the fairly large Koh Samui Island with the incomparable Bang Sak beach. On the west side there is even better, the Koh Phi Phi Island – just go and see for yourself. You might not want to come back.

This being Thailand, everything is unorganised, which is nice but within two hours of arriving somewhere, you have a car and driver for the next day or a fishing boat all to yourself. Naturally, apart from the odd night, you must stay somewhere and in this department it must be Phukhet, Songkhla or the bigger and uglier but more central city of Haadyai.

CITIES AND SIGHTS

In this chapter the two categories are inevitably mixed up since most of the great and famous sights are in two cities, Bangkok and Chiang Mai. Some people hate Bangkok. This huge city of five million people ranges in temperature from hot to hottest and is always so humid that the lens of your camera will go blurry within a few minutes. Bangkok is flat, immense, busy and almost as lethal as Tokyo when it comes to traffic. So you must be clear and disciplined when it comes to sightseeing. Just that, and no more. After all, there are over 350 'wat' or temples in the capital and one doubts whether you will have time for more than a few.

One you should not miss for anything is Wat Phra Keo, which is not especially distinguished apart from what it contains: the one and only Emerald Buddha. It's only 60 inches (153 cm) high but it is all emerald and it defies the most expert computations as to its value. It is part of the so-called Grand Palace, which is where the Kings of Siam used to live, a whole complex of pavilions and rotundas, VIP audience chambers, winged angels, fearsome Chinese-inspired giants and superb colonnades, all covered with gold leaf. Naturally, the Grand Palace is a photographer's paradise but, beware: it's hard on the feet too and several visits are indicated, especially at different times of day.

Not far away is Wat Po, the home of the world-famous Reclining Buddha, 160 feet (49 m) long and supposed to be the biggest statue in the world. But it pales for me when compared, at the right time, with Wat Arun, the Temple of Dawn on the other side of the Chao Prya River. Covered with mosaics, encrusted with gaudy orientalia of all types and yet infinitely mysterious, it has a lot of appeal. Also quite eyebrow-raising is the Golden Buddha housed in the Wat Trmitr. They discovered it was gold, all five and a half tons of it, only when they dropped it accidentally while trying to move it some years ago.

If you take my tip, you will miss Bangkok's celebrated floating market. Yes miss it altogether as one of the world's most overrated tourist traps. I was thoroughly put off it a few years ago when I discovered that it was so crowded with tourists, and Thais on the make, that it had virtually stopped moving, with Thai policemen and their very shrill whistles vainly trying to get the waterborne traffic moving. I suggest instead that you book a place aboard the Oriental Hotel's famous *Oriental Queen* boat and spend the day upriver in Ayutthaya. This largely ruined city is Thailand's past.

Another of Bangkok's attractions, if you are that way inclined, is the city's vice, which is rampant, all-pervasive and totally uninhibited. It forms a city within a city and anything goes from girls in massage parlours who are numbered for easy picking to any kind of drug you may wish. Compare this with staying a night or two in one of the suites of the Oriental's famous and original Author's Wing, all cane and ferns where Somerset Maugham and Joseph Conrad loved to stay.

Chiang Mai is worth visiting if only because this northern

hill city is reasonably accessible and is the home of some of the best crafts in Thailand. Anything made of teak, lacquer, gold and silver flourishes here and, yes, they still make those traditional gorgeous paper and silk umbrellas – not the Japanese plastic kind. Also worth a trip is the famous 'wat' of Doi Sutep, 1000 feet (305 m) high on its incredible hill. There are many other wat(s) in and around Chiang Mai and some are worth seeing. But, beware, tourism is creeping up there too.

CLIMATE

Thailand's weather, which should put off many travellers, happily does not. It's a hot country and it can be very humid too. March, April, May and June are either very hot (up to 100°F/38°C) or very wet because of the monsoon. Thais themselves think things are getting cold when the temperature goes below 75°F (24°C). By far the coolest and most pleasant areas are the northern hills and the thin peninsula to the south where sea breezes from both directions help a lot.

INTERNAL TRANSPORT

Thailand is basically a very well-organised country for the traveller who wishes to go to the obvious places and a hellish one the rest of the time. The roads are quite good if narrow but don't drive yourself because that borders on lunacy. The State Railway of Thailand is good by oriental standards, reasonable in price and the air conditioning works well. You can travel comfortably up to Chiang Mai, which takes 14 hours, and you can take the train all through Thailand and Malaysia down to Singapore, which takes 50 hours. Thai International, as everybody knows, is one of the best airlines in the world for service and inside the country the domestic equivalent, Thai Airways, is an extremely convenient airline, which can take you to most main cities.

HOTELS

Thailand has some of the finest luxury hotels in the world and some of the most basic.

SPECIALISED HOLIDAYS

There are very few – mostly because almost every long-haul tour operator includes Thailand in his brochure and thinks he is an expert because he has offered you Pattaya! Among those who at least know the country and will help devise something special for you are the ubiquitous Far East Travel Centre and Abercrombie & Kent.

Please see page 222 for addresses.

Indonesia

PROFILE

Salamat Datang – Welcome to Indonesia. I make no apology
for including this seemingly odd country in *A Guide for the
Independent Traveller*. On the contrary, I believe that
sooner or later the independent traveller is going to get
there. Can you think of an island or country which, if
stretched across the map of Europe, would reach from Ireland to the Caspian Sea? Can you imagine 13,777 islands,
not counting the rocks, and, yet, 90 per cent of the tourists
going to one island only – Bali?

Indonesia is the sixth largest country in the world and has
a population of 160 million. It's the world's largest producer
of natural gas. It has live and extinct volcanoes, 'green paddies', pale blue seas, marvellous coral reefs and quite a few
places that are not even on the map yet. It has lizards that
look like dragons, almost as many temples as India and acres
of batik, one of the world's last remaining folk art-forms. Its
carvers and sculptors are among the last good ones left
anywhere and so are its dancers. It has produced at least one
musical instrument, the 'gamelan', which is only just beginning to become known. Its mythology is filled with good-

natured beasts rescuing damsels in distress. Its people are good-looking, intensely expressive and eager to please. As a nation, Indonesia has one foot in the jet age and the other in a tradition going back 3000 years. Will Indonesia make it into the big world of international tourism? Having visited a mere five of the islands, Sumatra, Java, Bali, Lombok and Sulawesi, my own answer is an enthusiastic yes, simply because one cannot keep a secret for very long these days and, because tourism goes where the big jets go, as soon as the airport runways are finished.

To ask would it be a good thing if international tourism does come to Indonesia is an unfair and largely unanswer-able question. The only thing I can say is that if you, the independent traveller, have real expertise and real care for the aim in life which this book suggests you have, go now. Tomorrow might be too late. Already, the beer-drinking Australians who discovered Bali 25 years ago are in their second generation and widows with blue-rinsed hair spend-ing the insurance money are nibbling at Java's Borobudur or sending 'wish-you-were-here' postcards from that dreadful, but dreadful, Jakarta. The big cruise ships, like tamed piranhas, are already nosing around places like Nias Island and will without doubt one day make landfall wherever they can anchor. A few brave souls go to Sulawesi and, as far as the Bali lookalikes are concerned, the next one is bound to be Lombok, just across the Straits and complete with scenery that leaves you open-mouthed with astonishment. Of course, it is all a long way off. Or is it? An hour or two by jet will get you almost anywhere in Indonesia from Singapore, that Euston station of south-east Asia.

What is Indonesia good for? It is one of the real rewards of travel today, very little known and, apart from Bali, hardly tourist-polluted. So many islands, so many people, so much to see. A real traveller's country.

BEACHES

This is a big joke, of course. With almost 14,000 islands, the sea meets the sandy or rocky shore in so many places that it is hard to know where to start. I have personally seen some pretty good beaches in the islands I have visited, and that includes Sanur and Kuta on Bali – if you can ignore the headache-making Yamahas. From here, it is only a hop, skip, and a jump to that other Kuta village on Lombok where the sandy beach is a mere 62 miles (100 km) long. There are some good beaches too on Sulawesi, which unfortunately I hardly saw, and on Timor which, right now, is a little difficult politically since the largely Christian inhabitants are stoutly resisting the Indonesian takeover.

COUNTRYSIDE/ISLANDS

I have been looking up my own notebooks and the place that seems to recur most often is Sumatra. It is only a small island, roughly the size of California! And the memories come flooding back.

Here I am at 6 a.m. sitting on the verandah of my hotel room on Samosir Island in the middle of Lake Toba in northern Sumatra, and indulging in one of my favourite pastimes – watching a tropical dawn. Slowly, almost reluctantly at first, the night's many veils are clearing from the mountain tops that surround this amazing lake, which is 3000 feet (915 m) above sea-level. Then come wispy cirrus clouds, pink at first, then champagne-coloured and finally flaming orange as the sun makes its appearance and the lake's surface becomes a shining mosaic of light. And all the time I am thinking of the people back home. Especially those who keep telling me that now the joys of pure travel are over there are no places to go any more, no more personal discoveries to make. Perhaps they aren't looking in the right direction.

Samosir is a perfect example, a high green island of 400 square miles (1036 sq km) rising sheer out of one of the world's biggest and least-known lakes. Toba is 70 miles (113 km) long, filling the whole of a long-extinct volcanic crater. Until ten years ago, no tourist ever came here, only a few anthropologists and, in times gone by, the occasional colonial Dutchman. Now there are two small hotels on Samosir and I shared one with a handful of sentimental Dutch tourists and a few chirruping Chinese families from Singapore.

Not only is Samosir very beautiful and totally unexpected, it is unique. The island is the heartland of the several million-strong Batak tribe whose ancestors crossed over from Burma and Thailand 1500 years ago. On their easily-defended island home, the Bataks remained undiluted for centuries – short, wiry, cheerful people who often gave Malays, Dutch and, later, Indonesians, a good deal of trouble. Today, the Bataks remain Bataks, given to sentimental songs, much age-old ceremony and a mixture of their grandfather's animism and the missionary's Christianity.

The Bataks still live in their traditional houses, which are vast, gabled structures rising to fanciful pointed shapes and resting on enormous carved tree trunks. No Batak house has a single nail in it – only wooden pegs and rope – and some of them are 2000 years old. Every surface is decorated with some of the finest carving I have seen. Bataks live in family clans and are proud, independent and not at all bothered by the trickle of tourists now exploring their island. Go through a village anywhere on Samosir shouting the customary *Horas* – 'the Lord protect you' – and you will be greeted everywhere with smiles.

Here there are also great haughty mountains close to the equator, fantastic waterfalls and villages which differ marvellously from one another. Plus 60 pineapples for £1 or 12 bananas for ten pence or enough *rijstaffel* (a flavoured-down version of Indonesian food) to keep you going for three days at £2 a head. And, naturally, a superb climate.

What made me come to Sumatra? That is a long story which started when I became tired of hearing travel agents rave about a Bali which was already turning into a tropical Torremolinos when I first travelled there 20 years ago. 'What about your other islands?' I asked my Indonesian friends.

I was told about Sumatra. Tigers and leopards, water lilies the size of helicopter pads, and head-hunters of course. My imagination reeled. But was Sumatra really that big? Having now just covered about a quarter of it, I can assure readers that it is. It is 1000 miles (1610 km) long and 250 miles (403 km) wide and is a kind of south-east Asian Africa with 180-foot (55 m)-high trees, plus lots of oil, gold and bauxite. In short, it is a kind of treasure chest whose riches seem boundless.

Then there are the people and their history. Apart from Bali, where Hinduism reigns, most Indonesians are Muslims. Here in Sumatra, however, there are both Muslims and Christians. The island was the first landfall of conquering Indian kings, Arab sailors, Portuguese navigators and Dutch and British planters. It lies along the Straits of Malacca, blocking the way east and so near to the continent of Asia that you can almost smell it. You fly from Singapore to Medan and in a single hour you move from the frenetic, mercantile Orient into a curious *dolce far niente* land, whose people seem to have plenty of time to sit under the mango trees waiting for the fruit to fall.

Sumatrans see so few strangers that they are not yet used to dealing with them, and if the waiter brings you a lemonade when you have asked for tea with lemon, he does so with such a disarming smile that you forgive him. Hotels are simple, fairly basic but clean, rather tastelessly furnished and with chancey plumbing. I think people must eat bath-plugs in Sumatra, for I never saw one.

When you get outside the big cities, what passes for European food is like a lottery – you may win once but mostly you'll lose, with steaks fit only for cannibals with filed teeth, and chickens that seem to have passed away in writhing agony. Indonesian food, rice-based with Chinese, Indian and Malay touches, is fine occasionally and is the hottest thing east of Madras. Fish is fresh and good and there are an amazing 38 varieties of fruit. You won't find Beaujolais Nouveau in Sumatra but Indonesian beer is drinkable and Scotch and gin are available. You can't have everything. What there is is a divinely beautiful island with a kind of *plus ça change, plus ce n'est pas la même chose* feeling.

What does one do in Medan? The answer is to get out of this large, very hot and dusty city of more than a million people. It helps to have a friend or a good travel agent. I had both in the person of Ben Sukma, a wise and charming Indonesian who runs the largest travel agency in these parts. Ben took one look at me, decided that I would probably be a difficult customer and took me around himself in his car.

We departed for the hills and it was like moving from a sauna to an Alpine meadow – fresh and green, with cultivated terraces leading to the skyline of the mountains and the small town of Brastagi which, in Dutch colonial days was what Poona and Ootacamund were for the British raj.

This is the beginning of the Batak country and I received my first introduction to it in the small village of Lingga, where every house is a period piece and where every curved roof is a poem of elegance that has been lovingly painted and carved. An hour later Ben stopped the car on a high bluff. 'Turn around and look,' he said. Dutifully I did so and there was the vast, miraculous expanse of Lake Toba, like a sheet of silver as far as the eye could see with, in the middle, the great humpback shape of Samosir Island. We reached the small town of Parapat, which, with four small hotels, is the tourist centre in these parts, climbed on board what Ben Sukma called his navy and half an hour later we were having a drink at the Toba Beach Hotel on Samosir. This is Ben's pride and joy – a small, modern, clean and wonderfully relaxing place with a little beach on the lake.

Samosir is a remarkable island. Big as it is, there are virtually no roads – the Bataks don't like roads. You can hike right across in about 12 hours if you are fit. Otherwise, the best way of seeing it is by boat, calling at this village and that, visiting the stone tombs of long dead Batak kings and joking with the lively Batak children.

Almost every village spends the off-season carving and their artefacts are quite superb. Ebony, ironwood and splendid rosewood are so common here that they use them for packing cases, preferring to use plastic for restaurant chairs. Batak astrological calendars, called *porhalan*, are special. They tell people when rice-planting time is coming, when to get married and when to pray for rain. They bear a strong resemblance to south India's Tamil votive pieces – yet another proof of India's tremendous influence in the past. I am told that down in the south of the province at Gunung-tua, are 16 perfectly preserved Hindu temples so far almost unknown to the outside world.

Bataks weave their own cloth, which is quite unlike the traditional Indonesian batik. It is roughly homespun in dark colours with stripes and tassels and Batak beaux carry long swatches of it casually slung over one shoulder. Very fetching. Being naturally curious, I wanted to see more of Sumatra. 'Why can't we drive down to Padang?' I asked Ben Sukma. He laughed, 'You don't know our Sumatra roads,' he told me. 'It'll take you 18 hours.' I guessed prudence was the better part of valour so we drove back to Medan through endless rubber plantations and I caught a plane to Padang, flying over the virgin beaches of the Indian Ocean side. At the airport, the local tourist chief told me that I was the first British travel writer ever to get to Padang. Then, unwittingly, he possibly made me the last by taking me to a local lunch, in a rather superior *warung*, or roadside inn.

After the first mouthful, I leapt to my feet and, with my mouth open and voiceless, I began hopping from one foot to the other, to the great amusement of the local customers. By evening I had developed a bout of the Padang pangs – having accidentally swallowed a morsel of *deng deng*, which are thin strips of beef soaked in red chilli sauce. My advice to you is don't.

If north Sumatra is definitely other-worldish, west Sumatra could well be on the other side of the moon as far as tourists are concerned, as there are none to be found there. Padang itself is the island's hot spot and when it is not it's hotter which means that the locals move at a leisurely pace towards the shade of the nearest tree. The few foreigners who come here can't wait to get to Bukittinggi, which was once a Dutch hill station. And delicious it is too. A small town cradled in the mountains, it boasts a municipal clock tower called Big Ben, a few old Dutch houses, a lively street market heaped with instant death (red peppers), cocktail crisps made of cassava, and trotting horses with red pom-poms over their eyes pulling rickshaws up the sloping streets.

Wildlife is never far away. The next-door town of Padang-panjang lost five of its citizens shortly before I got there. Hungry tigers came slinking out of the misty night without warning and it is definitely not the place for a midnight stroll. This is the rural heart of the island, with towering mountains separating the sky from glistening paddy fields complete with plodding buffaloes. Then there are the lakes, four of them this time. I went to see the lovely Lake Maninjau, and came away with the realisation that Sumatra's lakes are its crowning glory.

With the exception of the shining, new, government-run Muara Hotel Padang where everything works and is in good taste, west Sumatra's hostelries are even less sophisticated than those in the north. Air-conditioning is a rarity, mosquitoes are not. All the courses of your dinner arrive at once and they are not what you ordered. If you ask for fruit, it comes in huge wobbly piles of papayas, bananas, mangoes or the evil-smelling but sweet-tasting durians which apparently have an aphrodisiac effect on women. A local saying has it that, 'When the durians are down, the sarongs are up' — though I cannot speak from experience. The room boy occasionally polishes your brown shoes with black polish and the refrigerator seems permanently out of action.

After a while you become used to it and, once you have passed the thin line that divides perpetual apoplexy from patient sanity, you begin to enjoy this vast luxuriant island, so different, so lush and so utterly devoid of the trappings of the most elementary tourism. People are charming and glad to see you, not because of what they can make out of you but because you are a stranger, an object of respectful curiosity.

The west is women's lib country, the homeland of the clever and articulate Maningkabau people who form a complete matriarchal and matrilineal society. Here women rule everything, decide on matters of money and politics and, though their men are not subservient, they are the recipients of a touching and amusing veneration. On feast-days one of the funniest things is to see the lady of the house lovingly dressing up her husband like a human doll. He wears the jewellery, she wears the pants. I found the west coast beaches absolutely sensational and among the finest in the world. I spent a morning on those just south of Padang, watching the fishing catamarans sailing to a string of little coral islets on the horizon, striped fish nosing close to the sand and gentle waves of pure turquoise eddying near the coconut palms. I did not see a single European.

The Sumatra tourist chiefs were most curious about my reactions. What did I think? Did I believe they stood a chance in the tourist stakes? For one, I was torn between my desire to see tourism, good tourism, flourish and the wish to see Sumatra remain as it is — a place of its own, quiet, beautiful, original and intensely desirable. As far as I am concerned, the dilemma will never be resolved.

CLIMATE

This is virtually impossible to define accurately. Since there are so many islands, any lowland is likely to be hot and humid while upland areas can be surprisingly temperate. In general, you should remember that much of Indonesia lies just north and south of the equator and should therefore be treated with respect. Generally speaking, the months from May to September plus October and November are the best. Rainfall during the rest of the year can be heavy if intermittent.

INTERNAL TRANSPORT

Considering the size and extent of Indonesia, local transport is not bad; just a little wayward when it comes to reservations. Garuda Indonesian Airlines is the national carrier with good connections in and out of the country. A local airline, Merpati, whose flights can be booked via Garuda, covers a great deal of Indonesia and can take you to some fairly untouristicated places.

Sea travel is also worth considering but do consult a local travel agent. The excellence of these, most of whom are based in the larger cities, almost offsets the universal lack of knowledge about Indonesia in the outside world.

HOTELS

Indonesian hotels are about as varied as the country itself and range from the top international ones in places like Jakarta, Yogyakarta, Bandung and Medan to extremely simple and informal places elsewhere. In far flung places the rule is always to make for the best, it won't cost you much, and you might be safer (prowling tigers and all that).

SPECIALISED HOLIDAYS

There are none! And it must be said here that Indonesia does not make it easy for the intending tourist. The Indonesian Tourism Promotion Board does not even have a London office though I did find that its Singapore branch office, which I consulted, was not only efficient but also helpful. In London, the source of all Indonesian tourism information remains the country's national airline Garuda.

Of the tour operators the best by far is Bales Tours Ltd who have been running packages to Indonesia for some years. Also active are Albany Travel and Fairways & Swinford. For the independent traveller, Indonesia remains very much a do-it-yourself country; so much the better. However, things are much easier to organise from cities nearer at hand, such as Singapore and, of course, Jakarta. For my own money, the best guidebook I have found in recent times is the new *Insight* guide to Indonesia.

Please see page 222 for addresses.

Hong Kong

PROFILE

It is an amazing fact that most people nowadays at least know just about where Hong Kong is and can put a finger on the right part of the map. It is also amazing that, God bless them, some actually go there. But the fact really is that there are still so many misconceptions about this Manhattan of the South China Seas. Tour operators are the biggest culprits. They send their charges there as a stopover on part of a 'See the Orient' package, for two days, or two and a half, if you are lucky. I have been going to Hong Kong on and off for years and it takes me at least that much time to cross the road and to find out what's new since I last went there.

Yes, Hong Kong is amazing, fantastic and unique. I was converted long ago but to this day I cannot think of another place anywhere in the world that can so easily act as a kind of battery recharge, a jolt to make you feel that you have been missing something all this time. Of course, you do not go to Hong Kong for a rest and it is difficult to sleep there because you might be missing something. The British sense of discipline and order and the Chinese gifts of ingenuity and hard work have produced a kind of phoenix city-state, hanging on to the underbelly of Mother China and revving up its engine to face each day's Monte Carlo Rally.

But, as I said, misconceptions die hard. Memories of the ten-dollar shirt and the instant suit, which go back to the 1940s and 1950s, when people were crying out for consumer goods, any consumer goods, still float around like a bad school report and yet all the time Hong Kong has been hitching itself up by its own bootstraps, doing better and better, living faster and more ritzily, showing the world that capitalism, out-and-out capitalism, can work if you will let it. Hong Kong today is everything that you do not find elsewhere – speed, ingenuity, business acumen, arts, antiques, design, banking, insurance, know-how, inventiveness, energy and a kind of super-charged atmosphere which sends you groping for another whiff. Two and a half days? A nice quick stopover? Those tour operators must be joking. They are joking because for the independent traveller Hong Kong must be a destination in itself – a place where you go for a certain type of holiday and come back reeling with excitement.

I am told that in the reports of the Hong Kong Tourist Association, which is one of the best tourist boards in the world, I am known personally as the nice old gent who knows every fire hydrant in the Western District. He likes to take five and sit on them. And how. Once I have walked down the canyons of this fantastic metropolis, I just have to breathe hard and rest a while. And resting, as I have said, is the hardest thing to do in this city of perpetual motion. People either sleep or work. Take your pick. You may also shop, or have your fortune told in 15 different ways, or take in the finest gastronomy this side of paradise. Yet, Hong Kong has its quieter moments, its quieter places and this chapter contains a few hints on what you could do if you tried. Hong Kong people are slowly discovering that they too have their own countryside, their own rustic retreats, their own spots where they can be quiet if they ever feel like it. Because, across the water from Hong Kong Island and past mesmeric Kowloon, are the New Territories where people farm, ducks glide across the ponds, the paddies shine with greenness, the islands stretch for almost as far as the eye can see and people go fishing. Travel agents always take visitors to Kam Tin, the famous walled village, but little do they know that on the north side of Tolo Harbour, for instance, there are 200 Kam Tins, most of them hardly ever visited and islands so remote that they could easily belong to another age.

Will it all last? After all, there is 1997 and all that and Hong Kong, let it be said, has China writ large. Maybe I should rephrase the question. How do you know that you are going to wake up tomorrow morning? I hope you do. Hong Kong is the same. It lives in the hope that there will be a tomorrow and that people will get its message, because if Hong Kong wasn't there, somebody would have to invent it.

What is Hong Kong good for? The acceptable face of capitalism? Possibly. But Hong Kong is also a place on its own, part of China with a strong Western veneer. A perfect place for shopping and for sightseeing, Hong Kong deserves more and longer-staying travellers.

BEACHES

On Hong Kong Island, you could have the perfectly lovely Shek O, or Repulse Bay or even Stanley. Lantau, which admittedly, is a bigger island than Hong Kong itself, has 10 beaches worth looking at and the shores of the 235 islands in the colony are dotted with nice sands, especially in the lesser-known New Territories. Altogether, the Hong Kong Tourist Association, which never hides its light under a bushel, lists 36 'official' beaches. But, you do not go to Hong Kong exclusively for a beach holiday. The climate, which is often humid and muggy, is not right for it and, besides, there are so many other things to do.

COUNTRYSIDE AND GREAT SIGHTS

Do I mean the fingers of concrete and glass that rise on both sides of the famous harbour? Or do I mean the almost frightening compactness of the great city itself? Or do I mean all the rest, of which there is quite a lot? I have been looking at my old notebooks to try and give you, the readers of this book, some of the feeling I have about Hong Kong. So here goes.

The Good Morning Company, Cissy Tailors, Hangover House, Tin Tin Motor Company, Real No Squek Shoes, Ping Pang Piano Factory, Front Gate Pants, Ladies' Tailor Shop, Ladies Have Fits Upstairs. Is this the cast for a new-style pantomime? No, just a few excerpts from the Hong Kong telephone directory. This incredible, astonishing, workaholic metropolis of the Orient has it all today and may have more tomorrow. For instance, it has 5500 shops, without counting the street stalls, and more interlinked, air-conditioned shopping malls than anywhere else in the world plus 350 banks, 92,000 cars on 150 miles (241 km) of urban roadway and 10,000 ships a year entering or leaving Fragrant Harbour (that's what the name Hong Kong means). Everybody's here. Valentino? You'll find him on the second floor of the lovely Landmark building with Gucci's just along the way. Christian Dior? You can see the shop from here. Diamonds? Hong Kong is the world's third-largest trading centre. Horses? Hong Kong Chinese put £800 million a year on the nose of those running at Happy Valley or Shatin. Do ships remind you of the Golden Greeks? Sir Y. K. Pao could buy them up on a Sunday afternoon; all together or one at a time.

Amazing? Perhaps, but true too. Hong Kong is the only city I know where the hotel doorman takes five minutes to hop across the road to see how his shares are doing on the computer generously donated by the Stock Exchange. The only city too, where, one suspects, the local tourist board pays the wages of the last three, very elderly rickshaw drivers to go and stand guard on the Star Ferry pier so that tourists can photograph them. Not being the national capital of anywhere in particular, Hong Kong is everybody's city; a place where the sea of human faces ebbs and flows around you along the concrete canyons and no one ever asks you what you are doing. A place where there are relatively few beggars and no unemployed. A place where anonymity is a virtue which means that you can make money or spend it or stand on your head. The goodies of the world here are duty-free, except for tobacco and alcohol, which last year did not prevent 5 million Hong Kong 'belongers' (HK Chinese) from drinking 8.6 million bottles of brandy because they believe it is an aphrodisiac. Less numerous than Londoners, they are the world's fourth-largest brandy consumers. It's the only place where your taxi may be following a lorry carrying a quarter of a million doll's eyes on their way to meeting the dolls. Blue jeans? Hong Kong exports 180 million pairs a year and that's the official figure. As for the tube stations, which are called MTR for Mass Transit Railway, each one is decorated with its own flowerbed over the entrance. Try that in Stockwell.

I do make a lot of fuss about Hong Kong; mostly because I find that the majority of people who have never been there don't believe me. Just go and see for yourself and you too will be converted. What grieves me most is that people who have not skimmed over the roof-tops and landed at Kaitak think that Hong Kong, being what it is, is bound to be ugly. All that concrete and so on. Let me say right away that apart from Rio de Janeiro, Hong Kong is the only place in the world where concrete has actually added to nature. Look at it on any day under blue sky, with an approaching typhoon or beneath the rolling cumulus clouds which are the rule – and Hong Kong makes you catch your breath. The skyscrapers literally scrape the sky and, depending on the time of day, it could all be a Bach fugue from the Götterdämmerung. The sea is glassy and the whole atmosphere is so charged with nervous energy that it makes you feel you haven't lived – yet.

Then there is the rest, the Hong Kong which so few people see. Of the colony's 400 square miles, a mere 13 per cent is built up. There are 235 islands and, of course, the New Territories. If you like fishy things, go to one of my favourite places, Lau Fau Shan, where oysters are the size of sideplates and fearsome creatures of the deep share stalls with some of the finest prawns in the world.

Not to see the islands would be a crime. Go to Cheung Chau, for instance, where people work at polishing jade, making enough noodles to feed most of Hong Kong and building superb junks without any blueprints at all. Lantau Island, the largest in the colony, is worth while too. It has a Trappist and a Buddhist monastery plus a lovely 2-mile (3.2-km) long beach. I personally like Lamma very much; it's a very quiet farming island whose people bring their produce to the city's market every morning. But, endlessly, the beehive city beckons: and it has many faces.

Old Hong Kong is in the Western District. What the locals call Central is the most swish and quality conscious. Going east, past the now rather unappealing Wanchai (Susie Wong's place), you come to the vibrant Causeway Bay where anything goes in any currency, plastic or otherwise. Across the harbour is the almost frightening Kowloon, fast-growing, tumultuous and raucous, where shop signs reach halfway across the road and where you can buy literally anything from a gem-studded snuff box to a Sony Walkman. At Tsim Sha Tsui, where the ferries arrive from Hong Kong Island, there are so many shopping precincts, all interlocked, that you sometimes emerge from an escalator or a moving ramp to find you have lost all sense of direction.

Shopping, of course, is the keyword. Last year, two million tourists left £600 million in the Hong Kong shops and though there are some fast boys there is less and less imitation and you are rarely taken for a ride. The Hong Kong Tourist Association is the world's expert on how to protect the tourist from unscrupulous traders. If you follow their rules, you can be 95 per cent certain that what you are

buying is the genuine article. Hong Kong is so fast in marketing that although it is no use trying to replace some gimmick
you bought two years ago as it is not being made any more,
there will be a new one available.

The people who still speak of fakes, sweated labour and
infernal factories are, I am glad to say, as out of date as last
year's diary. Hong Kong does not imitate, or not much anyway, for the simple reason that most of the great trading
names of the world, from Cartier to Davidoff, are here on the
spot and many of their products are made here. One man
who imports lovely Mikimoto pearls from Japan told me:
'We are here in Hong Kong because here you can feel the
pulse of things, the way the market is going, and you have to
be fast to catch the bus.' His pearls, by the way, are cheaper
than they are in Tokyo!

There are so many ways of shopping in Hong Kong that
each day brings new wonder. For myself I find that in the
shopping precincts I can only last for an hour or so and then I
must sit down for refreshments and think again. Those who
are younger and more hell-bent on an out and out bargain
make for the city's many factory outlets. Those catch-as-
catch-can markets are listed in the pages of the daily *South
China Morning Post* along with indications of what is the
best buy that day, and that can range from jewellery to rattan
furniture. Mostly, it is fashion and leisure wear, made up of
seconds or surplus requirements of an export order. Most
garments quite genuinely bear the name of a famous American or European fashion house whose goods are made in
Hong Kong. One of the biggest factory outlets is at the Kaiser
Estate in Kowloon. Another one, more picturesque, is in the
one-time fishing village of Stanley on the far side of Hong
Kong Island. This one is like a fair that never closes.

A few things don't change, such as the antique shops of
Hollywood Road, or the famous jade market in Kowloon's
Canton Road. In the Western District, markets abound and
the city's *amahs*, most of whom have Chinese bosses now,
still haggle over the day's supplies. They are among the
world's most canny shoppers. Some forms of trading don't
change either. Once, in the Western District, I walked into
one of those marvellous Chinese herbalists. A father and son
ran the place, with 4000 medicines in store and, happily,
one for my cold. The old man worked out a 'special' price on
his abacus. I asked him why he still used it when he could
have the most up-to-date calculator. He told me that he had
been brought up with the abacus, liked it and thought it
could beat the calculator anytime. He called to his son to

bring a calculator over and told me to choose any mathematical problem. I picked on the square root of a seven-figure number. The old man's fingers flew over the beads and his son worked the calculator with hardly a look. The abacus won.

Another Hong Kong perennial which no one would dare abolish despite the MTR, tunnels and flyovers, is the Star Ferry whose tubby, double-ended vessels have plied across the harbour from Hong Kong to Kowloon since 1898. They are unlikely to change because everybody loves them. About 110,000 people make the crossing each day comprising seven and a half minutes of Cinemascope sailing, past the liners, the tugs and the junks. The trip costs 6p for first class and 4p for second, making it the world's cheapest sea crossing.

But some things do change and in Hong Kong they do so faster than anywhere else. On my most recent visit in 1986, I looked out of my Mandarin Hotel window and realised that the skyline of the city was changing. Just behind the hotel was a new building reaching more than 500 feet (153 m) into the sky. Number One Queens Road Central, the new headquarters for the famous Hong Kong Bank, designed by a British architect, is one of the most unusual buildings in the world and has already become a place of pilgrimage for all those concerned with building. This one is different because of the brand new concept. Most large tower blocks are built around a heavy concrete core which demands thick columns thus creating a waste of space. Here the 52 floors are suspended from eight masts or towers – rather like a suspension bridge. The result is more uninterrupted space and a unique outline. There are 62 escalators and 23 lifts, 57,000 tons of steel, 35,000 cubic metres of concrete, 32,000 square metres (344,448 sq ft) of glass, 2000 miles (3220 km) of electric cable and room enough for 3500 office workers – plus the bank's money. Memorable too is the fact that the first girder was laid in January 1983 and the building was occupied last year.

Hong Kong is the place where superlatives are never quite super enough. Take hotels for instance. Once upon a time people went to Switzerland to study hotel keeping, and some still do, since the Lausanne School is the best. But to see it in perpetual motion they go to Hong Kong, where there are 18,000 hotel rooms in operation, several new hotels opening every year with almost every hotel company taking part for its own stake.

Hotels go from the sublime to the ridiculous with rooms

from £100 a night down to £15, with suites for a little more. And yet, after all that, one is left wondering about that deadline of 1997. Once, driving through the harbour tunnel to Kowloon, I asked my taxi driver about it as no doubt every foreign visitor does. He replied: 'We Hong Kong people are only interested in two things – working and making money!' I hope that those people in Peking feel the same way and, happily, I think they do. After all, as I said before, Hong Kong would have to be invented, wouldn't it?

CLIMATE

A tricky one this. Most Hong Kong people would like to have their home pad thought of as one of the marvellous tropical places but I fear there are a few snags. Typhoons of the Pacific variety are fairly frequent and the expression 'Typhoon shelter' was practically invented in Hong Kong. The colony lies just south of the Tropic of Cancer more or less on the same latitude as Calcutta, Jeddah or Hawaii. From March to May the average temperature works out at 68°F (21°C) with a fairly high humidity. From May to the middle of September, it rises by a good five degrees Centigrade; humidity is high and most of the rainfall takes place at that time and it can become pretty sticky. From late September to early December is the best season with the temperature at around 71°F (22°C). Winter can be quite cool in Hong Kong with the temperature dropping suddenly below 60°F (16°C). Winds can be high.

INTERNAL TRANSPORT

This is among the best in the world. One can go anywhere in the city-state at any time and often quite cheaply. Two aspects of Hong Kong transport are virtually features in themselves. One is the already mentioned 'Star Ferry' system and the other is the colony's trams. This almost extinct form of transport in the world goes from one end of Hong Kong Island to the other, meandering clatteringly down the canyons of concrete and providing the visitor with a marvellous introduction – the fare being a mere 0.30 HK$ for any distance. The Peak Tram is also unique to Hong Kong and it goes up or down the steep slope from the waterfront to the Peak District where the 'taipans' live in the magnificent villas, including the Governor of course. About 20 times a day Hong Kong's only real train covers the 20 odd miles (32 km) from Kowloon to the Chinese frontier at Lo Wu. The colony's pride and joy, however, is the Mass Transit Railway

(MTR), which is probably the fastest, cleanest underground/overground system in the world with superb trains and palatial stations at almost every corner of the big city. It goes from Hong Kong Island under the harbour to Kowloon and then branches east and west. Hong Kong taxis are ubiquitous and cheap, providing you don't take one from Hong Kong to Kowloon since the driver then has to pay the tunnel toll and drive by a roundabout route.

Don't let us forget the marvellous Hong Kong ferries which are in many ways the life blood of the city and go from Hong Kong or Tolo Harbour to practically every port and island where tourists short on time are likely to go. And finally there are 'wallah-wallahs', or bum boats to be exact, which will take you privately from one place to another. Good fun too if you hang on tight, unlike the American tourist I once saw losing his dentures in the middle of the harbour.

HOTELS

With almost two million tourists a year Hong Kong has a variety of hotels which is probably unbeatable anywhere else in the same space and that range from the best in the world to fairly humble places which were not there last time I looked. Which type and which locality to choose is of course up to you, and your wallet. From the Kowloon waterfront one has the best view of Hong Kong Island and, from the island, the lights of Kowloon blink on and on beckoning you to snap up yet another bargain.

SPECIALISED HOLIDAYS

Everybody can take you to Hong Kong in the style of a king or a beggar depending on your fancy and a few other things and at the last count I ticked off 35 major British tour operators whose packaged programmes cover the colony. Of course, as readers of *A Guide for the Independent Traveller* will have gathered by now, not one of them can truly be called a Hong Kong expert. Fortunately, you don't need to pay experts in this case since the Hong Kong Tourist Association will do it for you so well and for nothing. Just tell them what you want and, in my experience, they will turn up with the goods. In London, they can be found at 125 Pall Mall SW1, Telephone: 01-930 4775 and though they have several offices in Hong Kong itself, the central one is on the 35th floor of Connaught Centre (the Swiss cheese building which you can't very well miss). From basket ball to athletics by way of antique shopping and looking for jade, the HKTA recommend something like 20 different ways of passing the time — if you have had any spare!

Not long ago, I asked one of my friends, there to tell me, with his hand on his heart, what it was that the independent traveller could do that few other people do. Looking grave, he said: 'Eating'. I laughed it off and told him that I had indeed been to Food Street in Causeway Bay which specialises in gastronomic togetherness and is known all over the world. No, he told me, there are other things too. One can go for instance to the little known Po Toi Island where there are restaurants on stilts on the shore which specialise in seafood and seaweed soup. At Ley Yu Mon in the New Territories they also have very special seafood and in the typhoon shelter in Causeway Bay you settle yourself in the boat of your choice, have one course and see all the others floating by on offer. One boat brings you this, another boat brings you that. The experience is unique. Not bad for a start.

You could become an expert on tea. There are only 17 different kinds. There is even a Tea Museum at Flagstaff House and a genuine tea plantation on Lantau Island. You could have your fortune told according to at least 122 different ways. You could go and watch the horseracing either at Happy Valley or at the new course at Shatin — and you could do this from a private box too. You could go to Kennedy Town in the old Western District and see the famous 'go-downs' which made the early fortune of this amazing place. By following the advice of the Hong Kong Tourist Association you could even charter your own yacht and go where the fancy takes you amid the brilliant, sunlit waters of the South China Sea. And such activities are not in the guidebooks. So what are we all waiting for? The next Cathay Pacific flight? There is one every day without, of course, counting those of British Airways and a score of other world airlines. But do stay longer than two and a half days. That's an insult — both to Hong Kong and to you.

Please see pages 222–3 for addresses.

NORTH AMERICA

United States

PROFILE

Just in case anyone wants to know where I had one of my two best steaks ever, the answer is Ogilvie's 101 Broadway, Farmington, New Mexico. And if you don't know where Farmington is, I'm about to tell you. I didn't know either, till I went there. It's a small town, of about 40,000 people, with two principal streets, Broadway and Main, few supermarkets and some leather-jacketed cops who don't look anything like Starsky and Hutch. I don't know what people do there but I suspect it's mining. White Americans in cowboy boots, Levis and big hats dash about in beaten-up pick-up trucks. So do red Americans, mostly Navajos, the only difference between them being that the latter's clothes jingle with great turquoise and silver bangles. Farmington is where the great sagebrush-covered mesas meet the wide, wide sky, close to where New Mexico, Arizona, Colorado and Utah join.

But what about that steak? I'm coming to it. Apart from breakfast, which is superb anywhere, the worst value food in small-town USA is to be had in the ubiquitous eat-and-get-out-quick chain restaurants. The best value is usually found at the 'in' place. There is always one. The trouble is finding it in a country where a 'real' estate agent's office looks like a drugstore and the pharmacy could be something else altogether. And so, for 15 minutes, I kerb-crawled along the two main streets trying to fathom out where all those fancy locals with their frilly ladies got to.

The answer was Ogilvie's. It looked like the back entrance to a cinema and the sign on the door just said 'Cocktails—Dinners'. So, having parked my hired motorised leviathan, I walked in, only to fall flat on my face. My, these Americans do like their places dark. A pretty voice said: 'My name is Debbie and I am your waitress. What would you like? Cocktails or Dinner?' 'Both,' I replied hopefully, and followed her into the darker recesses of Farmington's 'in' place. Iced water arrived and so did a huge Scotch on the rocks with more water on the side. Then the menu. With the best will in the world and a flickering candle, I could hardly make out the headings. I asked Debbie if she could lend me a flashlight. Her laughter ran out. 'The English sense of humour ...,' she said. 'British', I said.

A year or so later I received a letter from the man who runs Ogilvie's. He wrote: 'We had a couple of Brits pass by the other day ... They had read your article and wanted to know if you were right. Next time you come, do let us know. Billie Donoghue is the man who tripped you up by putting his leg out from the bar and we'll put him in the jail for the night ... That's where he belongs anyway!'

The point of my telling this little story is simply this: with the exception of some airports and some city centres, all my anecdotal memories of the United States are happy ones. I have travelled more or less from New York to Northern California and from Texas to San Diego and nowhere do I remember anything but kindness, cheerfulness and hospitality. To the passing stranger, Americans rank in my mind among the two or three kindest people in the world. I remember the Florida road patrolman who went 25 miles (40 km) out of his way to put me back on the right road and said, 'Think nothing of it, we are glad to see you!' I remember the big rancher in Texas who put me up for three days just to show me that all Texans were not like the denizens of *Dallas*. I remember the waitress in a roadside eatery in Oklahoma who took her pinny off, dashed across the road to her own home to fetch me a piece of her own ' "real American apple pie", which is so much better than this shop stuff here.' And even in New York, supposedly the rudest place in the world, I recall once, in the middle of the night, the firechief lending me his crazy protective hat so that I could get a better view of the blaze. So, if you are USA-bound, and I hope you are, have no fear. You will be well received.

There are a few other pluses to. The size of the country for one. Everyone knows that America is huge but it is not until you get behind the wheel of a car and go, go, go that you truly realise the vastness of this incredible land. And it is not all parking lots either. Once, in the deserts of the west, I drove a whole morning and met nine cars. So much for pollution.

Furthermore, America is easy. Where else in the world would you meet a launderette proprietress who gives you a cup of coffee and the morning paper so you can while away the time? Where else would you get your car cleaned and polished by hand for less than you have to put into a parking meter in London's West End? America is cheap too. Where else would you get a salad for four dollars that would feed a family for a week? In America the customer is king and you are the customer. So prepare yourself for a few shocks. Nice ones.

What is the United States good for? Not knowing the United States these days is missing a good part of your education because this is the way the world is going, for good and for bad. The country itself is not only varied, but it is much more beautiful than you would expect and people are far more real than the Americans you see in Europe.

BEACHES

Anywhere you like, Atlantic or Pacific. There are magnificent strands outside most of those darling little New England towns, and yes, there are even some very good ones on Long Island. All the way from Georgia to Key West, the beaches are great, though perhaps they are not quite so marvellous on the western, Gulf of Mexico side of Florida. Out west, you could drive all the way from the Mexican border to Oregon and Washington without losing sight of the great ocean. In southern California, Santa Barbara and all that, the beaches tend to be 'arranged' and very well equipped. Elsewhere, especially in New England, Georgia and Northern California, a beach is just a place where the sea meets the land. Intense conservationists, Americans have really done their best to see that their great country remains as natural as could be.

COUNTRYSIDE

This is where I get into trouble. Where, in America? I have seen or inspected maybe 70 per cent of the United States and to this day I am unable really to decide on my favourite spots. Should one see Niagara Falls or make for those lovely plantation houses of the south? Should one give up the beauties of Florida for the beauties of the Rockies? Does one prefer sophistication à la New York or sophistication à la San Francisco? A few places can be disliked on sight – Los Angeles, for instance, with which I have never personally come to terms – and I would give a score of these great metropolitan centres for a few of those little towns across the length and breadth of this great land, places where people are people and church is the place where you meet on Sundays.

Over the years, I must confess that I have developed a sneaking affection for the south western states which, it seems to me, combine what we think of as America with the real thing. So what else is new? Lest you should think that travel writers go from one Farmington dinner to another, let me say right away: quite a lot. In New Mexico and Arizona, which are together two and a half times the size of Britain, I once drove more than 2000 miles (3220 km) and fell again under the spell of the old west: Billy the Kid and Kit Carson, Wyatt Earp and Doc Holliday, Cochise and Geronimo, Mexican bandits and Yanqui miners. Ghost towns, cow towns, ranches, canyons and eerie deserts, they are all there larger than one imagined – and unique. Yes, I did follow the Apache trail and, yes, I did become intrigued by mere names on the map and made endless detours to places like Coyote, Dusty, Moriarty, Truth or Consequences, Bagdad, Bumble Bee, Christmas, Inspiration, Mammoth, Oracle, Patagonia and, you might have guessed it, Surprise.

The whole country is physically grandiose, and haunted by the ghosts of former travellers: men such as Francisco Vasquez de Coronado, the Spanish *conquistador* who in the 1540s travelled thousands of miles looking for the legendary Seven Cities of Cibola – in what are now Texas, New Mexico, Arizona, Oklahoma and Kansas – complete with Spanish armour under the broiling sun, the first horses in America and a determination amounting to madness. He was the first European to see the Grand Canyon. Then there was Padre Kino, the Italian-Austrian Jesuit who, in the late seventeenth century, explored every corner of this vast land right up to the Californian coast, founding dozens of mission churches which are still standing today. And everywhere is the stunning physical beauty of a land which still seems almost untouched by man, and includes Indian reservations the size of Belgium or Holland, and 31 National Parks.

Since it would take a week or more to describe all there is to see, I will limit myself to the bare essentials. For a start, you must go to Santa Fe, capital of New Mexico, which calls itself the highest (7000 feet/2135 m) and oldest state capital in the Union. It was founded in 1609 by Don Pedro de Peralta, whose palace is still there – so Spanish it could be in Castile – looking out on to the plaza, where Indians sell jewellery under the arches and there are signs saying 'Keep Santa Fe Clean'. There, two centuries later, the first American Governor of New Mexico, Lew Wallace, sheltered behind barred windows because Billy the Kid had sworn to kill him and, to pass the time, wrote a book which became famous – Ben Hur. Santa Fe is a period gem, all adobe houses, patios and fountains, very Spanish and charmingly slow, with one or two impressive mission churches and a great cathedral. Nobody hurries, nobody shouts and you have to remind yourself that this is the United States. Inevitably, Santa Fe has become very art-orientated, with dozens of artists living and working down on the winding Canyon Road.

Even more Spanish and more art-bent is tiny Taos at the foot of the lovely Sangre de Cristo mountains. Its first famous citizen was Kit Carson, the great frontiersman whose house is still there. Another, later celebrity was D. H. Lawrence, who did some writing there in the 1920s, and a good deal of rather awful painting. I loved the ancient mission church of St Francis of Assisi, which is more like a fortress than a church. This is the country of the Pueblos – Indian communities which have existed for thousands of years and still do without bothering very much about the tourists. I went to see San Ildefonso, just north of Santa Fe, and especially the old Taos pueblo, a kind of Indian Manhattan with adobe buildings reaching to five storeys. Its inhabitants twice repelled the Spaniards and tried to keep out the Americans in 1847, but without avail.

Within an hour of leaving Santa Fe, I had to stop, look out

from a bluff and remind myself that there were other people alive. I was right in the middle of the Carson National Forest, which is half a million acres of 70-foot (21-m) high ponderosa pines stretching as far as the eye could see. One of my long-cherished aims had been to see Monument Valley, the site of countless cowboy movies. You know the stuff: the stage-coach rattles along the dusty trail, Indians erupt from behind a butte with blood-curdling cries and the chase begins. Fortunately, John Wayne is waiting with the Seventh Cavalry just behind the end of the Valley.

Monument Valley is now the private property of the Navajos. I reached the ranger-post just as the sun was beginning to sink in the afternoon sky. Down below, the Valley shimmered in the heat, dusty and deep red and totally unreal. I paid my dollar and the Navajo girl gave me a little map with a warning to look out for the signposts. It was easy to get lost.

I inched my car down into this incredible land of buttes and mesas and stunted trees, amid mountains sculptured by the winds of centuries into shapes that defy the laws of gravity. Some are the home of Indian deities and very holy indeed. The sun slid over, changing the colour of the mountains and, for an hour or two, the paleface outsider wandered speechless with awe. Since I was now in Arizona, the next stop should have been the Grand Canyon but having seen it twice before and in any case being more impressed by beauty than by size, I gave it a miss. Unless you have plenty of time and can indulge in one of those scary flights over the chasm or a mule train down to the deepest part, the Grand Canyon is almost too much to take in.

Instead, I raced across from Monument Valley to Page and my old favourite Wahweap Marina. There, for a few dollars, I hired a speed-boat with a skipper and went slicing across the incredible Lake Powell, where the Colorado River, dammed by the Glen Canyon complex, opens up into a world of enchantment consisting of monumental mountain walls dropping sheer into translucent waters.

After that I went south to see the lovely green Oak Tree Canyon and Jerome, the ghost town to end all ghost towns, which drapes its rickety and marvellous Victorian houses over 1500 feet (457 m) of hillside. Acting on a hunch, I turned east again and visited the vast Hopi Reservation where, on a fine crystalline morning, I had the privilege of driving 90 miles (145 km) through unbelievably grand country and meeting a total of 32 cars.

But, in what the Arizonians call the Valley of the Sun, which is Phoenix and its satellite cities of Scottsdale, Tempe and Mesa, one is back in the twentieth century. Two million people live in this latter-day American dreamland with 40 golf courses and so many swiming-pools that no one has ever bothered to count them. In Phoenix everything gleams, credit cards flash in the sun, and Scottsdale has more Rolls Royces to the square mile than London W1. Plus clubs, palatial pads, manicured lawns, dude ranches and all the goodies of the world's most affluent society. Undoubtedly, Phoenix has a lot to offer, but it is just a trifle rich for me and I could not wait to leave for my favourite western city.

Over the years I have tried hard to analyse the reasons for my love-affair with Tucson. And I can conclude only that it is due to a combination of things about this city which just appeal to me. The weather comes first. Tucson has the driest and sunniest climate in the United States – 3800 hours of sun a year – and a kind of shining clarity, which I have only ever found elsewhere in Greece and the Middle East. The rainfall is minimal and the greenness comes from underground. The temperature has an average maximum of 82°F (28°C), though it can be a lot hotter, and an average minimum of 52°F (11°C): in other words there is no winter. Then there is size. Tucson has just half a million people, which is still enough to become engulfed in. And it is the only city of its size in the United States to have its own professional theatre company, opera and symphony orchestra. Finally, there is the atmosphere of the place: heartily Western, genteelly Spanish, friendly and unpretentious, open-hearted and tremendously hospitable. People are cheerful, polite, extrovert, without being vulgar, and endlessly helpful.

The old side of Tucson is part adobe, part extravagant *fin de siècle*, where at eleven o'clock any morning, you can stand and watch a real-life Western unfolding before your eyes: there is bedlam in the saloon, two or three guys come tumbling out with their guns flashing. One rolls off the roof, the sheriff appears and everybody is off to the 'hoosegow'. It is all good clean fun. Then there is the splendid Arizona University and a short drive away, the Arizona-Sonora Desert Museum where you can see the world of the desert preserved and beautifully explained.

A lot of worth-while sights lie within reach of Tucson. On my way there from Phoenix I drove to Apache Junction and turned off along the Apache Trail. Before I knew what was happening, the tarmac ended and the road climbed into the most beautiful mountain scenery in this part of the west and, in second gear and with my foot on the brake, I found out the reason why the Apaches climbed up here, apart from to avoid the palefaces down in the valleys. Peaks and mesas, buttes and canyons, springs and lakes succeed each other in the kind of diorama one sees only through those children's 3D spectacles. I caught up with a man driving the biggest bulldozer I have ever seen. He shut off his engine and said: 'Hold on there, bud. You won't get through until I have cleared a way.' He roared forward, picked up a rock half the size of my car and casually tossed it over the side. It rolled down and down, ending up in Navajo Lake with a magnificent splash. I passed three houses and a post office, discovered that this was indeed Tortilla Flat, and ended up on the shining shores of Roosevelt Lake. I recommend the Apache Trail to all those who think that America is all drugstores and caravans.

Tucson, at the foot of the Santa Catalina Mountains, is in real Padre Kino country, and I revisited with pleasure the lovely mission church at San Xavier del Bac, and another at Tumacacori. From there I simply had to make a detour via Nogales on the Mexican frontier to see the ranch village of Patagonia, with its Museum of the Horse and its Santa Fe and Western Railroad station which saw its last train 20 years ago and has hardly changed since 1880. Two of the real prizes lie to the west. The first is Tombstone, 'the town too tough to die', once as rich as San Francisco and the home of the OK Corral where Wyatt Earp and Doc Holliday had their epic gunfight with the Clantons: corny but nice. Less well-known but in my opinion even more interesting is the old mining town of Bisbee, which in its day produced 41 million tons of copper ore from the Copper Queen and Lavender Pit mines. Saturday nights up Brewery Gulch are still sung about in the old west and Bisbee, not dead by any means, carefully preserves its charming fretworked and galleried houses rising up the steep hills like dolls' houses.

It is for things like this that I love the south-western states. There are other areas of America that I remember with pleasure but none has for me quite the same rare blend of history, folklore and wide, wild open space. So, go south-west, traveller. With any luck you won't see me there – it's big enough for both of us.

CLIMATE

Americans are very weather-conscious. This is not just because they dislike rough weather more than we do but simply because in this huge country, more of a continent, the weather is just one of the facts of life. It could be snowing in Milwaukee (it often does) and tropical in San Diego. California could be catching the tail-end of a typhoon and in the mid-west the sky could be blue and limpid. What Americans mostly do about the weather is listen to their car radios. There are over 5000 local radio stations across the United States and all give their own forecasts at regular intervals during the day. You can't go far wrong.

INTERNAL TRANSPORT

America is the country of mobility *par excellence*. People travel any time, anywhere and with the greatest of ease. The country's airlines are the most integrated, most efficient and cheapest in the world and although most of the big ones cover all major destinations, each one tends to cover its own patch for visitors.

Car hire is the cheapest in the world by a long way and the choice is often bewildering. So do shop around, consult the local Yellow Pages or ask the Visitors' Bureau. Taking it here and leaving it there is second nature in the American car hire plan and you don't have to book. When you arrive at your destination airport, take a good look around at what is on offer – then make up your mind. The big multinationals may have some advantages but they are not always the cheapest. Price competition is fierce and the rates change all the time.

Quite apart from the ease of car hiring, driving yourself in the United States is child's play – the whole country is made for the car driver. Apart from the very large cities, self-drive presents no problems for those used to the congested roads of Europe. American traffic moves fast and safely, the maximum speed on main roads is a low 55 mph (88 kph) and is sometimes strictly enforced. Signposting and directions vary a good deal from state to state and can be rather upsetting for Europeans. Americans often signpost their highways by numbers instead of destination, for instance US80 North or Interstate 13 West, and unless you know what direction you are making for you can get lost, especially with named or numbered exits as you approach the big cities. Make sure you've got the right one because the worst mistake you can make is taking the wrong exit. The second worst fault, especially in cities, is changing lanes too quickly or too hesitantly. Americans are sticklers for lane discipline so when you are in a city study the street plan carefully and count the number of stop intersections before you turn right or left. Many cities, and states, have their own driving regulations, especially with regard to lighting.

Long-distance buses in America are ideal, if you don't

want to drive yourself. They are frequent, flexible and go literally everywhere. There are several companies but the best known is Greyhound Lines. They have a variety of all-in packages at prices that make the mind boggle.

HOTELS

Some of the finest hotels in the world are in America and a few are listed on page 223. But if you are travelling around, motels offer the best value and almost every small town has two or three. Some are independent and some are affiliated to chains like Best Western, Holiday Inns, Ramada or Travelodge. How much you pay and what you get depends on how hard you look.

SPECIALISED HOLIDAYS

America is one of the few countries to which you can just go, go, go, and make up your mind as you bowl along. Yet, inevitably, most tour operators can get you organised if that is what you want. There are a few specialists, mostly in particular areas, like Mark Allan Travel Ltd, Albany Travel Ltd and Cox & Kings. Most will be willing to help but don't count on getting a lot of generalised advice.

Tourism is a state business in America, or even more frequently a matter for the city's Visitors' Bureau and they are never represented in London. There is no American Tourist Office as such except for the trade and there is no point in looking for it. On the other hand, the wealth of guidebooks on this fascinating land makes up for the lack of official help.

Please see page 223 for addresses.

The Caribbean

The Caribbean islands are all things to all people. That incorrigible pen-pal, Madame de Sévigné, once wrote that they were: 'The most shining, most astounding, most wonderful, most miraculous, most triumphant, most amazing, most incredible things in the world.' One Italian tourist we met recently in Guadeloupe had other words for it. 'The food is awful,' he said, 'and there is no culture.' Pointing to the gleaming strand that faced us, we asked: 'Don't you like the beach?' Grudgingly, he admitted that it was 'all right'. Obviously, he was a Mediterranean man out of his element.

The truth, of course, lies somewhere between the two. And, unfortunately for the intending visitor, the truth is often hidden behind a screen of clichés, forests of adjectives, bagfuls of misconceptions all wrapped up in a kind of 'metooism' which has obscured the real facts. Travel agents and tour operators who trade on expectations rather than personal fulfilment are guilty of many such sins. It is obvious that if you like walking around Venice, visiting the Taj Mahal or steaming up the Nile, you may not like the Caribbean. It is not your scene and this, let's face it, is what holidays are all about. Discovering what is your scene is the beginning of travelling wisdom.

The first thing to remember about the Caribbean islands is that they are not all the same. The secret lies in knowing this difference and making it play a part in your choice. Someone who likes the 'Platinum Coast' of Barbados will probably hate messing about in boats in the Grenadines. And if you tell someone in Jamaica that he reminds you of someone you met in Trinidad, you are likely to have a war on your hands. Tiny though some may be, the Caribbean islands are intensely separate and nationalistic. Isolation, historical remoteness, different masters in bygone years and the different origins of those who came as slaves from Africa have all contributed to a remarkable island identity.

Caribbean people don't even speak the same language. There is French Creole and English Creole, which often overlap. There is the soft English of Barbados and the harder one of Antigua. There is old-fashioned Normandy French in

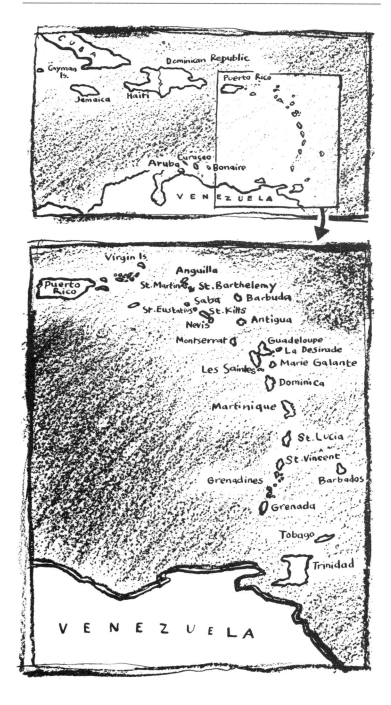

Guadeloupe, but across the water in Les Saintes everyone sounds like a Breton. They speak American in Puerto Rico, Papiamento in Trinidad, Dutch in Curaçao and Spanish in the Dominican Republic. As for Haiti, they speak Haitian, which most people think is French but is not.

Quite apart from their sizes, which vary from Switzerland to Hyde Park, the islands don't even look the same. Some are parched and dry, others lush and tropic green. Some are so lofty you can't even see the top of their mountains 10,000 feet (3050 m) up in the clouds and others are as flat as yesterday's Crêpe Suzette. Some are sugar islands and others are banana islands and these are differences that are enormously important. So don't speak of 'the Caribbean'. Say St Lucia or Jamaica or Barbados. Speak even of Marie Galante or Saba — though no one will know what you are talking about.

A few things, however, are common to all Caribbean islands. One is the most reliable and superbly tropical climate in the world. Another is some of the finest beaches to be found anywhere and the best and most experienced resort hotels. In recent years, the popularity of West Indian destinations has declined for a number of reasons, the most important being that the whole of the world is now competing for your travellers' cheques. Today, the pendulum is beginning to swing back and we believe we know why: because in the tropical beach holiday business, the Caribbean wins every round in the long run. If this is what you are looking for, read on and choose your patch. I will try and take you step by step through 1300 miles (2093 km) of sunlit sea in what someone once called 'This naive, pristine Eden'.

BEACHES

You are, of course, joking since the excellence of the beaches is more or less synonymous with Caribbean islands. Almost every island — with the exception of that lovely Dominica — has a beach or beaches which both locals and visitors will call the best. I would probably disagree since I have seen, in other parts of the world, such as Bali, Thailand, the Philippines and Greece, beaches that rival the Caribbean except that they do not have that *je ne sais quoi* which makes a Caribbean beach special. It is a blend of the sophisticated and the natural, a human-made combination which goes a long way towards making life easy and, above all, as I have already mentioned, there are some of the best beach hotels anywhere. With ups and downs in between, Caribbean hoteliers have been at it a long time and they know what makes a great beach hotel. No one can take that away from them.

Which is the best beach? It is hard to say. Some believe that Pigeon Point on Tobago is the world's finest strand and they might well be right. But then Antigua, which is an island I do not particularly like, has beaches that are quite superb and so have St Lucia and Grenada. For those who like small islands, the Grenadines and their beaches, for instance the so-called 'Princess Margaret Beach' on Bequia, are quite marvellous. On some of the Grenadines you can actually walk around the island without ever leaving the beach at all, as on Palm and on Barbuda, which is next door to Antigua and where I once recall walking a good mile and a half in ankle-deep soft blond sand until I thought that maybe it was time to go back. I have also often thought that I could go a long, long way around the world before finding the equivalent of the private beach of Jamaica Inn in Ocho Rios.

So what follows is an 'ABC' of Caribbean islands plus, at the end, a slice of purple prose about one or two of my real favourites. So, please read on.

What is the Caribbean good for? Everybody's tropic dream and why not? When the weather is ugly elsewhere, the Caribbean islands are a cornucopia of blue skies, blue seas, golden sun and superb beaches. They are very well organised for the holiday-buyer. There is not much genuine culture but they are a good place to forget everything.

Anguilla

LANGUAGE: ENGLISH.

STATUS: BRITISH DEPENDENCY WITH INTERNAL SELF-GOVERNMENT.

SIZE: 35 SQUARE MILES. POPULATION: 6000.

A long, thin coral island, never more than 200 feet (61 m) above sea level and 2 miles (3.2 km) across, which one can reach via Antigua or St Kitts by plane. In 1967, it made headlines by breaking away from St Kitts/Nevis federated state and calling in British troops. It is very quiet and bucolic. The capital is called The Valley. Anguilla has many good beaches, especially Rendez-Vous Bay and Sandy Island and about half-a-dozen hotels of which the best is the Malliounana.

Antigua

LANGUAGE: ENGLISH

STATUS: ASSOCIATED STATE WITHIN COMMONWEALTH.

SIZE: 108 SQUARE MILES. POPULATION: 64,000.

Harpers & Queen's own phrase, 'A beach with an island in the middle' has stuck through the years. Antiguans maintain that there are 365 beaches around their penny-shaped island, though we have never counted them. Most are extremely good. Antigua is a dry, sugar-growing island, which is quiet and peaceful though not particularly attractive in the scenic sense. Very interesting, however, is the famous Nelson's Dockyard at English Harbour in the south, which is one of the finest shelters in the entire Caribbean and if you see it you will understand Caribbean history. Horatio himself built it and much of the original is still standing. Antiguan waters are very clear and calm, and perfect for swimming. The best hotel is Curtain Bluff and the next best Half Moon Bay.

Aruba

LANGUAGE: DUTCH/ENGLISH/PAPIAMENTO.
STATUS: PART OF NETHERLANDS ANTILLES.
SIZE: 71 SQUARE MILES. POPULATION: 62,000.

Most oilmen know Aruba for it's only 15 miles (24 km) from Venezuela and its huge refinery deals with a lot of Venezuela's oil. As it happens Aruba also has some very fine beaches – if you are upwind of the oil. It is deliciously Dutch, especially in Oranjestad, the capital. The locals still bear some resemblance to the first inhabitants, the gentle Arawaks (those who were not murdered by the not-so-gentle Caribs). Divi-divi trees are an Aruba speciality – they lean away from the breeze. It's a very dry island, apart from the bars. Aruba has splendid duty-free shopping and five casinos, plus marvellous Dutch/Indonesian food. There are good beaches too – especially Palm Beach. The best hotels are Aruba Concorde and the Aruba Caribbean, which are both quite big. The Divi-Divi Beach Hotel (cottages) is most attractive. You can fly to Aruba from Amsterdam or New York and/or neighbouring islands.

Barbuda

LANGUAGE: ENGLISH.
STATUS: DEPENDENCY OF ANTIGUA.
SIZE: 62 SQUARE MILES. POPULATION: 1100.

Barbuda is 32 miles (52 km) from Antigua and 15 minutes by plane. It is very flat and scrubby. It was once the private property of the Codrington family who ruled in paternalistic fashion and engaged in genetic hanky-panky trying to produce the best slaves. Every other name is Codrington! The island's tourist appeal lies in its one enormous beach at Coco Point, which never seems to end. The best hotel is Coco Point Lodge, which is simple and quiet.

Bonaire

LANGUAGE: DUTCH/ENGLISH/PAPIAMENTO.

STATUS: PART OF NETHERLANDS ANTILLES.

SIZE: 112 SQUARE MILES. POPULATION: 8500.

Bonaire is very quiet and simple. The great curiosity here is flamingos and a hundred other species of bird life. It has superb coral reefs and is one of the best scuba-diving locations. The beaches are nice too and there is duty-free shopping. Access is via Amsterdam and New York and/or Curaçao. The best hotel is Flamingo Beach.

Cayman Islands

LANGUAGE: ENGLISH.

STATUS: BRITISH CROWN COLONY.

SIZE: 99 SQUARE MILES. POPULATION: 12,000.

These consist of three small islands, 180 miles (290 km) north west of Jamaica, called Grand Cayman, Little Cayman and Cayman Brac. Once the haunt of pirates and buccaneers, it is now the home of 390 banks and 14,000 offshore companies (no income tax at all). Very up-and-coming touristically but not spoilt yet. Nice, friendly people of mixed racial origins. There is a place called Hell, so named by a governor who hated the islands and made the fortune of the local post office. The beaches are very good with lots of wrecks and coral and great fishing. The best hotels are the Caribbean Club, West Indian Club and Cayman Kai.

Curaçao

LANGUAGE: DUTCH/ENGLISH/PAPIAMENTO.

STATUS: PART OF NETHERLANDS ANTILLES.

SIZE: 130 SQUARE MILES. POPULATION: 145,000.

Holland home and away: it is one of the cleanest places in the Caribbean. There are pretty Dutch houses in Willemstad, which are mostly eighteenth century and also the oldest synagogue in the Western hemisphere. It is a very cosmopolitan island with representatives of 79 nationalities, who are mostly there because of a huge oil refinery – Venezuela is 35 miles (56 km) away – and sundry businesses, all of them duty-free. Perhaps Curaçao is the best place in the Caribbean for this. A flat and dry island, with some old plantation houses, it's also the birthplace of Curaçao liqueur made from secret recipes. The best beaches are at the west end of the island. The best hotels are the Curaçao Hilton and the historical Curaçao Plaza, which was once a Dutch fortress. There is superb food everywhere.

Dominica

LANGUAGE: ENGLISH AND FRENCH CREOLE.

STATUS: ASSOCIATED STATE WITHIN COMMONWEALTH.

SIZE: 290 SQUARE MILES. POPULATION: 71,000.

If you want to visit an island that's different and not overrun with tourists, go to Dominica. They don't come any stranger. With only one white beach – the others are volcanic black – it's no island for beach softies. The island is one vast tropical Garden of Eden, some of it almost vertical. It is absolutely wild and untamed and a kind of botanical madness. This is also the home of the last Carib Indians who now live in a large reservation.

Grenada

LANGUAGE: ENGLISH.

STATUS: INDEPENDENT STATE WITHIN COMMONWEALTH.

SIZE: 120 SQUARE MILES. POPULATION: 110,000.

It's pronounced Gre-nay-dah and is one of the two or three most beautiful islands in the Caribbean with waterfalls, flowers, jungle green and superb beaches. St George's, the capital, is the nicest-looking little city in the area with, next door, the famed Grande Anse beach – among the tops anywhere. Unfortunately, politics work in Eden too and for the past few years Grenada has been in the doghouse, touristically-speaking. Its dogmatic, left-wing government was strongly allied to that of Fidel Castro. Called the Spice Island, Grenada is the world's biggest producer of nutmeg, vanilla and so on. The island changed hands many times from French to British and back again. The only time they co-operated was in an eighteenth-century drive against the last Caribs who, rather than surrender, dived to their death from the Morne des Sauteurs. You fly to Grenada from London via Barbados and connecting flights. The best hotels are the Spice Island Inn, the Calabash and Secret Harbour.

The Grenadines

LANGUAGE: ENGLISH AND CREOLE PATOIS.

STATUS: OVER 100 SMALL ISLANDS, FOUR-FIFTHS BELONGING TO
ST VINCENT AND THE REST TO GRENADA.

POPULATION: 1867.

'The heavenly microdots' – my own long-ago phrase has stuck here too and I still firmly believe that they are the most beautiful small islands in the world. It is a paradise for sailors – you are never out of sight of land – and is perfect for quiet beachcombing. Only ten islands are inhabited, the rest are just for picnics! There is a charming *dolce far niente* atmosphere with nothing much happening except the sun rising and setting. The swimming and diving is superb. The biggest island is Bequia, pronounced Beck-wee, which is the sort you fall in love with at first sight and may never wish to leave, especially if you remember the notoriously rough crossing from St Vincent for there is no airport. Lovely people, among the finest sailors in the Caribbean and famous as whalers — they'll have a go at anything as long as it floats. Mustique (you know who has a house there) is very pretty and pastoral and privately owned. Palm belongs to round-the-world-single-handed sailor John Caldwell and is just a round dot with a beach on the midriff. Canouan is bigger, almost unknown, and so are Union, Mayero, Petit St Vincent and the Tobago Cays (nothing to do with Tobago). All are quite unique. You can share a yacht charter from St Vincent or, as I did once and will never forget it, spend a week on an inter-island schooner and sleep on the beaches. The best hotels are the Cotton House on Mustique, Palm Island Beach Club, Crystal Sands on Canouan (simple), Petit St Vincent Resort, the Anchorage Yacht Club on Union and the legendary Frangipani on Bequia. There are airfields-of-sorts on Union, Mustique, Palm and Petit St Vincent.

Haiti

LANGUAGE: FRENCH/CREOLE.

STATUS: INDEPENDENT REPUBLIC.

SIZE: 10,700 SQUARE MILES. POPULATION: 6 MILLION.

Once the parish of 'Baby Doc' (slightly less sinister than his father 'Papa Doc' and his *tontons macoute*, unfortunate Haiti is one of the most politically battered and impoverished nations in the world. It is a pity. It was the world's first black republic, Toussaint L'Ouverture and all that, plus the megalomaniac Henri Christophe whose own Versailles you can still see. It is the home of voodoo, cockfighting and famous Haitian primitive painters ranging all the way from Douanier Rousseau to bad Walt Disney. Yet, Haitians are not downhearted for they are full of *joie de vivre*, music and song and are very charming people. The country has high mountains and deep valleys and some superb beaches, especially around Jacmel on the south coast. Try the famous Kenscoff market not far from Port-au-Prince, it's the greatest for colour. You can reach Haiti from Paris with Air France, or via Miami, or from Kingston with Air Jamaica. The best hotels are the sensationally luxurious Habitation Leclerc, which seems almost disgusting in the circumstances, and the gingerbread Grand Hotel Oloffson.

Les Saintes

LANGUAGE: FRENCH.

STATUS: FIVE SMALL ISLANDS FORMING PART OF GUADELOUPE.

POPULATION: 2234.

The site of a famous naval battle when Rodney clobbered the French, they are very unusual, off-beat small islands. Only 2 miles (3 km) of road and two taxis (different colours). The two main islands are Terre de Bas, whose inhabitants are black, and Terre de Haut, where they are white, descendants of Normans and Bretons who settled there 300 years ago. Most wear a huge hat made of bamboo and called salako, though nobody knows why, and are superb sailors and fishermen. The best hotels are two small ones, the Hotel du Bois Joli and La Saintoise. Superb seafood is to be found everywhere. You can fly in from Guadeloupe or take the ferry, which is much more fun.

Marie Galante

LANGUAGE: FRENCH/CREOLE.

STATUS: PART OF GUADELOUPE.

SIZE: 61 SQUARE MILES. POPULATION: 7000.

If you tell people you have been to Marie Galante, they won't believe you – they don't know what it is! It is one of the last totally unspoilt small Caribbean islands, which has been making sugar and rum by the same methods for 300 years. Very quiet and bucolic, with lovely beaches. You can fly from Guadeloupe or, more interesting, take the boat to St Louis, a small town where the local housewives lie in wait on the doorsteps banging saucepans together and shouting: 'Dejeuner, dejeuner!' and provide superb Creole food. The capital is Grand Bourg, which has an untouched 3-mile (4.8-km) beach next door that is always empty except at weekends. Marie Galante is the Caribbean as it was.

Martinique

LANGUAGE: FRENCH/CREOLE.

STATUS: DEPARTMENT OF FRANCE.

SIZE: 425 SQUARE MILES. POPULATION: 345,000.

Martinique is very French and sophisticated. It is mountainous in the north where, in 1905, the Mont Pelee volcano erupted and wiped out the old capital, St Pierre, and turned it into the Pompeii of the West Indies. Softer and flatter in the south where the best beaches are, such as Ste Anne and Le Diamant, with, offshore, the cone-shaped rock which Rodney commissioned into the Royal Navy as HMS *Diamond Rock*. Martinique is a very sensuous island, soft and yet proud. Its women are legendary for their beauty and two of them made history – Madame de Maintenon, Louis XIV's mistress, and Napoleon's Josephine whose house you can visit. The island's restaurants serve the best food in the West Indies. The best hotels are: Bakoua Beach, Meridien-Martinique and two historical reconstructions, the Manoir de Beauregard and the Plantation de Leyritz. Fly Air France.

Montserrat

LANGUAGE: ENGLISH.

STATUS: BRITISH CROWN COLONY.

SIZE: 39 SQUARE MILES. POPULATION: 15,000.

Difficult Irishmen were exiled there in the seventeenth century and the population still speaks with an Irish brogue. Montserrat is very quiet, the vegetable garden of the Caribbean. Most beaches are volcanic black or grey. People who love Montserrat and its quiet, unspoilt charm never stop talking about it. It's an acquired taste. The best hotel is the Vue Pointe. Island-hops from Antigua.

Nevis

LANGUAGE: ENGLISH.

STATUS: PART OF ST KITTS/NEVIS INDEPENDENT STATE WITHIN COMMONWEALTH.

SIZE: 36 SQUARE MILES. POPULATION: 13,000.

Columbus first called it 'Las Nieves' meaning the snows, because of the white ring of clouds around its high central mountain. Apart from being very beautiful, this lofty island has one claim to fame: here Horatio Nelson met his wife, Frances Nesbitt, and married her at the Montpelier Estate. The capital, Charlestown, still has an eighteenth century feel. Nevis is a very green and jungly island with at least one super beach – Pinney's. You fly in from St Kitts. The best hotels are Nisbet Plantation Inn and Montpelier Estate.

Puerto Rico

LANGUAGE: AMERICAN, ENGLISH AND SPANISH.

STATUS: SELF-GOVERNING COMMONWEALTH WITHIN USA.

SIZE: 3423 SQUARE MILES. POPULATION: 2,800,000.

America in the Caribbean, all the way from the Miami/Las Vegas syndrome to little 'ole Spanish America – an island with a split personality. But great efforts are being made to preserve the Spanish heritage, which is second only to Santo Domingo. The island is lush and green in the north and much drier in the south past the central cordillera. The old part of San Juan is very pretty with Spanish houses and the famous El Morro fort built in 1591. There are a dozen really fine beaches, especially Luquillo, east of San Juan, and some delightful fishing villages on the south coast. British tourists are rare. 'You spik funny English,' a local once told me and I could have said the same of him. Puerto Ricans in their island are sweet, smiling people. Direct flights from New York and Miami or connections from Antigua and Barbados. The best hotels are the Caribe Hilton in San Juan, which is on the beach, and the huge and smart Dorado Beach in the south.

Saba

LANGUAGE: DUTCH/ENGLISH.

STATUS: PART OF NETHERLANDS ANTILLES.

SIZE: 5 SQUARE MILES. POPULATION: 1000.

A perfect volcanic cone, Saba is one of the great landmarks of the Caribbean and locals are said to navigate by it. It's almost vertical and the capital, The Bottom, is, you have guessed it, at the bottom of the crater and 'The Road' (there is only one) leads you in from the airport once you've got your breath back. Half the population is white – mostly ex-Shetlanders. Saba is a curiosity if you are collecting islands. The best hotel is Captain's Quarter.

St Barthelemy

LANGUAGE: FRENCH.

STATUS: PART OF GUADELOUPE.

SIZE: 15 SQUARE MILES. POPULATION: 2450.

St Bart's – everybody calls it that – is one of the best kept secrets in the Caribbean for it is a very small world and quite unique. The French got there first, though most of them were eaten by the Caribs. France sold it to Sweden and the latter sold it back to France, which is Caribbean history all right. The capital, Gustavia, is quaint and pretty and still rather Swedish in appearance, but the women wear Normandy bonnets. There are some fine beaches, totally untouched on the north coast. Shopping is French and good. You fly in from St Martin or Guadeloupe. The best hotels are the PLM and Jean Bart.

St Eustatius

LANGUAGE: DUTCH.

STATUS: PART OF NETHERLANDS ANTILLES.

SIZE: 8 SQUARE MILES. POPULATION. 1300.

Call it 'Statia' – everybody does. In the seventeenth century, Statia made a vast fortune from being the world's first free port. Rodney sacked it and became rich but now it's very quiet and subdued. There is some very good surfing on the north coast. The best hotel is the Old Gin House (cotton, not drink), which is simple and islandish.

St Kitts

LANGUAGE: ENGLISH.

STATUS: ASSOCIATED STATE WITHIN COMMONWEALTH.

SIZE: 65 SQUARE MILES. POPULATION: 40,000.

Historically, St Kitts is very important for it was the first British colony in the West Indies (1623) and was the principal base in countless wars. See the vast Brimstone Hill Fort and from there you can gaze at six different islands. Basically, St Kitts is a sugar island and is not very good on beaches, but there is some interesting colonial architecture in Basseterre, the capital. You island-hop there from Antigua. The best hotel is The Golden Lemon, which is a superb revamping of an old colonial house.

St Lucia

LANGUAGE: ENGLISH/FRENCH CREOLE.

STATUS: INDEPENDENT STATE WITHIN COMMONWEALTH.

SIZE: 238 SQUARE MILES. POPULATION: 112,000.

Call it 'St Loosha' – it's nowhere near Naples! People often ask me which is the most beautiful island in the Caribbean and I always ask 'Big, medium or tiny?' Of the medium ones, St Lucia takes the prize. Scenically, it is matchless: jungle-green, up and down, beautifully profiled. The two Pitons mountains are world famous on all travel posters. So is the tiny bay of Marigot, the scene of many films, and the bubbling Soufrière volcano plus countless banana plantations. Sixty-seven shipwrecked English sailors landed there first in 1605 and forty-eight of them made a main meal for the Carib Indians. The English and French fought like farmyard animals over St Lucia and the island changed hands 13 times. The beaches, which include Vigie, Choc Bay and Reduit, are among the best anywhere. There are direct flights from London three times a week. The best hotels are Anse Chastanet, La Toc and St Lucian.

St Martin /Sint Maarten

LANGUAGE: FRENCH/DUTCH.

STATUS: TWO-THIRDS FRENCH (GUADELOUPE) AND ONE-THIRD DUTCH.

SIZE: 37 SQUARE MILES. POPULATION: 23,000.

How can you divide such a small island? Yet, greed and politics managed it and St Martin is the world's smallest piece of shared property. The French and Dutch were there at the same time, placed two men back to back, told them to run around the island and then drew a line between departure and arrival point. The Frenchman ran faster. The Dutchman (too much gin) lost. The great attraction of the island is the dual nationality. You go shopping in the free port of Philipsburg on the Dutch side and eat on the French side around Marigot. There are some very good beaches and tourism is booming but not yet spoiling the roost. The best hotels are the superb La Samanna on the French side, though do bring your money with you, and Mullet Bay on the Dutch side.

St Vincent

LANGUAGE: ENGLISH.

STATUS: INDEPENDENT WITHIN COMMONWEALTH.

SIZE: 198 SQUARE MILES. POPULATION: 94,000.

One of the tourism Cinderellas of the Caribbean for most beaches are black and they put people off. Why? A quiet and dignified island with charming, hard-working people much given to emigration when their crops, for example bananas and sea-island cotton, fail or are nobbled by speculators. Captain Bligh brought his first breadfruit trees there on the second attempt. St Vincent's best bet is its ownership of most of the Grenadines. The best hotels are Young Island (on an islet) and the Cobblestone Inn, which is 200 years old.

Tobago

LANGUAGE: ENGLISH.

STATUS: PART OF TRINIDAD & TOBAGO INDEPENDENT STATE WITHIN COMMONWEALTH.

SIZE: 177 SQUARE MILES. POPULATION: 37,000.

Tobago is paradise, full stop, or as near as one can get to it. Green and jungly, with the tallest coconut palms in the business, some dreamy beaches including the world-famous Pigeon Point and Buccoo Reef, which has the best coral in the Caribbean. Offshore little Tobago has a bird of paradise sanctuary. It is certainly one of the prettiest islands of all. The best hotels are the Mount Irvine Bay, which has super golf, and Arnos Vale.

Trinidad

LANGUAGE: ENGLISH, HINDI, URDU AND ALMOST ANYTHING.

STATUS: SENIOR PARTNER IN INDEPENDENT STATE WITHIN COMMONWEALTH.

SIZE: 1864 SQUARE MILES. POPULATION: 1 MILLION.

The Caribbean's Tower of Babel — raffish and industrious, rich, well governed, totally polyglot and multi-racial with Africans, Portuguese, Spaniards, British, Indians, Pakistanis, Chinese and Lebanese who are all mad on cricket and steel bands (they invented the things). Strictly speaking, Trinidad is not a holiday island but it is well worth sampling as the liveliest and noisiest place in the West Indies. You never go to bed here. It's the second-richest island after

Puerto Rico with oil, natural gas and the biggest pitch lake in the world containing enough bitumen to tar the roads of the world. It's only 8 miles (12.8 km) from the Venezuelan coastline and it has a tremendous variety of bird (feathered) life. Port-of-Spain is a gingerbread jungle of architectural styles, mosques and churches and Hindu temples and even a German castle. Trinidad has very good shopping and eating and lots of night-life. Maracas Beach, not far away, and other beaches on the more distant east coast are not at all bad. The national airline, BWIA, has scheduled flights from London. The best hotel is the Trinidad Hilton, known as the Upside Down Hilton for you go in through the top floor.

Virgin Islands (American)

LANGUAGE: AMERICAN/ENGLISH.

STATUS: US TERRITORY.

SIZE: 76 SQUARE MILES. POPULATION: 75,000.

There are three of them, St Thomas, St John and St Croix (pronounced St Croy) purchased from Denmark in 1917 and they have made the fortune of US cruise lines since they are easy destinations. St Thomas is the most crowded since the capital, Charlotte Amalie, is largely a free port. It is pretty but is not really worth the trip. St John is for it has over 30 gleaming beaches, superb blue seas and charming, quiet villages. St Croix is even quieter, pastoral and rather like a tropical vegetable garden. There are lots of flowers and very nice old houses. You can fly to St Thomas from virtually anywhere. The best hotel is the celebrated Caneel Bay Plantation built by Laurance Rockefeller with great taste. It's on St John.

Virgin Islands (British)

LANGUAGE: ENGLISH.

STATUS: INTERNALLY SELF-GOVERNING BRITISH CROWN COLONY.

SIZE: 69 SQUARE MILES. POPULATION: 12,000.

After the Grenadines, these are the second most interesting small islands in the Caribbean. There are over 60 of them, of which 17 are inhabited, dotted on both sides of the Francis Drake Channel. All of them rather scrubby and dry but with magnificent beaches and lots of places to get lost. One friend (or was he?) once got me marooned on a desert island for the day. It was a salutary experience. The British Virgin Islands are a paradise for sailors and all who like messing about in boats since you can go in and out of deserted little coves or have a picnic on some islet. One of them is the original Dead Man's Chest, Yo-ho-ho and all that. One of the world's finest beaches is unromantically called The Baths – on Virgin

Gorda. It is quite superb. There is little night-life anywhere, even in Road Town, the capital, on Tortola but these are splendid islands for a quiet holiday. You can fly only from St Thomas. The best hotels are the super luxurious but beautifully built Little Dix Bay on Virgin Gorda and Peter Island Yacht Club on Peter Island.

Most readers will, by now, have gathered that I am not anti-Caribbean. So I make no apologies for enlarging on two islands, Guadeloupe and Jamaica. It could have been St Lucia or Tobago but these two came more readily to mind. At least, they will give you something to think about.

My love affair with the strange island of Guadeloupe (this time around) did not start when I discovered the fast and scary motorways that now lead out of Pointe-à-Pitre or when I saw French gendarmes looking the way French gendarmes do everywhere. It began when I pointed the car in the nowhere direction and ended up on the Plage du Souffleur near the little old town of Port Louis. It's on the Caribbean side of Grande Terre, which is one half of Guadeloupe, an island that looks like an inebriated butterfly. No one ever goes to Port Louis – there are no signposts to heaven. There was a great white sand beach dappled with sunshine under the sea grape trees. Little boys and girls played in the surf and no travel poster was ever like this.

It was at the end of the beach that I found Myrna, the Creole cook. She stood, arms akimbo, in the dark recesses of a large beach hut. Could I have some lunch? She seemed doubtful. 'I don't have much today,' she apologised and in the end agreed that she could offer me stuffed crab, langouste with Creole rice and apricots. Apricots in April? I saw her go into the kitchen and start work on a charcoal brazier. Behind her stood a brand-new, gleaming, electric cooker. Why didn't she use it? She giggled. '*Ça n'a pas le même goût*', she said. I agreed with her.

As she prepared the meal, I talked to Myrna about Port Louis. There were no tourists here she told me and I was the first stranger she had seen in two weeks. It was not sophisticated enough. Don't change it, I told her, some people like it that way. The greengrocer called in his van; he gives two hoots if he has tomatoes, one hoot if he has not. The fish? You get up early, go to the beach, and wait for the fishermen to return from their night's labour.

I walked on to the terrace. It was haphazardly filled with bits of driftwood, each one holding a fresh red hibiscus. Palm fronds dropped into the sea in front of me and the radio whispered soft Creole songs. The sea, all colours from pale blue to dark green, seemed to change every five minutes and even that was almost completely forgotten when the food came, which was absolutely delicious. At St Francis on the other end of the island, they are wearing the latest French beach fashion – mostly without the top bit – and holding a different gastronomic evening every day and a video after that. The starry night is the same but that is where the resemblance ends. I'll have the Port Louis end of Guadeloupe.

Any traveller who leaves an Anglophone Caribbean island and arrives in a Francophone one is in for a culture shock, for they are worlds apart. For one thing, the French islands, Martinique, Guadeloupe and the others, are far more developed – the roads are superb and the food is unbeatable. They are, of course, an integral part of France and receive all the state benefits that *les metropolitains* receive such as family allowances. That is why Guadeloupe, for instance, has a large population of 325,000. One restaurant owner told me: 'Apart from "le sucre", making children is the biggest industry here. Guadeloupe people think it's a wheeze. Now they get paid for doing what they have always liked doing anyway.'

After Trinidad, Guadeloupe is the largest island in the Lesser Antilles – 584 square miles – which gives you some elbow-room. But it's really two islands separated by the Rivière Salée, a salt-water channel crossed by a causeway, and nature, always fanciful, has made them as different as they could possibly be. In the west is Basse Terre which, inevitably, is high – it's 4500 feet (1372 m) up to the top of its great volcano, La Soufrière. Grande Terre, the other half to the east, is undulating and low, with endless fields of sugar-cane and the finest beaches on the island. That's where tourism started and that's where it's staying.

Christopher Columbus, as inevitable in these parts as the rising tide, discovered the island on 3 November 1493 and named it after the famous Spanish monastery, Santa Maria de Guadalupe de Extremadura. For 150 years nothing happened. Then the French happened. Five hundred 'colons' landed in 1635 but not stay long. Half of them, it seems, were eaten by the Carib Indians who had their own form of Creole cooking.

The British captured Guadeloupe and then gave it back to the French and so on several times over as with so many Caribbean islands. Martinique, smarter and quicker off the mark, stole most of the limelight: after all, one of its favourite daughters was Napoleon's Josephine. Guadeloupe slumbered on and woke up only when it became part of France and now I personally find it infinitely more attractive than Martinique for it is softer, quieter and less grasping. I am sorry I have never been there in August because that is the time when Guadeloupe ladies in all their finery, and with those gorgeous madras turbans on their heads, congregate to celebrate '*la fête des cuisinieres*'. For three days they cook their best, sing and dance and make whoopee and, as the Michelin Guide might say, it is worth a detour.

I have a great weakness for Guadeloupe. I once covered no less than 550 miles (885 km) which, in a middle-sized island, is not bad going. I started with the toughest part, Basse Terre, which needs some perseverance. The island is one big mountain, craggy, jungle-green and tortured into a thousand shapes so that the road hugs the shore and the corners are so vertiginous that I sometimes had to stop at the bottom to get my breath back. It's grandly beautiful in a wild sort of way and dotted with little towns such as Petit Bourg, Goyave, Capesterre, Basse Terre itself which is the former capital, Vieux-Habitants and Pointe Noire. All of them are quiet and old-fashioned and so remote that you would swear no one ever leaves – that is until you cross paths with some smart 'planteur' screaming his Citroen around a hairpin bend. In the southern part, there are no roads at all across Basse Terre – you'd have to move the mountains to build one. One little side road goes up to St Claude where the Guadeloupe hotel-school teaches its promising chefs at the Relais de la Grande Soufrière and you are able to sample Creole cooking as it should be.

Some 15 years ago the French decided that it went against national pride not to have a road across Basse Terre at all. So they built one, along the traces of an old smugglers' path. Called the Traversee, it runs right through Guadeloupe's National Park where the jungle is filled with giant ferns 20 feet (6 m) high, mahoganies with their heads in the clouds and a hundred varieties of orchids, and from the top the Caribbean spreads at your feet, with the dark blue of the sea meeting the green of the jungle. It is quite a sight and well worth seeing.

Grande Terre is easier, at least on your driving muscles. Le Gosier, not far from Pointe-à-Pitre, is the oldest resort in Guadeloupe where there are several good hotels. There are a few boutiques, one or two night-clubs and two of the island's most celebrated Creole restaurants, Honore and Hortense. Next to the village is a new and not unpleasant marina development which, believe it or not, even has a branch restaurant of Prunier of Paris.

For myself, what I liked to do best of all was to get away in the car and explore Guadeloupe, an island which is distinctive, amusing, gently old-fashioned in the more remote corners and absolutely charming. The whole of the coast is sprinkled with splendid beaches, mostly in little coves that are sometimes hard to reach. The eastern side of Grande Terre facing the Atlantic is, of course, grand and rough and in places like Le Moule, a lovely old fishing town, you can see the great rollers crashing on the beach in their final fling from the big ocean. At La Mahaudière, I went to see one of the oldest sugar-mills on the island dating back to the early 1700s and, a little further, I saw a signpost leading to a place called Malgré Tout, meaning Despite Everything. Unable to resist, I drove into a tiny hamlet with a few old houses and a store house and the first man who greeted me, a local hardly visible below his vast straw hat, was quite sure that I had lost my way. '*Il n'y a rien par ici,*' he kept saying. I said never mind, I liked seeing places with nothing to show, but why the name of the place? He took his hat off, scratched his head, smiled and said: 'I remember my grandfather telling me about the name but, you know, I have forgotten.'

Further along the south coast is Ste Anne, up-and-coming and with a very long beach, where I liked the Relais du Moulin and even admired the Club Méditerranée. On again and you come to St François, which I suppose is destined to be the St Tropez of Guadeloupe but, thank goodness, not yet. It is a charming fishing village.

If you are brave, darling little coves beckon you everywhere, such as Anse Ste Marguerite, Anse à la Barque or Anse Maurice, and after a mile or two you reach the tiny beachlet where you are alone with the Caribbean. A better-known one is the Porte d'Enfer which is what paradise must be like, for it is a superb, almost land-locked little bay with lively, pale blue water lapping against the sands in the rock cleft. Not far away is La Grande Vigie and from there you can just see Antigua and Montserrat on the horizon. And so I went on to Anse Bertrand and its magnificent beach, to Port Louis and Petit Canal and Vieux Bourg and Morne-à-l'Eau, each one a place with a history and a continuity of traditions which are remarkable. Everywhere are old plantation houses, sugar-mills or jetties with a plaque to say that the *intendant* of King Louis XVI built it.

People everywhere are surprised to see you and more than once I was stopped by locals telling me that obviously I had got lost. Tourism in Guadeloupe is happily only skin-deep.

One of the most interesting things about Guadeloupe is that it has colonies or dependencies of its own on offshore islands, which are sometimes very offshore, like La Désirade, Marie Galante, Les Saintes, St Barthelemy and St Martin, so one is never short of a new destination for a day or two. La Désirade, just off St François, is a long, thin, dry island, which used to be a leper colony long ago. Quiet and pastoral, it's worth risking if you are collecting islands.

Guadeloupe? Please, don't hesitate – go now before tourism takes over completely and spoils an island, which is truly itself. Jamaica is worth sampling too.

The rafter pushed his long pole into the light-green, sun-dappled water of the river, turned to me and said: 'Them bamboos ... they have a voice. Listen.' It was true. As the breeze eddied past, the tall bamboos creaked as though they were crying. Then, in a sibilant murmur, the leaves called out 'Sch ... Sch ...'. By the banks of the Martha Brae, a blue heron stood on one leg and watched us pass – oblivious. John Crow glided high overhead without ever moving its wings. Two turtles sunbathed on a log. The world was primeval, silent, serene. The Martha Brae flowed on under its canopy of jungle green and I could have been a continent away from the bright spots of Montego Bay or Ocho Rios. Was this the sophisticated, goldplated paradise the holiday posters advertised?

I love all islands, especially tropical ones. Tiny islands delight me, as long as I can get off after 24 hours. Small islands, say 20 or 30 miles (32 or 48 km) long, do too, except that I am by nature incapable of staying put in one place and I very quickly run out of places to go. That will never be a problem in Jamaica.

If you placed Jamaica over a map of Britain, it would stretch roughly from London to Cardiff and from north to south it would go from Hertfordshire to Brighton. And, as Christopher Columbus told Queen Isabella when she asked him what Jamaica was like, you could crumple a piece of silver paper, throw it on a floor of shiny blue tiles and say: 'That's it'. Except that you would have to clothe it with almost impenetrable forest, add soft pastures and great waterfalls and line its shore with some of the finest beaches in the world.

Jamaica is at the same time an island for tourists and not a tourist island. One morning, during a recent visit, I pointed the car west through Montego Bay, drove to the darling little town of Lucea where children in their Sunday best and women wearing cream-puff hats were lining up for church, went on to Negril and its 7-mile (11-km) beach, which is the longest in the Caribbean, passed through the soft, fertile cattle country around Savanna-la-Mar, on past Chichester and Content over the hills and back to my starting point. The car groaned through the pot-holes and my arms ached with the twisting of the steering wheel. I passed villagers who waved or asked for lifts or tried to sell me mangoes but never once did I see a single non-Jamaican.

That in a way is the trouble with tourists in Jamaica. They stay close to their tall frosted drinks under the shade of the seagrape trees on the beach and never both to find out what Jamaica is really like. They never go to Good Hope, one of the finest plantation houses in the West Indies, or even catch a glimpse of the privately-owned Arcadia, all tropical timbers and wrought iron curlicues, with its regal terrace over-looking the distant sea. No, they never go to Anchovy or Balaclava, Big Bottom or Maggoty, Paradise or Rat Trap, Tranquillity or Wait-a-Bit. Even less are they likely to go to that village in the half-forbidden Maroon country called so eloquently Me-No-Call-You-No-Come. They have not seen the unforgettable Blue Mountains cascading down to the ocean around Port Antonio, or visited Highgate where the locals still make furniture as they did in the eighteenth century. And, with few exceptions, tourists have never swum off a north shore beach at 7 a.m., when the sky is cloudless, the sea calm and translucent and you can see your toes 6 feet (1.8 m) down.

I understand that but I regret it. I know that holiday people go to Jamaica for the weather, the beach and a good rest. Quite so. But I do feel they are missing Jamaica and espe-cially the differences that make travel worth while, because Jamaica is Jamaica, not just another island in the sun.

Right now, Jamaica is just emerging from a political and economic nightmare. The tourists stayed away. Now they are back – 70 per cent up on 1985 – and the Jamaicans are glad because they need the work. But if anyone thinks that Jamaica is one of those Yes-Sir-No-Sir-Three-Bags-Full places where the only contact a visitor has is with servile waiters, well, Jamaicans are not like that. They are gay, happy-go-lucky and even a trifle shiftless, independent (one might even say stroppy), argumentative and often prickly. But they are not mass-produced people. Years ago, I remember having the unenviable task of introducing a friend called Wilmot, a tough, short and bunchy Jamaican, to a toffee-nosed Englishman also called Wilmot. Brightly, I said: 'Mr Wilmot, meet Mr Wilmot!' The Englishman looked at my friend up and down and said 'That's funny, how did you get that name?' My Jamaican drew himself up trying hard to keep his temper and replied: 'As a matter of fact, my father had it before me.'

On one occasion, driving out of Palisadoes Airport into Kingston along a road choked with honking traffic, I suddenly saw a strange man, all arms and legs and very thin and wearing one of those incongruous woolly caps, walking blithely along the white line in the middle of the road. Cars swerved, buses jangled, drivers called out obscenities but the man just kept walking along as if on a tightrope. 'What on earth is he doing there?' I asked my driver. 'Man,' he replied, 'he just likes walking along the white line. Why no?' I knew I was back in Jamaica, the country of the individual who won't be a carbon copy of anyone. In Jamaica, the barman who serves you talks to you on a plane of total and unstudied equality. Some visitors don't like this and my advice to them is that they should go somewhere else. This would be a great pity since they would miss one of the loveliest island-countries in the world.

Scenically, the most beautiful part of Jamaica is at the east end of the island around Port Antonio, a banana port which never quite made it into the tourist big league, perhaps because of the distance and the state of the roads leading to it. Errol Flynn loved Port Antonio and made it his home for years and it was he who saw the tourist potential of river rafting and got it going on the Rio Grande, which is by far the best of all Jamaican rivers for this contemplative pastime. Years ago Port Antonio had Jamaica's first tourist hotel, the old Titchfield. Then came Garfield Weston and the once legendary Frenchman's Cove and other hotels like Dragon Bay, Trident and Goblin Hill.

It is Jamaica's second largest tourist centre after Montego Bay but what makes it, as everywhere else, is the exclusive property of the great hotels, those islands of luxury well hidden from the chaff of ordinary life. Most of them have their own beach, great terraces and a life-style which you can become used to. Here in Ocho Rios development has gone on vigorously if not always happily. But that need not bother those staying in plush hotels like Jamaica Inn or the beautiful Plantation Inn.

Tourist life in Jamaica is hotel-centred. Apart from the occasional dinner out in a good restaurant (Moxon's in Ocho Rios is an example), you stay in your hotel because it has everything; your room faces the great sweep of beach beneath the tall palms, the swimming pool is there, the bar around the corner and the candlelit terrace are not far away. Evenings offer a good deal of entertainment and though this is life in golden isolation, it is what millions of people dream about.

There are tourist attractions of course, like plantation tours or visits to Dunn's River Falls where, swimsuited, you pit your muscles against the great cascade of white water coming down the hillside. Along the coast you stop at Discover Bay where Columbus landed on 4 May 1494 and very soon you reach Montego Bay, the country's premier 'resort'. Montego Bay is lively, not unattractive, and very tourist conscious with lots of facilities and many shops and restaurants. But here again it is the hotels that make the place, though for me it is just being in Jamaica — knowing that my food will range from the acceptable to the great, my drinks will be as I want them and the material trappings of tropical living will be up to the mark. I also like to know that if the urge takes me, I can get into the car and just go, knowing that there is enough country for me to turn around in and enough local life to make the going interesting.

As elsewhere in the Caribbean, I can rise in the morning without having to think about what I shall wear or whether I will be cold. The temperature hovers around the 78° to 82°F (26° to 28°C) mark all year round and in the winter when the rest of the world freezes, I must admit getting a certain kick out of being anti-social. This is the good life and a little of it will surely help to forget strikes, late trains and the inspector of taxes. Sheer escapism and very good it is too.

Over it all is the divine beauty of the great island, its mountains, its rivers, its delicious hidden valleys and of course its beaches, so numerous and each so beautiful that the very sight of the tide eddying in over the sand like a spreading white tablecloth is guaranteed to turn you into another person. That is what the Caribbean is for, and I sincerely hope that it will remain that way.

CLIMATE

This is where the Caribbean scores. The temperature hardly ever changes from a minimum 75°F (24°C) to a maximum 82°F (26°C). The traditional season is from December to mid-April but that is not because the weather is better then than at any other time. It is simply because it is more fashionable, and more anti-social, to go away from nasty northern climes when the Joneses can't get away. In the summer, say from June to late September, it rains quite a lot in the islands but rainfall is on the whole short and hard and quickly over. It would be a great mistake for the independent traveller to pay top prices in the 'in' season and miss good bargains at other times.

INTERNAL TRANSPORT

Virtually every major British and American airline tries to get a Caribbean foothold, so there is no shortage of seats or variations. A good bet is the Trinidad-owned BWIA which has many good services to and from the UK and among the islands. When it comes to island-hopping (please excuse that dreadful phrase) the ubiquitous Leeward Islands Air Transport (LIAT) is still the most generally used though its schedules sometimes happen to be a little fanciful. They can be booked via British Airways. Coming up fast for any island within reach of Antigua is the excellent Carib Aviation. For those who like boats, Caribbean islands excel. The best, with or without crew, can be chartered from places like St Vincent, Antigua and the British Virgin Islands. Rates can be quite accessible during the so-called off-season.

HOTELS

Caribbean hotels are among the best and most sophisticated in the world and some of the best are London-represented.

SPECIALISED HOLIDAYS

Tourist-wise, Caribbean islands are very badly represented. Among the exceptions are the Jamaica Tourist Board, the Barbados Tourist Board, the Trinidad & Tobago Tourism Centre and, happily enough, little Anguilla's Tourist Board.

Strange as it may seem, very few people really know the West Indian islands and when I say 'know' I mean know in every detail, island by island. Some people who can help are Windotel Ltd and Tradewinds Faraway Holidays. Otherwise, and apart from reading up and digging hard, most British tour operators have comprehensive programmes. Among the safe bets are Speedbird and Sovereign Holidays. Avoid if you can the man who describes Antigua, for instance, as a new discovery. It's only new because he's just been there himself.

Please see page 224 for addresses.

APPENDIX I

Travel Agents

Thomas Cook Ltd, Thorpe Wood, Peterborough PE3 6SB.
Telephone: (0733) 63200. Also 45 Berkeley Street, London W1A
1EB. Telephone: 01-499 4000. Branches throughout the country.
Pickfords Travel Ltd, 400 Great Cambridge Road, Enfield,
Middlesex. Telephone: 01-366 1211. Branches throughout the
country.
Hogg Robinson (Travel) Ltd, 106 Bishopsgate, London EC2N 4AX.
Telephone: 01-628 3333. Branches throughout the country.
Mark Allan Travel Ltd, 130 Mount Street, London W1Y 5HH.
Telephone: 01-491 3200.
Far East Travel Centre, 3 Lower John Street, London W1.
Telephone: 01-734 7050.
Sole Bay Travel, 10 Market Place, Southwold, Suffolk 1P18 6EE.
Telephone: (0502) 723 915.
Sheringham Travel Centre Ltd, 17 Church Street, Sheringham,
Norfolk NR26 8QR. Telephone: (0263) 822 095.

Tour Operators

Bales Tours Ltd, Bales House, Barrington Road, Dorking RH4 3EJ.
Telephone: (0306) 885 991.
Abercrombie & Kent Ltd, Sloane Square House, Holbein Place,
London SW1W 8NS. Telephone: 01-235 9761.
Serenissima Travel Ltd, 21 Dorset Square, London NW1 5PG.
Telephone: 01-730 9841.
Time Off Ltd, Chester Close, Chester Street, London SW1X 7BQ.
Telephone: 01-235 8070.
The Best of Greece (Travel) Ltd, Rock House, Boughton
Monchelsea, Maidstone, Kent ME17 4LY. Telephone: (0622)
46678.

Specialist Map Shop

Edward Stanford Ltd, 12/14 Long Acre, London WC2E 9LP.
Telephone: 01-836 1321.

Specialist Publications

ABC Air Travel Guide, World Timetable Centre, Dunstable,
Bedfordshire LU5 4HB. Telephone: 0582 600 111.
The Business Traveller, Perry Publications, 49 Old Bond Street,
London W1X 3AF. Telephone: 01-629 4688.
The Airline Passenger Tariff (£32.50), World Timetable Centre,
Dunstable, Bedfordshire LU5 4HB. Telephone: 0582 600 111.
The Financial Times World Hotel Directory (£35), Business
Publication Division, Munster House, Arthur Street, London
EC4R 9AX. Telephone: 01-623 1211.

Egon Ronay's *Lucas Guide*, Egon Ronay Organisation, Greencoat House, Francis Street, London SW1P 1DH. Telephone: 01-630 0861.

Travel Trade Directory, Morgan-Grampian Book Publishing Company Limited, 30 Calderwood Street, London SE18 6QH. Telephone: 01-855 7777.

Bucket Shops

Euro-Asian Travel, 27 Old Bond Street, London W1X 3AA. Telephone: 01-499 8485.

Wingspan, 6 Great Queen Street, London WC2. Telephone: 01-242 3652.

Bestways, 56/58 Whitcomb Street, London WC2. Telephone: 01-930 3985.

Travel Mart Ltd, 126 Uxbridge Road, London W12 3SL. Telephone: 01-740 0660 and branches.

Hotel Specialists

British Association of Hotel Representatives (BAHREP), Suite 19, College House, 29/31 Wrights Lane, London W8 5SH. Telephone: 01-730 7144.

The Leading Hotels of the World, 15 New Bridge Street, London EC4V 6AU. Telephone: 01-583 4211.

Windotel Ltd, Suite 19, College House, 29/31 Wrights Lane, London W8 5SH. Telephone: 01-730 7144.

Room Centre (UK) Ltd, Kingsgate House, Kingsgate Place, London NW6 4HG. Telephone: 01-328 1790 (UK only) and 01-625 8691 (overseas).

Reliance Tours (UK) Ltd, 62 Shaftesbury Avenue, London W1V 7AA. Telephone: 01-439 2651.

Value Travel, Africa House, 64/78 Kingsway, London WC2. Telephone: 01-402 0535.

Trinifold Travel, 1/3 Spring Gardens, The Mall, London SW1A 2BB. Telephone: 01-930 5466.

National Tourist Offices

Anguilla Tourist Board, Suite 19, College House, 29/31 Wrights Lane, London W8 5SH. Telephone: 01-937 7725.

Barbados Tourist Board, 6 Upper Belgrave Street, London SW1. Telephone: 01-235 2449.

Cyprus Tourism Organisation, 213 Regent Street, London W1R 8DA. Telephone: 01-734 9822.

Egyptian Tourist Information Centre, 168 Piccadilly, London W1. Telephone: 01-493 5282.

French Government Tourist Office, 178 Piccadilly, London W1V 0AL. Telephone: 01-491 7622.

German National Tourist Office, 61 Conduit Street, London W1R 0EN. Telephone: 01-629 1664.

National Tourist Organisation of Greece, 195/197 Regent Street, London W1R 8DL. Telephone: 01-734 5997.

Hong Kong Tourist Association, 125 Pall Mall, London SW1. Telephone: 01-930 4775.

Government of India Tourist Office, 7 Cork Street, London W1. Telephone: 01-437 3677.

Israel Tourist Office, 18 Great Marlborough Street, London W1V 1AT. Telephone: 01-434 3651.

Italian State Tourist Department, 1 Princes Street, London W1. Telephone: 01-408 1254.

Jamaica Tourist Board, 50 St James's Street, London SW1. Telephone: 01-499 1707.

Japan National Tourist Organisation, 167 Regent Street, London W1R 9FD. Telephone: 01-734 9638.

Kenya National Tourist Office, 13 New Burlington Street, London W1X 1FF. Telephone: 01-839 4477.

Tourist Development Corporation of Malaysia, 57 Trafalgar Square, London WC2N 6DU. Telephone: 01-930 7932.

Mauritius Tourist Information Service, 49 Conduit Street, London W1. Telephone: 01-437 7508.

Moroccan National Tourist Office, 174 Regent Street, London W1R 6HB. Telephone: 01-437 0073.

Seychelles Tourist Information Office, 30 Woburn Place, London W1R 9TE. Telephone: 01-631 4104.

Spanish National Tourist Office, 57 St James's Street, London SW1. Telephone: 01-499 0901.

Sri Lanka, Ceylon Tourist Board, c/o Marketing Services Ltd, Suite 433, High Holborn House, 52/54 High Holborn, London WC1V 6RB. Telephone: 01-405 1195.

Tanzania Tourist Office, 77 South Audley Street, London W1Y 5TA. Telephone: 01-499 7727.

Tourist Authority of Thailand, 9 Stafford Street, London W1X 3FE. Telephone: 01-499 7679.

Trinidad & Tobago Tourist Board, 20 Lower Regent Street, London SW1Y 4PH. Telephone: 01-839 7155.

Tunisian National Tourist Office, 7a Stafford Street, London W1. Telephone: 01-930 1103.

Turkish Tourism and Information Office, 170/173 Piccadilly, London W1V 9DD. Telephone: 01-734 8681.

United States Travel Service, 22 Sackville Street, London W1X 2EA. Telephone: 01-439 7433 or 01-439 7744.

APPENDIX II

FRANCE

French Railways Ltd, 179 Piccadilly, London W1V 0BA.
  Telephone: 01-493 9731 or, for passenger inquiries, 01-493 4451.
Air France, 158 New Bond Street, London W1Y 0AY. Telephone:
  01-499 9511.
UTA French Airlines, 166 Piccadilly, London W1V 0LX.
  Telephone: 01-493 4881.
Air Jet, Air Languedoc, Air Littoral and Air Vendée: inquiries with
  Air France as above.

Hotels

Les Hospitalliers, Le Poet-Laval, Drome. ££
Château Le Scipionnet, Les Vans, Ardèche. ££
Château du Besset, St Peray (Ardèche). £££
Château Le Violet, Peyriac-Minervois (Aude). ££
Cheval Blanc, Sept-Saulx (Champagne). ££
Ste Foy, Conques (Aveyron). ££
Host. Le Prieuré, Villeneuve-les-Avignon. £££
Host. du Bas-Bréau, Barbizon (Fontainebleau). £££
Cap-Eden-Roc, Cap d'Antibes. £££
Château de Marçay, Chinon. £££
Cap Estel, Eze sur Mer. £££
Ritz, Paris. £££
Lancaster, Paris. £££
Remparts, Kaysersberg (Alsace). ££
Hermitage, Quimperle (Britanny). ££
Moulin des Templiers, Avallon. ££
Château de Pray, Amboise. ££
Host. du Château, Chaumont-sur-Loire. ££
Livradois, Ambert. ££
De la Marine, Caudebec. £££

Relais et Châteaux, c/o Gravetye Manor, Near East Grinstead, West
  Sussex RH19 4LJ. Telephone: (0342) 810 567.
Relais du Silence, c/o Hotel Les Oiseaux, F. 38640 Claix, France.
  Telephone: (76) 98 35 79.
La Vie de Château (inquiries with the French Government Tourist
  Office).
Château Accueil, Mme La Vicomtesse de Bonneval, Château de
  Thaumiers, Thaumiers, 18210 Charenton-du-Cher. Telephone:
  (48) 61 81 62.
Logis and Auberges de France (inquiries with the French Tourist
  Office).
Gîtes de France (inquiries with the French Government Tourist
  Office. Special telephone number 01-493 3480).

Fédérations Equestres, 164 Faubourg St Honore, 75 Paris.
Telephone: 1 42 25 11 22. Or contact French Government Tourist
Office.
Billington Travel Ltd, 2a White Hart Parade, Riverhead, Sevenoaks
TN13 2BJ. Telephone: (0732) 460 6666.
Blackheath Travel Ltd, 13 Blackheath Village, London SE3 9LD.
Telephone: 01-852 0025.
Alec Bristow Travel Ltd, 84/86 Guildford Street, Chertsey, Surrey.
Telephone: (09328) 611 55.
Celebrity Holidays, 18 Frith Street, London W1. Telephone: 01-734
4386.
French Leave Holidays, Travelpoint House, 21 Fleet Street,
London EC4Y 1AA. Telephone: 01-353 9681.

ITALY

Italian State Railways, 50 Conduit Street, London W1. Telephone:
01-434 3844.
Alitalia, 27 Piccadilly, London W1. Telephone: 01-745 8200.

Hotels

Villa Cipriani, Asolo (Venice). £££
Cipriani, Venice. £££
Gritti Palace, Venice. £££
La Residenza, Venice. £
Grand Hotel Villa Serbelloni, Bellagio. ££
Grand Hotel Villa d'Este, Cernobbio (Como). £££
Gd. Hotel & La Pace, Montecatini Terme. £££
Le Sirenuse, Positano. £££
Certosa di Maggiano, Siena. ££
San Domenico Palace, Taormina. £££
Hassler Villa Medici, Rome. £££
Cardinal, Rome. ££
Alexandra, Rome. ££
Villa Azalee, Florence. £
Villa San Michele, Fiesole (Florence). £££
Corallo, on the beach near Ravenna. £
Rubens, Milan. ££
Due Torri, Verona. £££
Umbra, Assisi. ££
Capuccini, Gubbio. ££
Marina-Riviera, Amalfi. £
Palumbo, Ravello. ££
Le Axidie, Vico Equense (Naples). ££
San Michela, Cetraro (Calabria). £££
Santavanere, Maratea (Calabria). £££
Villa Athena, Agrigento. ££

Citalia Ltd, Marco Polo House, 3/5 Lansdowne Road, Croydon CR9
1LL. Telephone: 01-686 0677.
W. F. & R. K. Swan (Hellenic) Ltd, King's Court, 216 Goodge Street,
London W1P 2EU. Telephone: 01-636 8070.

Page & Moy Ltd, 2 Hatfields, London SE1 9PU. Telephone: 01-928 4833.

Serenissima, 21 Dorset Square, London NW1 5PG. Telephone: 01-730 9841.

Villas Italia, 93 Regent Street, London W1. Telephone: 01-439 8547.

SPAIN

Iberia International Airlines of Spain, Venture House, Glasshouse Street, London W1. Telephone: 01-437 9822.

Hotels

Landa Palace, Burgos. £££
Parador Nacional del Castillo de Santa Catalina, Jaen. ££
San Marcos, León. £££
Villa Magna, Madrid. £££
De la Reconquista, Oviedo. £££
De Los Reyes Catolicos, Santiago de Compostela. £££
Parador Nacional Raimundo de Borgogna, Avila. ££
Monasterio de Piedra, Zaragoza. ££
Parador Nacional Conde de Orgaz, Toledo. ££
Parador Nacional Via de la Plata, Merida. ££
Huerto del Cura, Elche. ££

Cox & Kings Travel Ltd, Vulcan House, 46 Marshall Street, London W1V 2PA. Telephone: 01-734 8291.

Sovereign Holidays, Victoria Terminal, Buckingham Palace Road, London SW1W 9SR. Telephone: 01-834 2323.

Mundi Color Holidays, 276 Vauxhall Bridge Road, London SW1. Telephone: 01-828 6021.

Fairways & Swinford Travel Ltd, Sea Containers House, 20 Upper Ground, London SE1 9PF. Telephone: 01-261 1744.

PORTUGAL

Hotels

Pousada dos Loios, Évora. ££
Ritz, Lisbon. £££
York House, Lisbon. ££
Reid's, Madeira. £££
Palacio dos Seteais, Sintra. ££
Estalagem do Mestre Alfonso Domngues, Batalha. ££
Estalagem do Conde, Colares. £
Pousada da Rainha Santa Isabel, Estremoz. ££
Estalagem de Monsaraz, Monsaraz. £
Pousada do Castelo, Obidos. ££
Pousada de Sao Gens, Serpa. £

Harlen Travel, Harlen House, 42/46 London Road, Staines, Middlesex. Telephone: (0784) 62606.

GREECE

Olympic Airways, 164/165 Piccadilly, London W1. Telephone: 01-846 9966.

Hotels

Athens Hilton, Athens. £££
Astir Palace, Corfu. £££
Elounda Beach, Agios Nikolaos. £££
Minos Beach, Agios Nikolaos. ££
Akti Myrina, Lemnos. £££
Galaxy, Kavalla. £
Atlantis, Santorini. ££
Calypso, Rhodes. ££
Royal Olympic, Athens. ££
Koukounaries, Skiathos. £
Astir Galini, Kamena Vourla. ££
Sirene, Poros. ££
Xenia, Lesbos. ££
Makriammos, Thassos. ££
Xenia, Olympia. ££

The Best of Greece (Travel) Ltd, Rock House, Boughton Monchelsea, Maidstone, Kent ME17 4LY. Telephone: (0622) 46678.
Wanderways Holidays, 51a London Road, Hurst Green, Sussex TN19 7QP. Telephone: (058 086) 607.

CYPRUS

Hotels

The Annabelle, Paphos. £££
Paphos Beach, Paphos. £££
Amathus Beach, Limassol. £££
Churchill, Limassol. £££
L'Onda Beach, Limassol. £££

Cyprair Tours Ltd, 27/31 Hampstead Road, London NW1 3JA. Telephone: 01-388 7514.
Sunvil, 7/8 Upper Square, Isleworth, Middlesex TN7 7DJ. Telephone: 01-568 4499.

TURKEY

Turkish Airlines (THY), 11/12 Hanover Street, London W1. Telephone: 01-499 9249.
Turkish Maritime Lines, Orwell House, Ferry Lane, Felixstowe, Suffolk IP11 8QL. Telephone: (03942) 73161.

Hotels

Istanbul Hilton, Istanbul. £££
Pera Palace, Istanbul. £££

Buyuk Efes, Izmir. £££
Eutan Oteli, Cesme. ££
Mehmet Posa Kulup Kervanseray, Kusadasi. ££
Tusan Motel, Pammukale. ££
Atlantik Oteli, Marmaris. ££
Likyo Oteli, Fethiye. ££
Pansyon Olimpyat, Antalya. ££
Aphrodite, Side. ££
Bulvar Palas, Ankara. ££

Aegean Turkish Holidays, 53a Salisbury Road, London NW6 6NJ.
  Telephone: 01-629 4148.
Cricketer Holidays, 4 The White House, Beacon Road,
  Crowborough, East Sussex TN6 1AB. Telephone: (08926) 64242.
Fairways & Swinford Ltd, Sea Containers House, 20 Upper Ground,
  London SE1 9PF. Telephone: 01-261 1744.

MOROCCO

Royal Air Maroc, 174 Regent Street, London W1. Telephone:
  01-439 8854.

Hotels

Palais Jamai, Fez. £££
La Mamounia, Marrakech. £££
La Gazelle d'Or, Taroudant. £££
Le Zat, Ouarzazate. ££
Grand, Tinerhir. ££
Du Sud, Zagora. ££
La Roseraie, Ouirgane (Marrakech). ££
Chaouen Hotel, Chaouen. ££

Twickers World, 2 Chester Row, London SW1W 9JH. Telephone:
  01-730 5268.
Fairways & Swinford Ltd, Sea Containers House, 20 Upper Ground,
  London SE1 9PF. Telephone: 01-261 1744.
The Best of Morocco Ltd, Rock House, Boughton Monchelsea,
  Maidstone, Kent ME17 4LY. Telephone (0622) 46678.

TUNISIA

Tunis Air, 24 Sackville Street, London W1X 1DE. Telephone:
  01-734 7644.

Hotels

Tunis Hilton, Tunis. £££
Carlton, Tunis. ££
Dar Zarrouk, Sidi Bou Said. ££
Sheraton, Hammamet. £££
Les Orangers, Hammamet. ££
Les Aghlabites, Kairouan. ££

Port El Kantaoui, Sousse. £££
El Menzel, Djerba. £££
Jugurtha Palace, Gafsa. £££
Sahara Palace, Nefta. £££

Cadogan Travel Ltd, 9/10 Portland Street, Southampton SO9 12P.
  Telephone: (0703) 332 661.
Hove Travel Agency Ltd, 139 Church Road, Hove BN3 2AE.
  Telephone: (0273) 732 139.
Sussex Travel, 12/14 Terminus Road, Eastbourne, Sussex.
  Telephone: (0323) 645 111.

EGYPT

Egyptair, 296 Regent Street, London W1. Telephone: 01-580 5477.

Hotels

Mena House Oberoi, Cairo. £££
Nile Hilton, Cairo. £££
Hurghada, Hurghada. ££
Aswan Oberoi, Aswan. £££
Cecil, Alexandria. ££
Ibis, Kharga Oasis. ££

Abercrombie & Kent (Europe) Ltd, Sloane Square House, Holbein
  Place, London SW1W 8NS. Telephone: 01-235 9761.
Hayes & Jarvis (Travel) Ltd, 6 Harriet Street, London SW1X 9JP.
  Telephone: 01-235 3648.
Bales Tours Ltd, Bales House, Barrington Road, Dorking RH4 3EJ.
  Telephone: 0306 885 991.
Fairways & Swinford (Travel) Ltd, Sea Containers House, 20 Upper
  Ground, London SE1 9PF. Telephone: 01-261 1744.
Twickers World, 22 Church Street, Twickenham TW1 3NW.
  Telephone: 01-892 7606.
Nawas Tourist Agency, 19 Great Portland Street, London W1N
  5BD. Telephone: 01-580 6405.

EAST AFRICA

Hotels

Peponi, Lamu. ££
Norfolk, Nairobi. £££
Mount Kenya Safari Club, Nanyuki. £££
Samburu Game Lodge. ££
Diani Beach, Near Mombasa. ££

Abercrombie & Kent (Europe) Ltd, Sloane Square House, Holbein
  Place, SW1W 8NS. Telephone: 01-235 9761.
United Touring International, Carrington House, 930 Regent
  Street, London W1R 6HD. Telephone: 01-734 4246.
Flamingo Tours of East Africa, Kingsland House, 122 Regent
  Street, London W1R 5FE. Telephone: 01-734 5832.

Nilestar Tours (Africa) Ltd, 623 Grand Buildings, Trafalgar Square, London WC2N 5HN. Telephone: 01-930 1895.

Wexas International, 45 Brompton Road, Knightsbridge, London SW3 1DE. Telephone: 01-589 3315.

Holiday Planners Ltd, 240 West End Lane, London NW6 1LG. Telephone: 01-435 8071.

ISRAEL

Hotels

Dan, Caesarea. £££
King Solomon Sheraton, Jerusalem. £££
Tel Aviv Sheraton, Tel Aviv. £££
American Colony, Jerusalem. ££
Dor, Jerusalem. ££

Homtel Ltd, Suite 604, Triumph House, 189 Regent Street, London W1R 7WF. Telephone: 01-437 2892.

Peltours Ltd, Mappin House, 156/162 Oxford Street, London W1V 9DL. Telephone: 01-637 4373.

W. F. & R. K. Swan (Hellenic) Ltd, King's Court, 216 Goodge Street, London W1P 2EU. Telephone: 01-636 8070.

Bales Tours Ltd, Bales House, Barrington Road, Dorking RH4 3EJ. Telephone: 0306 885 991.

Egged Tours, 59 Ben Yehuda Street, Tel Aviv, Israel. Telephone: 242271.

Galilee Tours, 3 Ben Sirast, Jerusalem 94181. Telephone: 02 246858.

Kibbutz Representatives (Inquiries with the Israel Tourist Office — please see page 214 for address).

INDIA

Air India, 17/18 New Bond Street, London W1Y 0BD. Telephone: 01-493 4050.

Hotels

Mughal, Agra. £££
Oberoi Towers, Bombay. £££
Taj Mahal InterContinental, Bombay. £££
Fort Aguada, Goa. £££
Rambagh Palace, Jaipur. £££
Lalitha Mahal, Mysore. £££
Oberoi InterContinental, New Delhi. £££
Taj Mahal, New Delhi. £££
Lake Palace, Udaipur. £££
Centaur Hotel, New Delhi. ££
Sealord Hotel, Cochin. ££
Umaid Bhawan, Jaipur. ££
Kovalem Beach, Kovalem. £££
Pandyan Hotel, Mahabalipuram. ££
Oberoi Clarkes, Simla. ££

Cox & Kings Travel Ltd, Vulcan House, 46 Marshall Street, London
W1V 2PA. Telephone: 01-734 8291.
Holiday Planners Ltd, 240 West End Lane, London NW6 1LG.
Telephone: 01-435 8071.

THAILAND

Thai International Airways, 41 Albemarle Street, London W1X
3FE. Telephone: 01-491 7953.

Hotels
Dusit Thani, Bangkok. £££
Erawan, Bangkok. £££
Oriental, Bangkok. £££
Princes, Bangkok. ££
Chian Inn, Chiang Mai. ££
Lak Huang, Phangna. ££
Phuket Island, Phuket. £££

Far East Travel Centre, 3 Lower John Street, London W1.
Telephone: 01-734 7050.
Abercrombie & Kent Ltd, Sloane Square House, Holbein Place,
London SW1W 8NS. Telephone: 01-235 9761.

INDONESIA

Garuda Indonesian International Airlines, c/o KLM Royal Dutch
Airlines, Time & Life Building, New Bond Street, London W1Y
0AD. Telephone: 01-493 1231.

Hotels
Mandarin, Jakarta. £££
Transaera, Jakarta. ££
Segara Village, Bali. ££
Bali Oberoi, Bali. £££
Pusi Saren, Ubud, Bali. ££
Suranadi, Lombok. ££
Astari, Prapat, Sumatra. ££
Pulo Tao, Lake Toba, Sumatra. ££
Alaska, Sulawesi. £

Bales Tours Ltd, Bales House, Barrington Road, Dorking RH4 3EJ.
Telephone: 0306 885 991.
Albany Travel Ltd, 3 Broadway, London SW1H 0BA. Telephone:
01-222 0881.
Fairways & Swinford Ltd, Sea Containers House, 20 Upper Ground,
London SE1 9PF. Telephone: 01-261 1744.

HONG KONG

Cathay Pacific Airways, 2 Berkeley Street, London W1. Telephone:
01-930 7878.
British Airways: any British Airways shop.

Hotels
Mandarin. £££
Peninsula. £££
Regent. £££
Hong Kong. ££
Hyatt Regency. ££
Excelsior. £££
Hilton. £££
Lee Gardens. ££
Repulse Bay. ££

USA

Most major American airlines represented in London have their own visit-the-USA tickets and/or can construct a package with local affiliated airlines.
Greyhound Lines, 14/16 Cockspur Street, London SW1Y 5BL. Telephone: 01-839 5591.

American hotels are too numerous to mention in the context of a book of this kind. Please refer to specialist publications.
However, in the area covered in this chapter I should mention two outstanding hostelries:
Arizona Inn, 2200 E. Elm Street, Tucson, Arizona 85719. Telephone: (602) 325 141.
Tanque Verde Ranch, RT8 Box 66, Tucson, Arizona 85748. Telephone: (602) 296 6275.

Below are the London addresses of US or British combines, which operate excellent motels all over the country and will be glad to help you with an itinerary.
Best Western, 26 Kew Road, Richmond, Surrey. Telephone: 01-940 7566.
Holiday Inns, 10 New College Parade, London NW3. Telephone: 01-722 7755.
Ramada Hotels, 50 Curzon Street, London W1. Telephone: 01-235 5264.
Travelodge (part of the THF chain), 86 Park Lane, London W1. Telephone: 01-493 4090.
Mark Allan Travel Ltd, 130 Mount Street, London W1Y 5HH. Telephone: 01-491 3200.
Albany Travel Ltd, 3 Broadway, London SW1H 0BA. Telephone: 01-222 0881.
Cox & Kings Ltd, Vulcan House, 46 Marshall Street, London W1V 2PA. Telephone: 01-734 8291.
United States Travel Service (please see page 214).

CARIBBEAN

British Airways: any British Airways shop.
Carib Aviation, Suite 19, College House, 29/31 Wrights Lane, London W8 5SH. Telephone: 01-730 7144.

Hotels

Cobblers Cove, Barbados. £££
Coral Reef Club, Barbados. £££
Little Dix Bay, Virgin Gorda. £££
Half Moon Club, Jamaica. £££
Golden Lemon, St Kitts. £££
Maliouhana, Anguilla. £££
Lond Island, Antigua. £££
The Inn, Antigua. ££
Springfield Plantation, Dominica. ££
Calabash, Grenada. ££
Bakoua Beach, Martinique. £££
Montpelier Plantation, Nevis. £££
Anse Chastanet, St Lucia. ££
Frangipani, Bequia. ££

Windotel Ltd, Suite 19 College House, 29/31 Wrights Lane W8 5SH. Telephone: 01-730 7144.
Tradewinds Faraway Holidays, 66/68 Brewer Street, London W1. Telephone: 01-734 1260.
Speedbird Holidays, 200 Buckingham Palace Road, London SW1W 9TJ. Telephone: 01-930 3422.
Sovereign Holidays, 200 Buckingham Palace Road, London SW1W 9SR. Telephone: 01-834 2323.